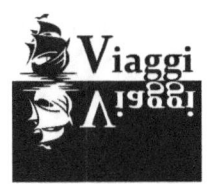

Author: Franco Purini

Title: Talking Canvases:
Subtitle: The Painting of Nino Saggio

Book Series: "I Viaggi"
Publisher: Vita Nostra Edizioni
Piazza Grecia 61, 00196 Rome
Tel. +39 06 97615923
Email: VitaNostraEdizioni@nITrosaggio.net
Website: www.VitaNostraEdizioni.it

Layout by: Chiara Corsetti
First Edition: November 2024
Second Edition: January 2025

Published on the occasion of the exhibition at Cappella Orsini in Roma from October 16 to 22, 2024.

Special thanks to Roberto Lucifero d'Aprigliano, Director.

https://www.cappellaorsini.net/
https://www.fondazioneoperalucifero.org/
+393336240517

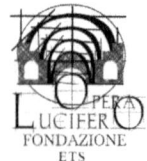
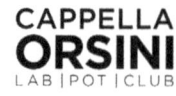

FRANCO PURINI

Talking Canvases:
The Painting of Nino Saggio

Vita Nostra Edizioni

VIAGGI

"Viaggi" should be called "Trips." In fact, only the English term effectively opens up the plurality of connotations that this series aims to convey. The first, naturally, concerns the intellectual adventure shared between an author and a reader. We often forget about this pair, this true thread of Ariadne: the best one known to escape the labyrinth of a depressed world that empties and depresses. Guided by the poet of the moment, the Dante-reader follows him to discover and think. This is an intimate adventure for two. If others, perhaps at our invitation, follow and undertake their own journey, so much the better.

Come to think of it, the second aspect naturally derives from the first. Isn't it the journey, after all, the primary place of storytelling and therefore of the book? Naturally, we think of Homer and his Ulysses, and after him, many others, countless others, up to Gulliver and Peter Pan. Two heroes, one of enlightened thought, the other of the perpetual rediscovery of the world of elsewhere.

The third aspect is again contained in the second. How did James Joyce title his masterpiece? He called it Ulysses, but by then, we are deep into the twentieth century, and the journey has become syncopated, fragmented, a journey between dream and wakefulness, a journey that delves into the true unconscious of Freud or Jung, or even one induced artificially. No, not the one of all-consuming artificial intelligence, but that of substances. These are the journeys, between the fumes of opium or lysergic acid diethylamide, that suddenly reveal other worlds, other designs, other projects.

The greatest and most brilliant among us know how to land them and change real life.

Steve Jobs, as is well known, was a great traveler and had visions that he then materialized, against all odds, in the contemporary world: the first personal computer for the rest of us, the Lisa, the first Macintosh, the Apple music store with the iPad, and later the iPhone and iPad.

The series began with a book on *Boullée* by Claudio Catalano, which holds both historiographical and dreamlike value. It continued with *Mari*, a writing suspended between real travels and those in the past. The third volume is *Lemuel*, which almost literally takes up the program of the series. Like the new Lemuel Gulliver, Lorenzo Casavecchia travels with the social critique spirit of his predecessor, and somewhat like *Boullée* and Nicolas *Ledoux*, the fourth book in the series, also by Catalano, creates a world of images on the border between the real and the dream, between the utopian, dystopian, and syntopic. This fifth volume, signed by Franco Purini, one of the most prominent architects of today, is particularly noted for combining unflagging graphic research with theory and design. To our surprise, he presents an exhibition that is a curatorial work much more than an authorial one. This small catalog contains what he deemed necessary to write for the occasion.

The book presents two parallel paths, one of words and one of images. They deliberately do not intertwine in the book. The reader will see how to make the journey their own, as there is white space to add their own notebooks of notes. To rediscover the path or to trace one of their own.

Table of Contents

Talking Canvases	9
Illustrations	13
I. Primordiums	14-19
II. Shadow series	20-25
III. Light Impressions	26-33
IV. White City	34-41
V. Back in Sicily	42-45
VI. Vincent and Paul	46-51
VII. Wandering Magic	52-59
VIII. Abbey of the Tre Fontane	60-63
IX. Hills	64-69
X. New City	70-77
XI. Past Lives	78-83
XII. Tevere	84-89
XIII. Urban Glimpses	90-99
XIV. Landscape Glimpses	100-109
XV. Italian Landscapes	110-115
XVI. Sangue Miu!	116-121

XVII. Sicily Sea	122-131
XVIII. Santa Caterina	132-139
XVIII. Sicilian Villages	140-147
XIX. Abaué	148-157
Note	158-159

Talking Canvases

Nino Saggio is a magical presence bridging the past, present, and future. His thoughts are indeed oriented toward the transformations necessary for the near future in a prophetic dimension—and it is not excessive to believe so—while he is also deeply attentive to preserving the sacredness of the past. For him, memory is a space for reimagining the elapsed time, which brings to mind Marcel Proust and paraphrases Paul Valéry in a famous verse: "the sea, the sea, always beginning anew." In the present, he is a generous and experimental teacher, one who believes that students should not depend on him but should share a common journey in an exchange of progressive ideas, transcending common beliefs, widespread habits, and repetitive conceptual formulations as they evolve into architects.

Nino Saggio is an explorer of the new, having begun his journey many years ago with a painting style that held no uncertainty, imitation, or initiatory qualities; instead, he approached and understood it in its sincere artistic essence. In his figurative adventure, already mature at its inception, where one perceives the influence of Paul Cézanne and later Henri Matisse, his painting emerges as definitively tonal and timbral. His painting is tied to his central idea of embracing in his imagination the mythical landscape of Sicily's northern shore, where cities punctuate the relationship between sea and land on a border of golden hills with mysterious geography. One might say that light, as a native energy, is the subject of young Nino Saggio's painting, sublimating reality by dissolving it into color as if inventing a new language. Each of his paintings becomes a musical transcription of light in a color order that renders it eloquent.

In the summer meetings held in Gioiosa Marea, in the historic family palace, Nino Saggio, along with his young students, constructs a genuine architectural ritual celebrating an environment with a primal character, as if freshly created. This picturesque setting, simultaneously sublime, hosts architectural interventions like the Wind-Pierced Tower, signaling the emergence of beauty in a land that had always awaited it. And it is from the paintings of the young Nino Saggio that all this began and continues to manifest, in a constant and mysterious metamorphosis. The five paintings in this exhibition represent a native journey that has unfolded over time in search of itself, along with his rigorous work as a teacher, discovering and solving extraordinary enigmas in a visionary and utopian journey. All of this is expressed in the signs and colors of these talking canvases.

— Franco Purini, Rome, October 10, 2024

Tele Parlanti

This small book has been published in the context of the exhibition:

Franco Purini presents Five Unpublished Paintings by Nino Saggio
At the Cappella Orsini, Roberto Lucifero Foundation, Rome
From October 16 to 22, 2024

The following paintings were exhibited:

Santa Croce, Roma 1969 Oil on canvas 25x35 cm p. 14
Villa Celimontana, Roma January 1972 Oil on canvas 50x70 cm p. 30-31
Santa Maria Maggiore, Roma May 1971 Oil on canvas 60x70 cm p. 34-35
Fiumara, Sicily 1972 Oil on canvas 50x70 cm p. 45
Dona and Lele, Roma August 1987 Oil on canvas 25x30 cm p. 121

The Painting of Nino Saggio

Primordiums

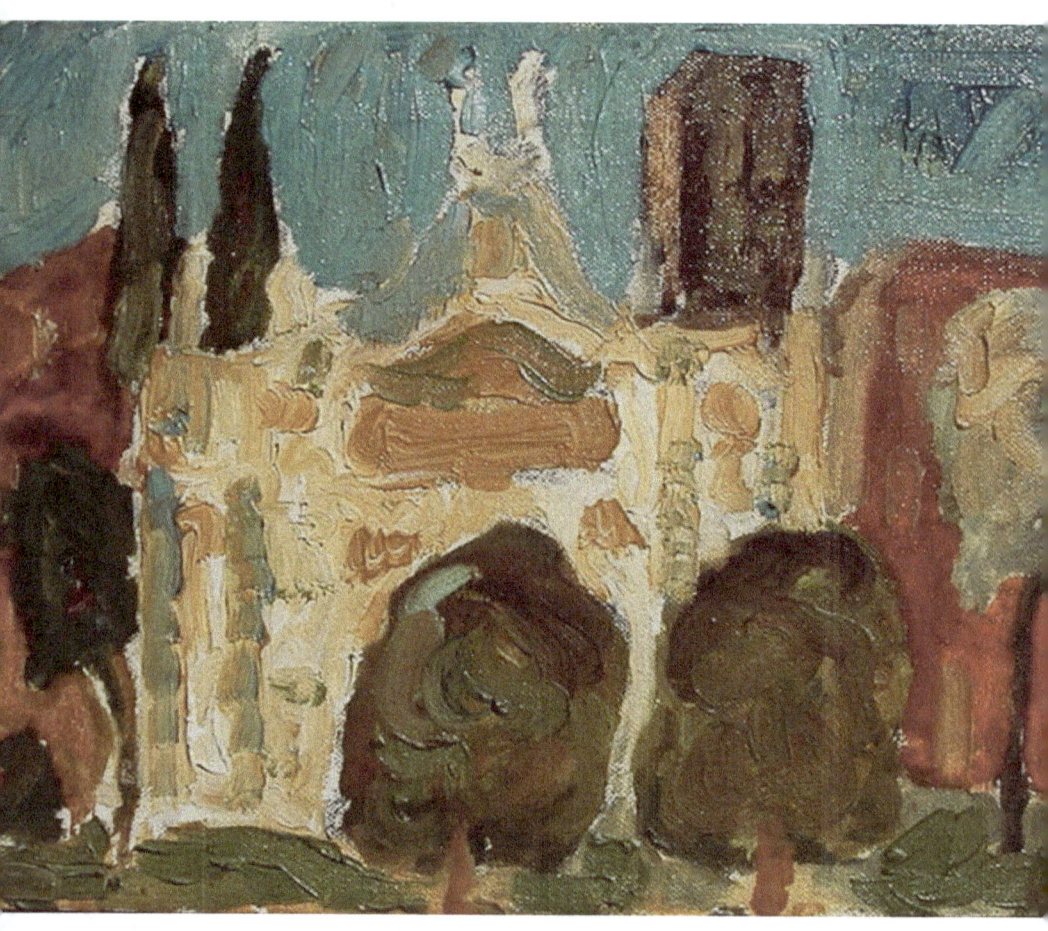

1.1 Santa Croce, Roma, 1969
   Oil on canvas, cm 25x35
1.2 Aventino, Roma, March 1970
   Oil on canvas, cm 30x40

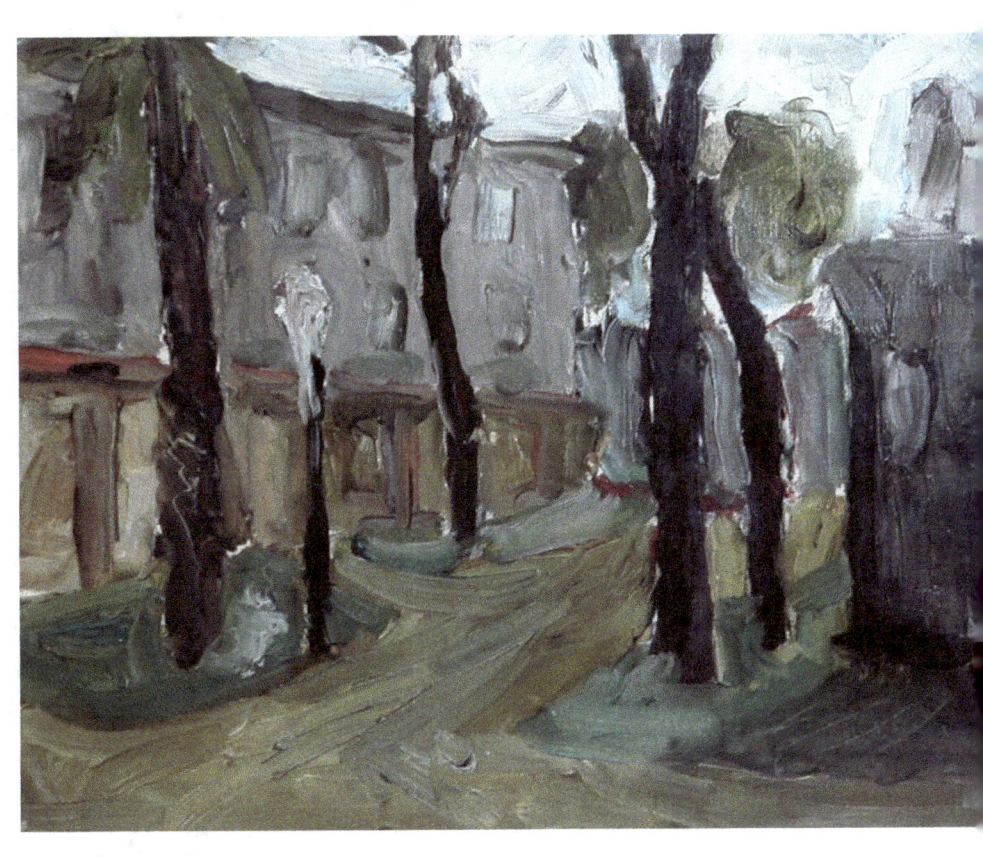

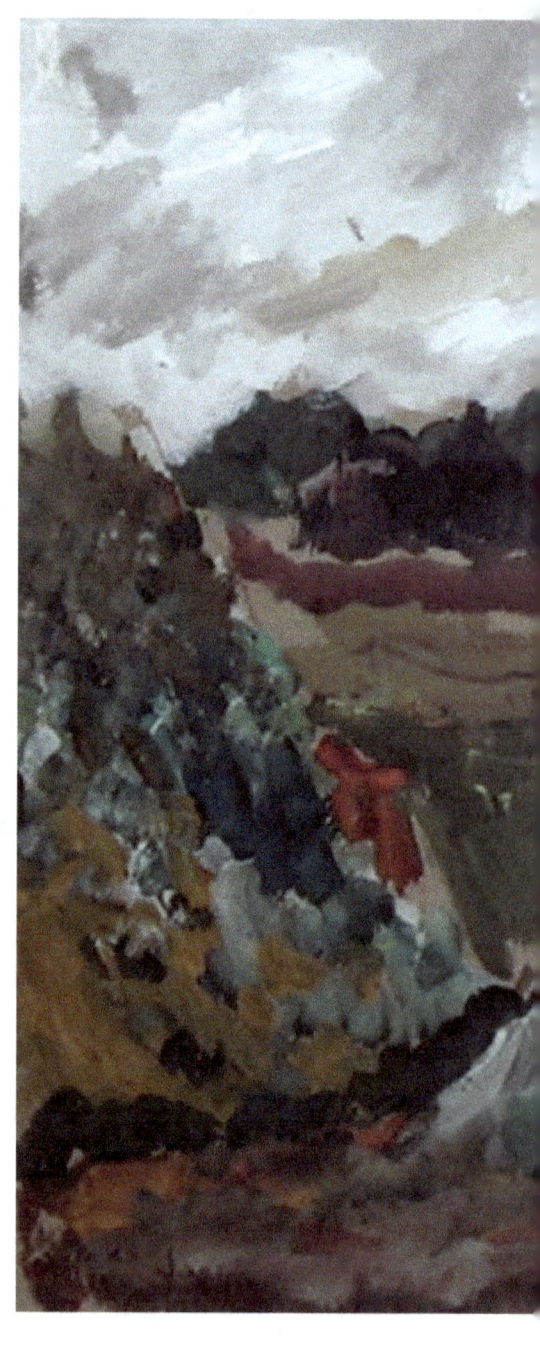

1.3 Crocifissione in Sicilia ("Crucifixion in Sicily"), Roma, 1971
Tempera on cardboard, cm 35x50

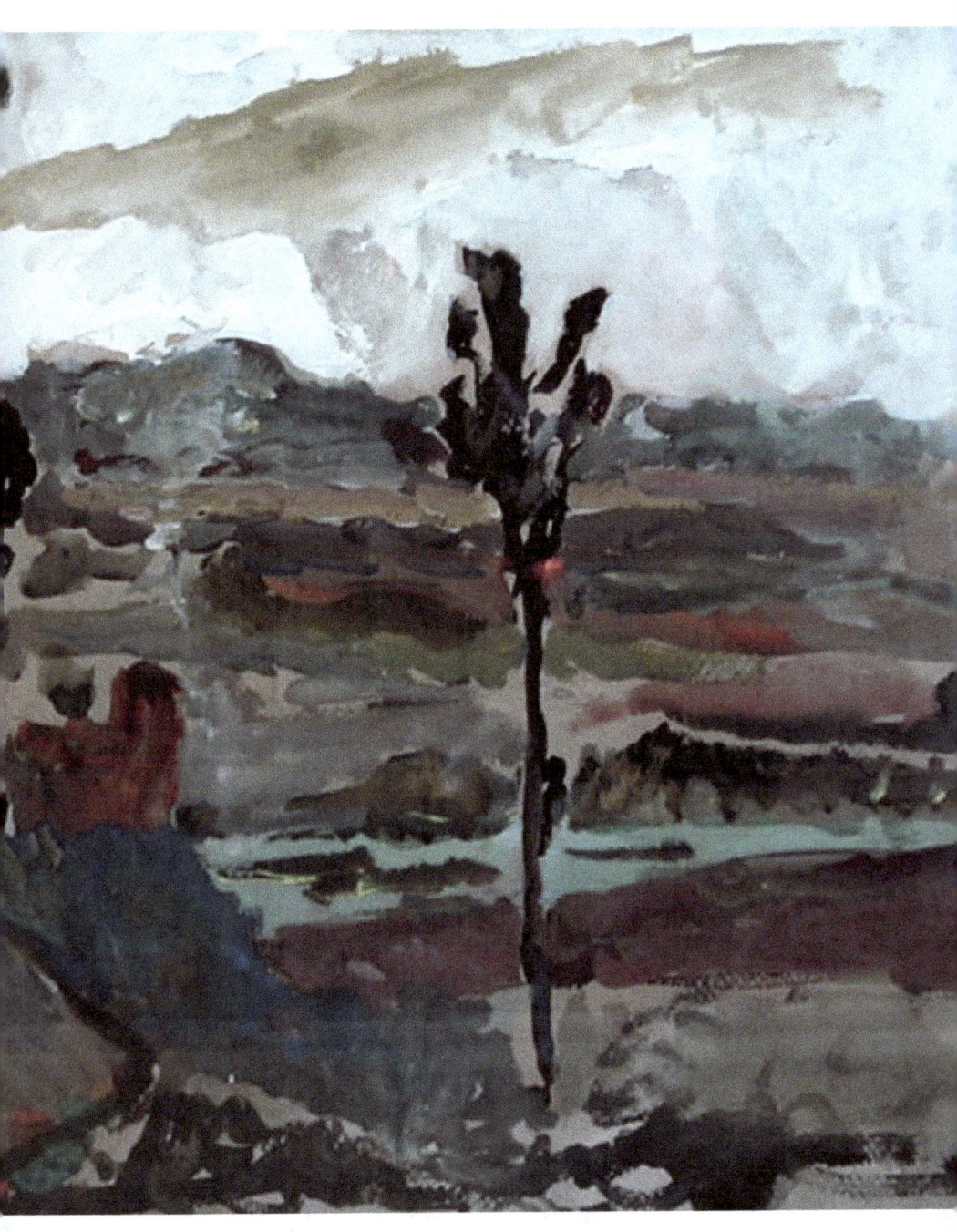

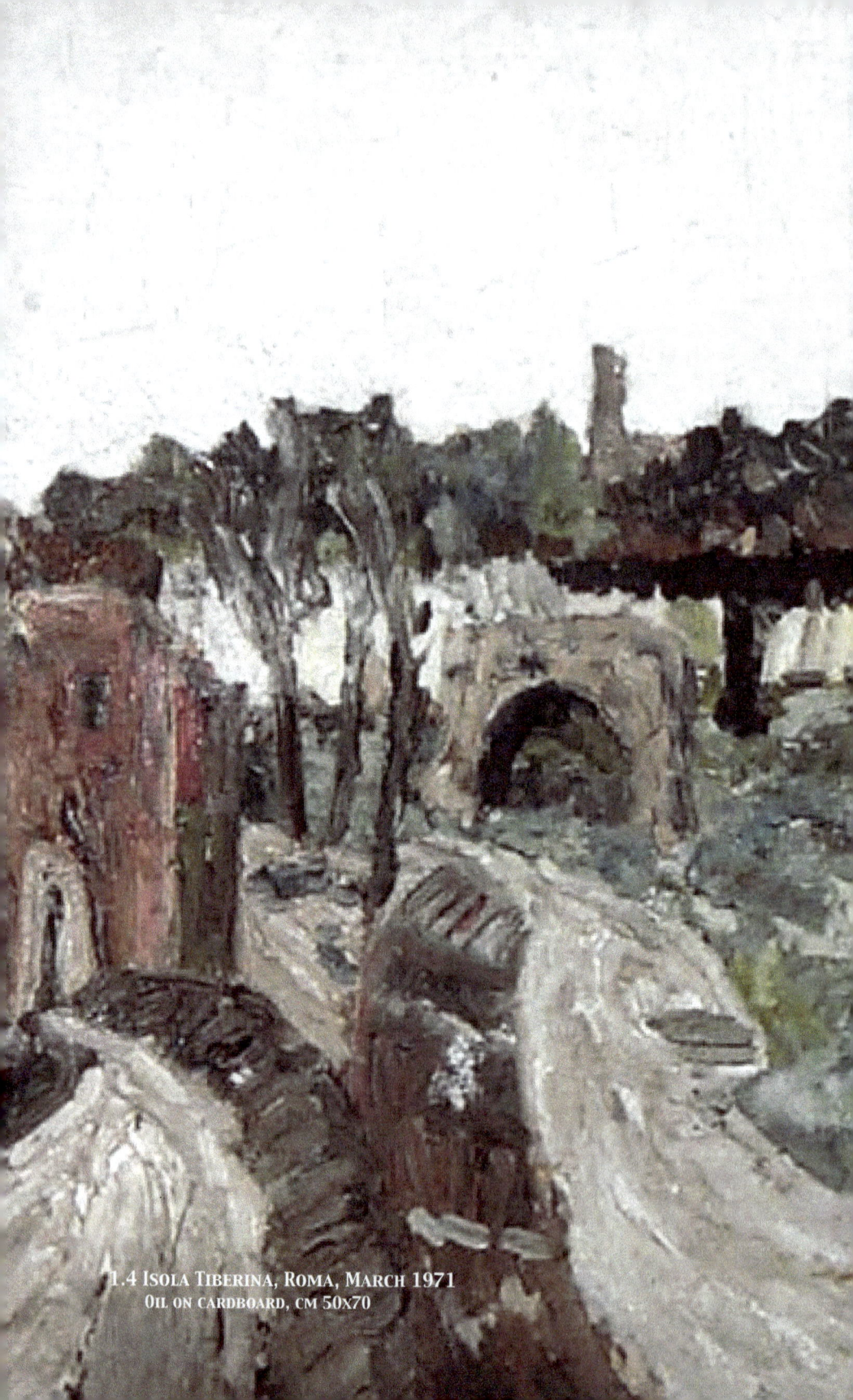

1.4 Isola Tiberina, Roma, March 1971
Oil on cardboard, cm 50x70

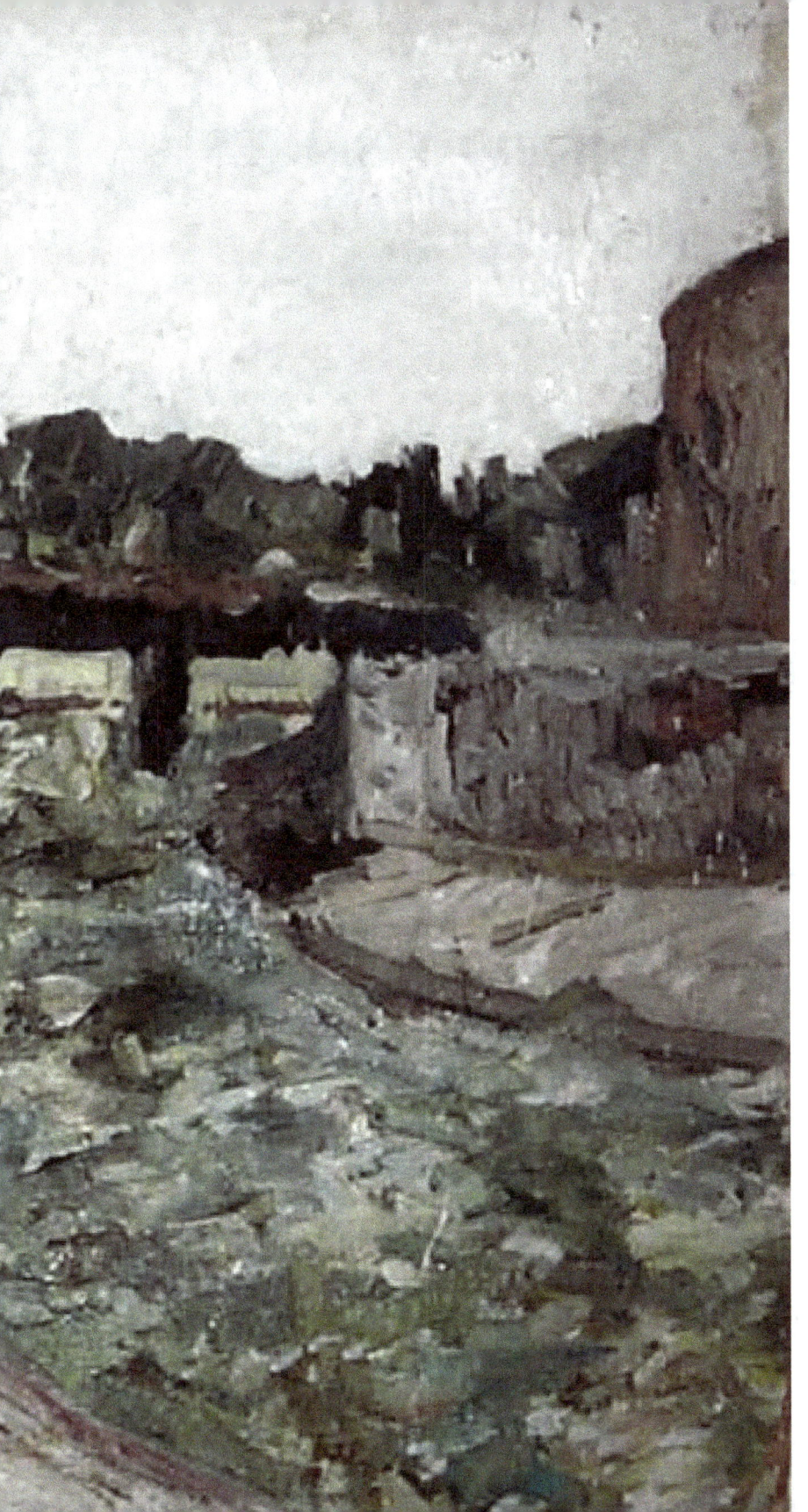

Shadow series

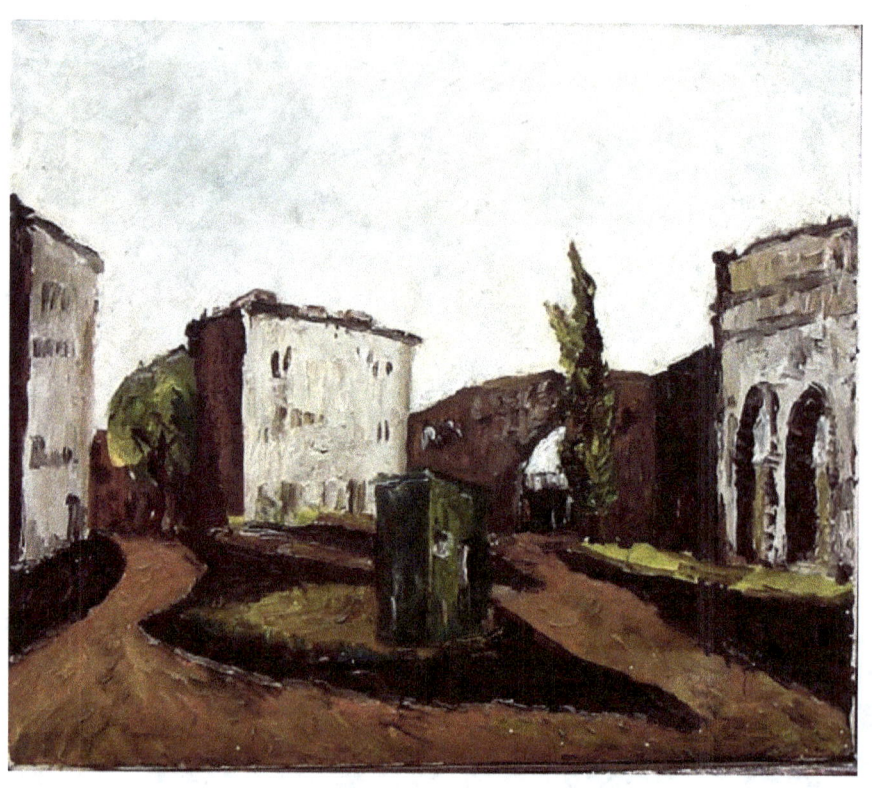

2.1 Porta Maggiore, Roma, January 1971
   Oil on canvas, cm 60x70
2.2 Santa Croce, Roma, January 1971
   Oil on canvas, cm 60x70

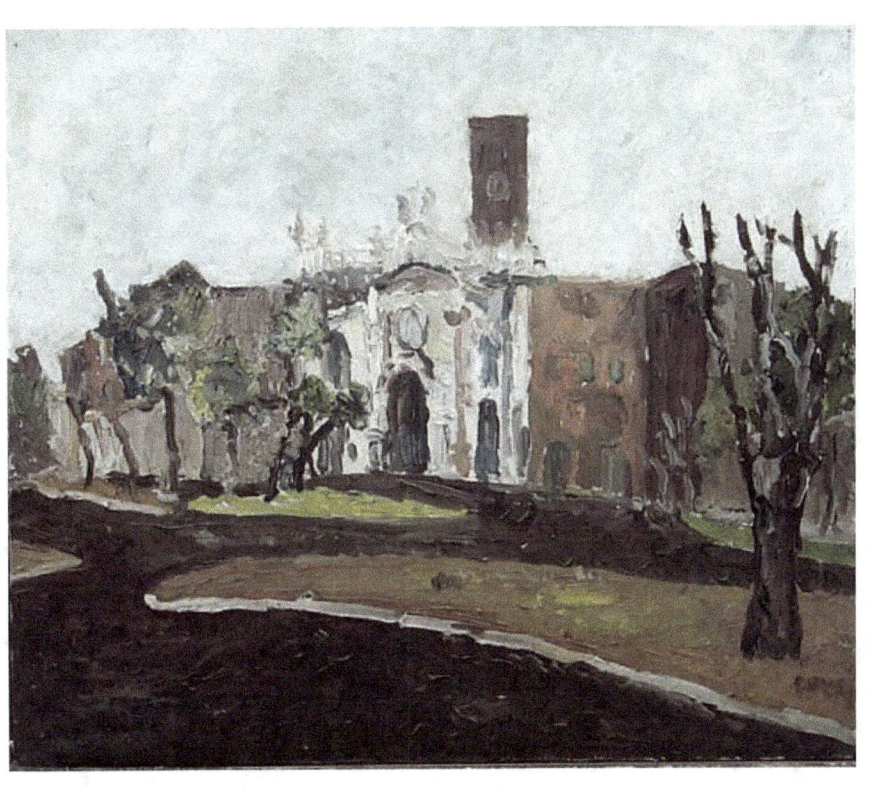

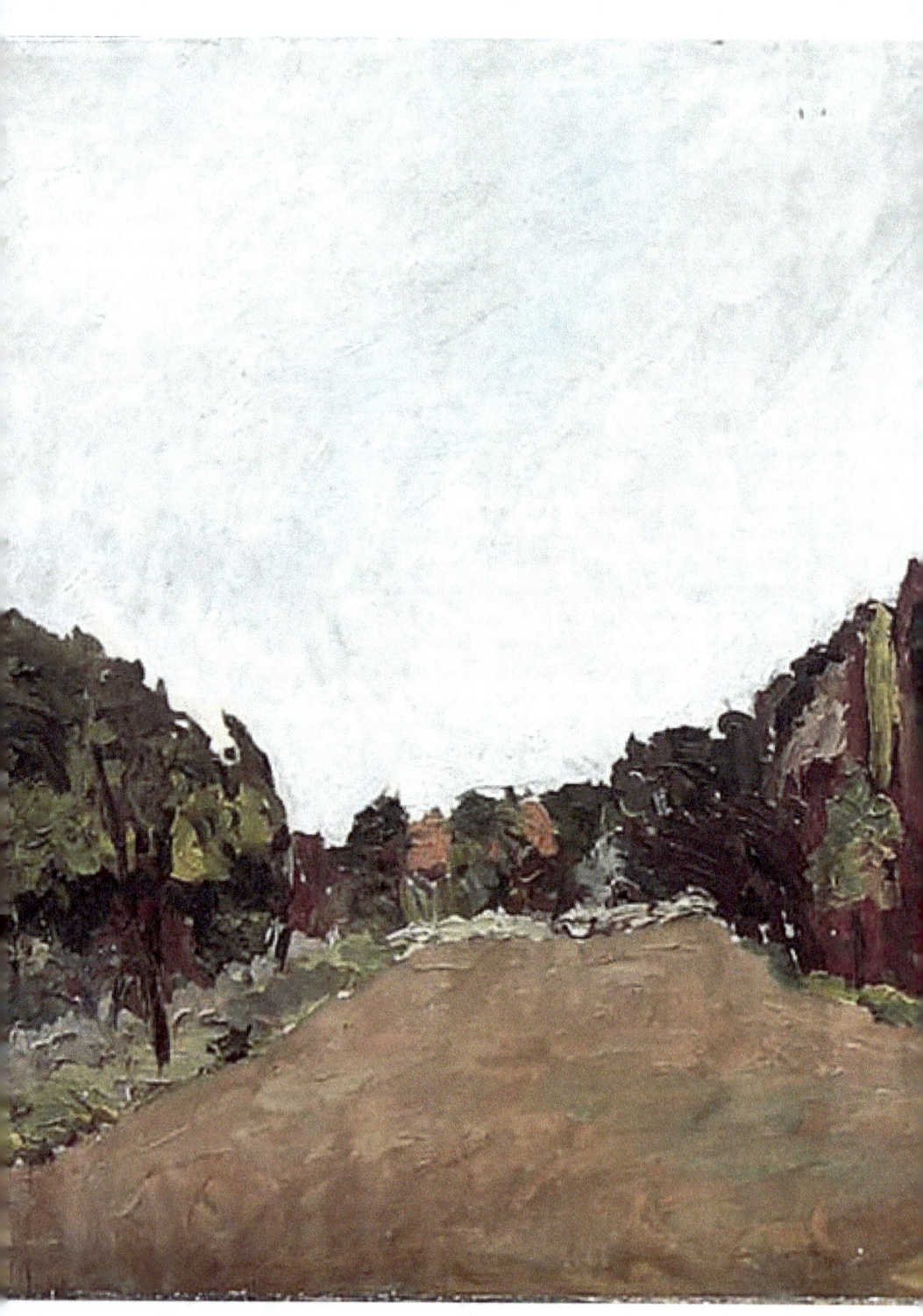

2.3 CARACALLA, ROMA, DECEMBER 28, 1970
OIL ON CANVAS, CM 50x70

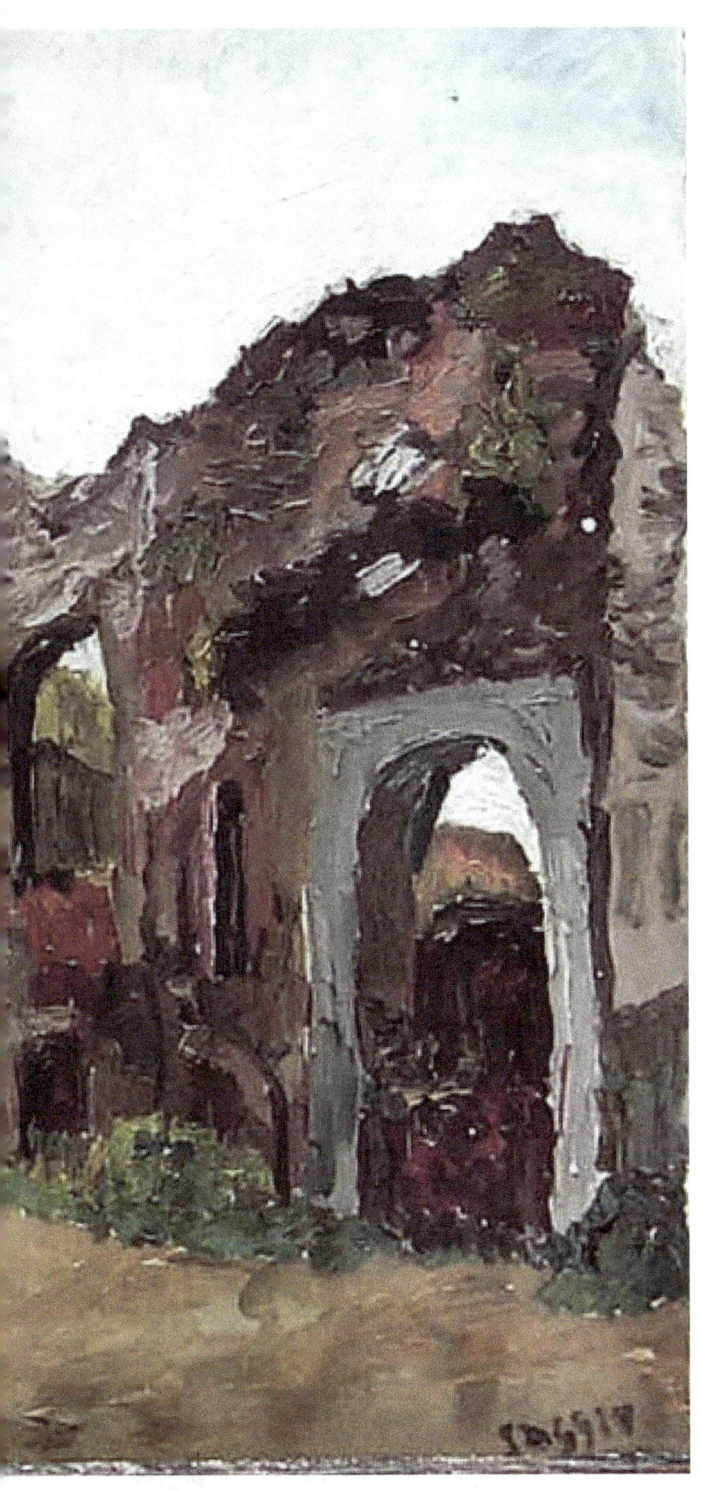

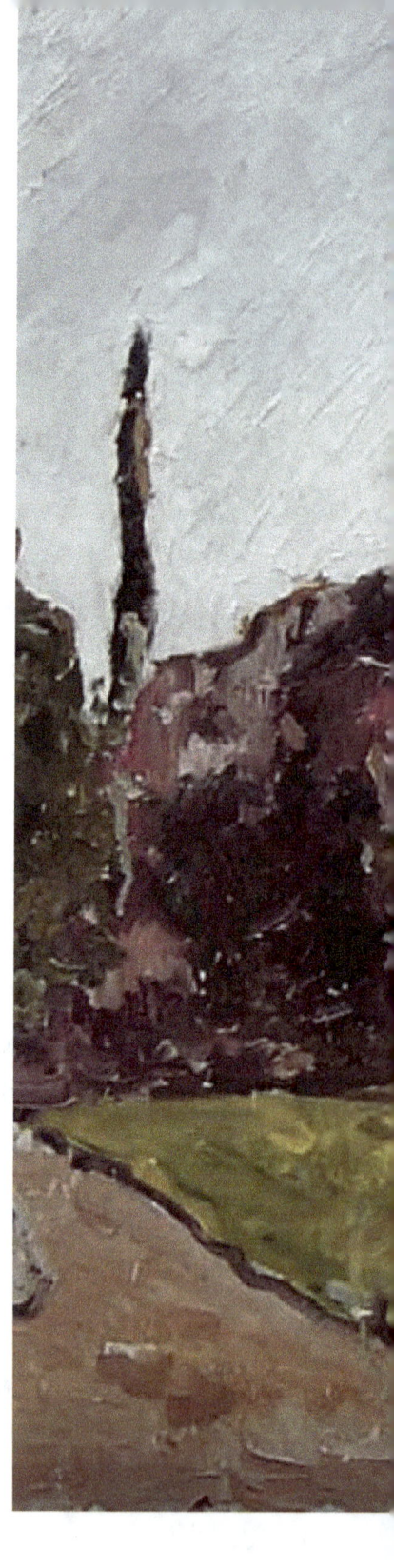

2.4 ANFITEATRO CASTRENSE, ROMA, DECEMBER 23, 1970
OIL ON CANVAS, CM 60X70

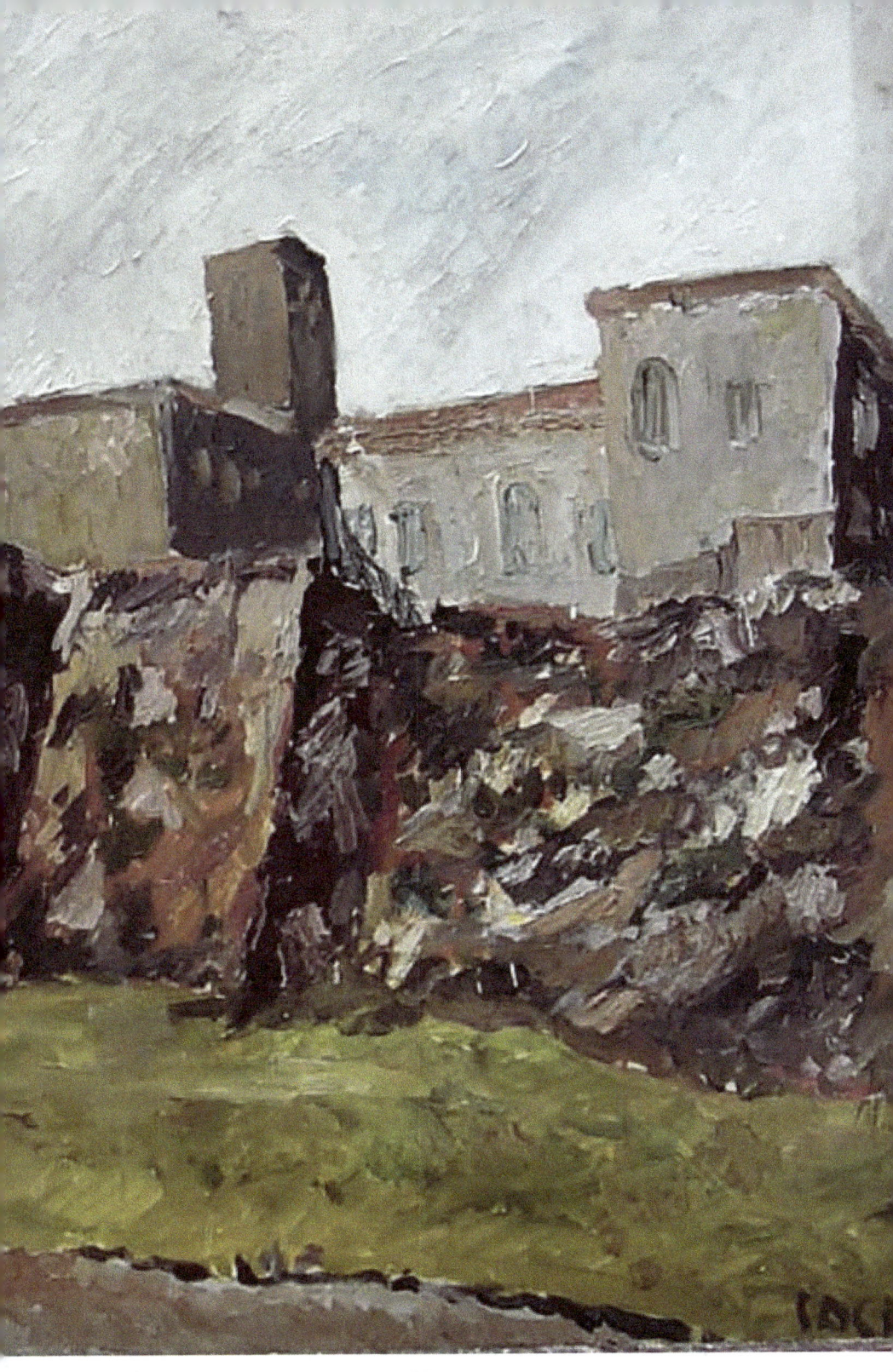

LIGHT IMPRESSIONS

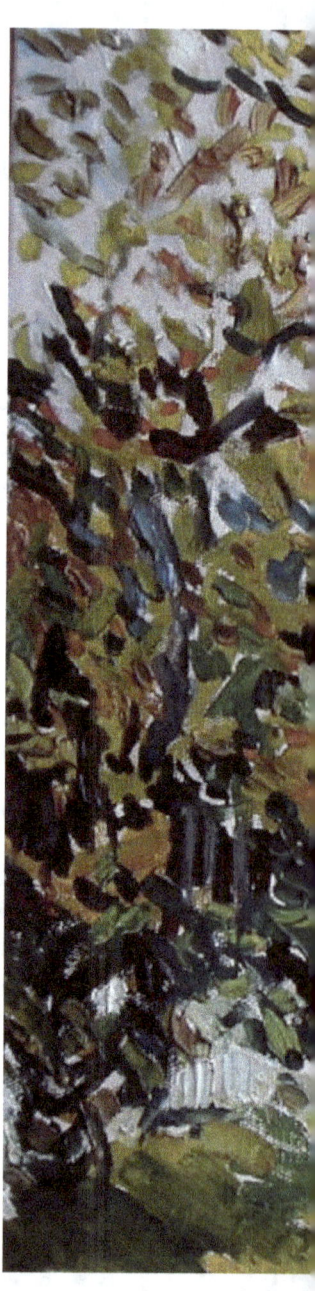

3.1 FOREST ON SAN GREGORIO STREET,
ROMA, OCTOBER 1970
OIL ON CANVAS, CM 40x50

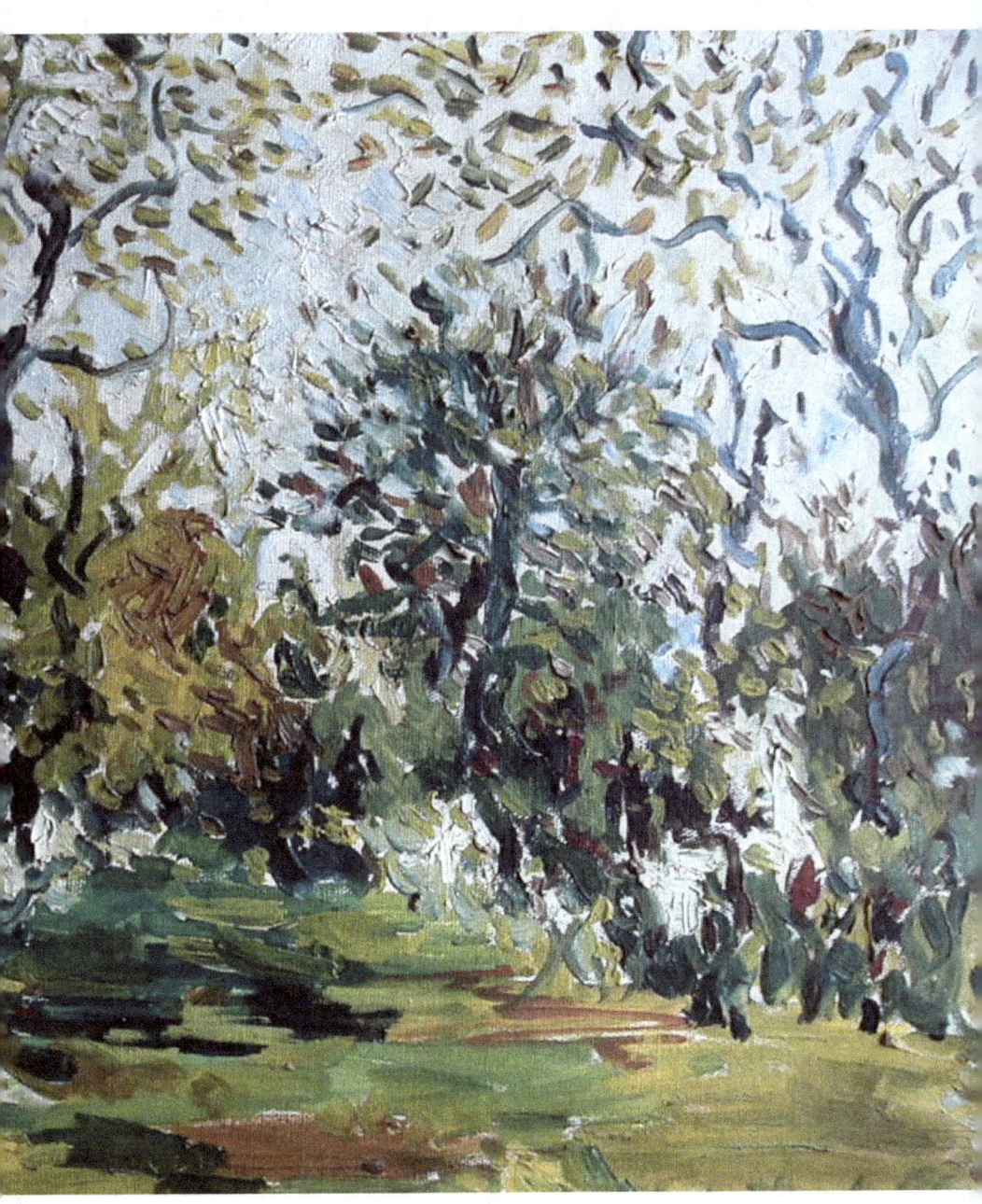

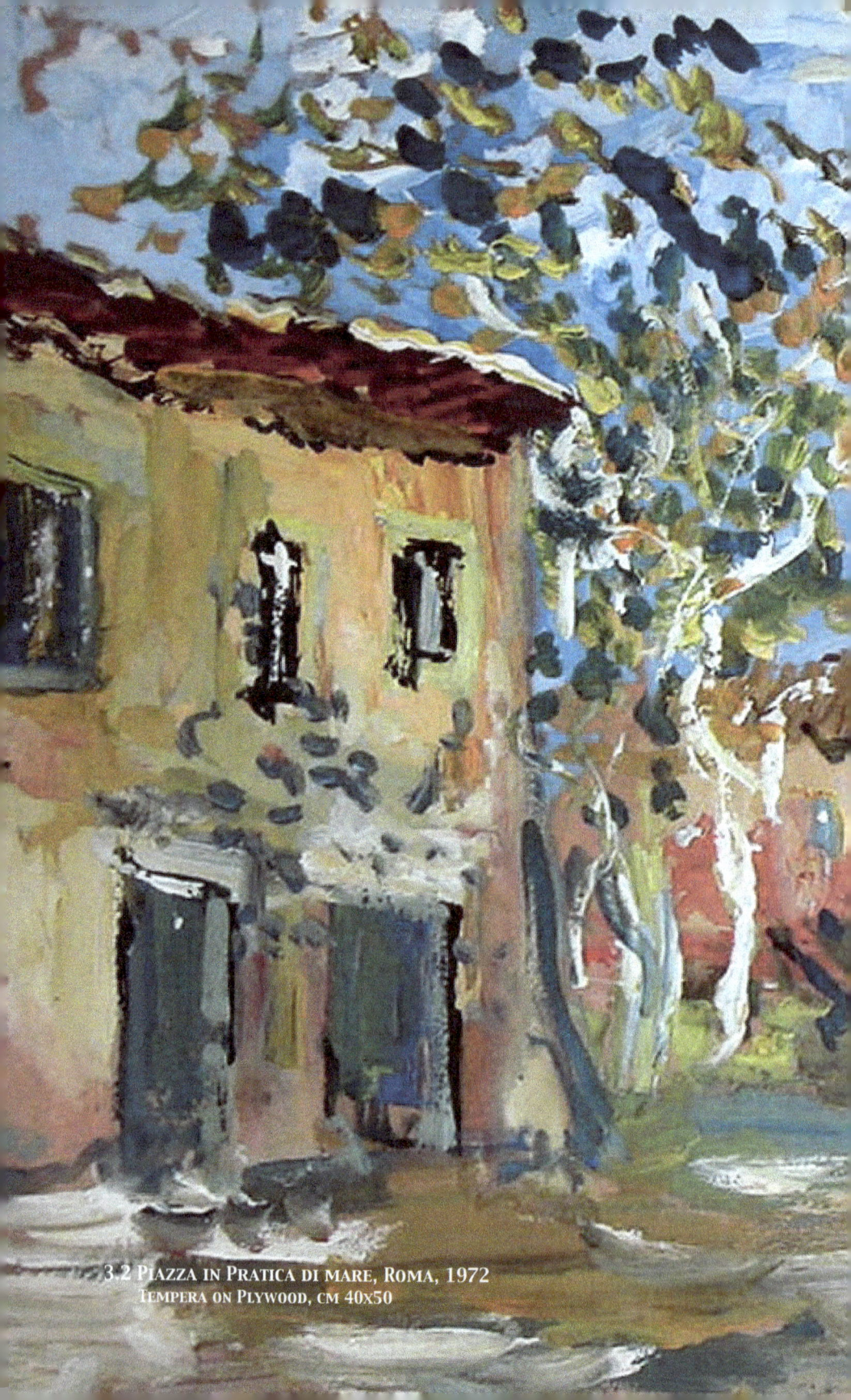

3.2 Piazza in Pratica di mare, Roma, 1972
Tempera on Plywood, cm 40x50

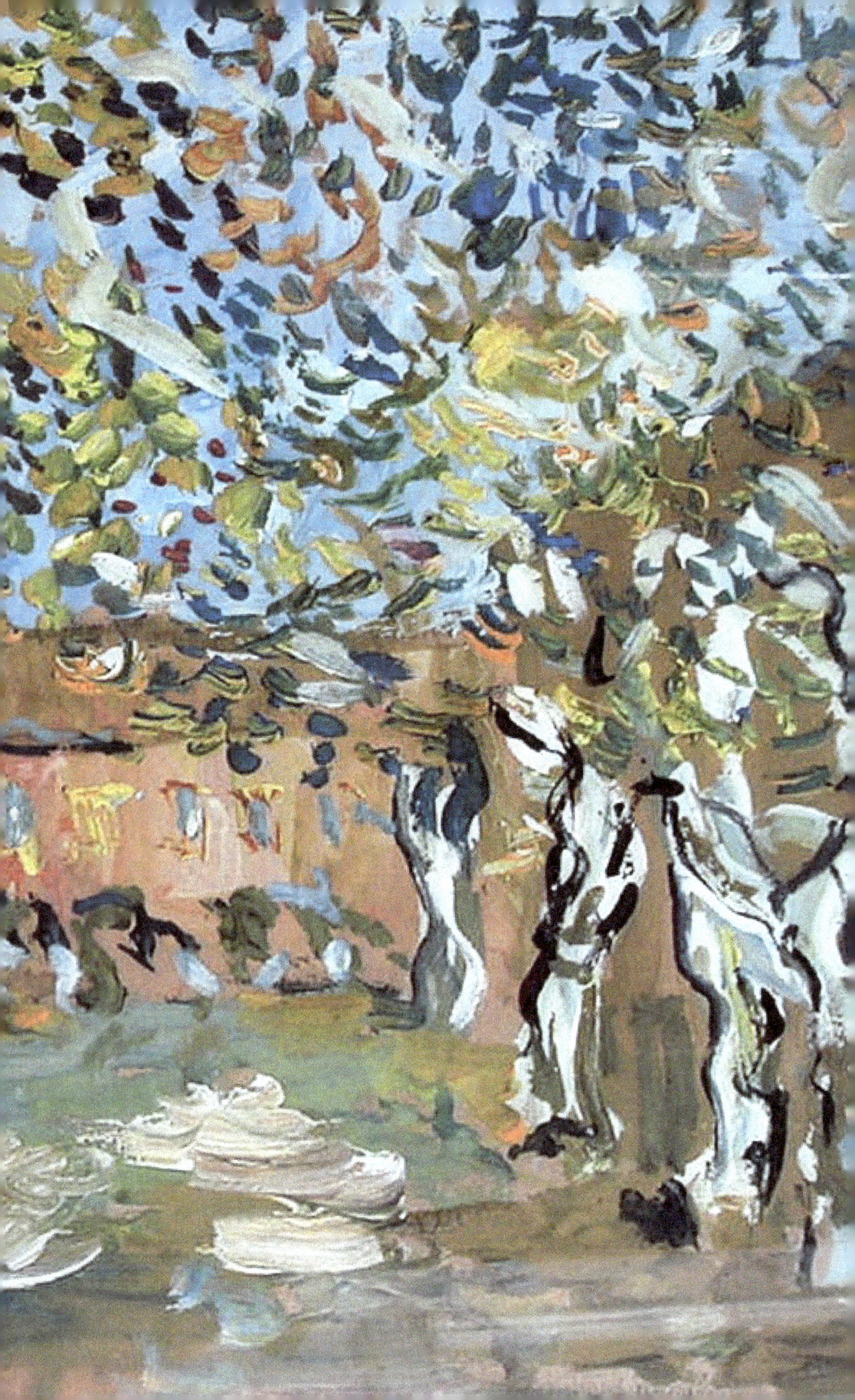

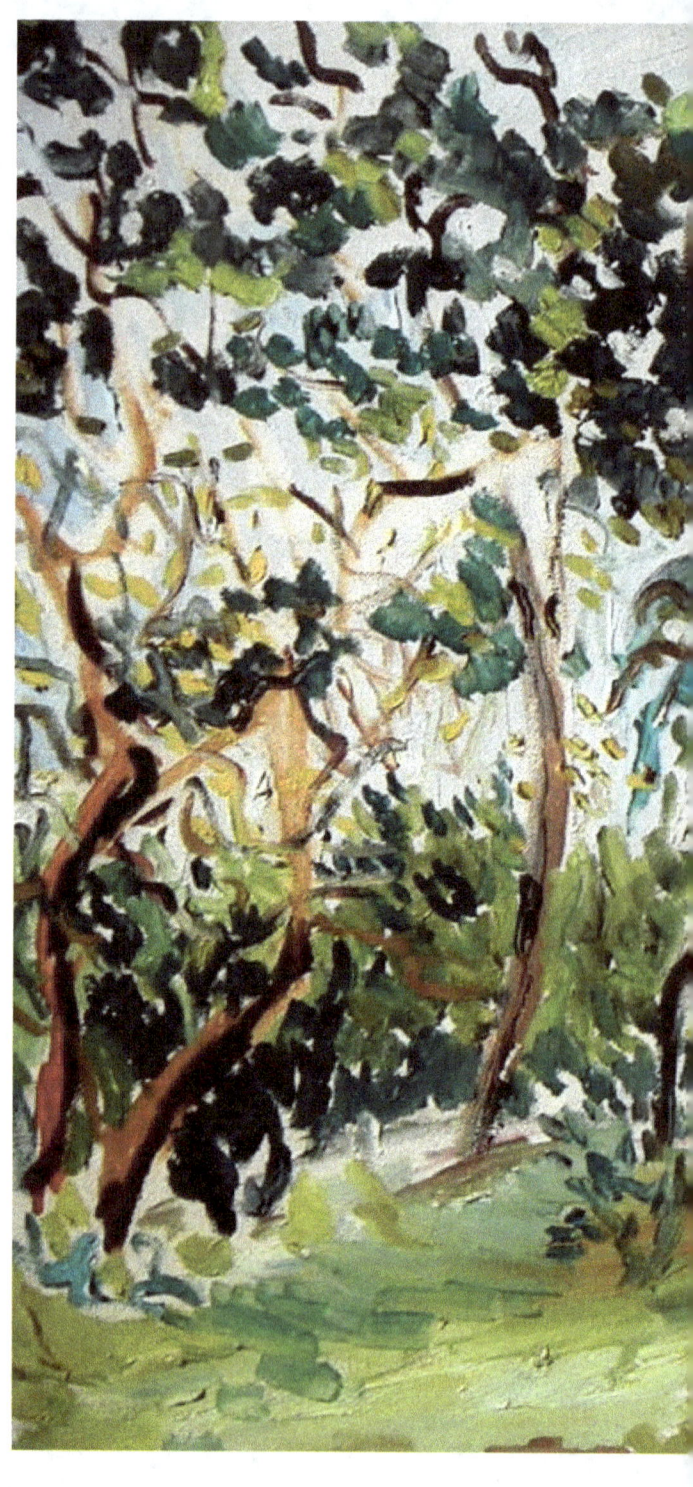

3.3 Villa Celimontana, Roma, January 1972
Oil on canvas, cm 50x70

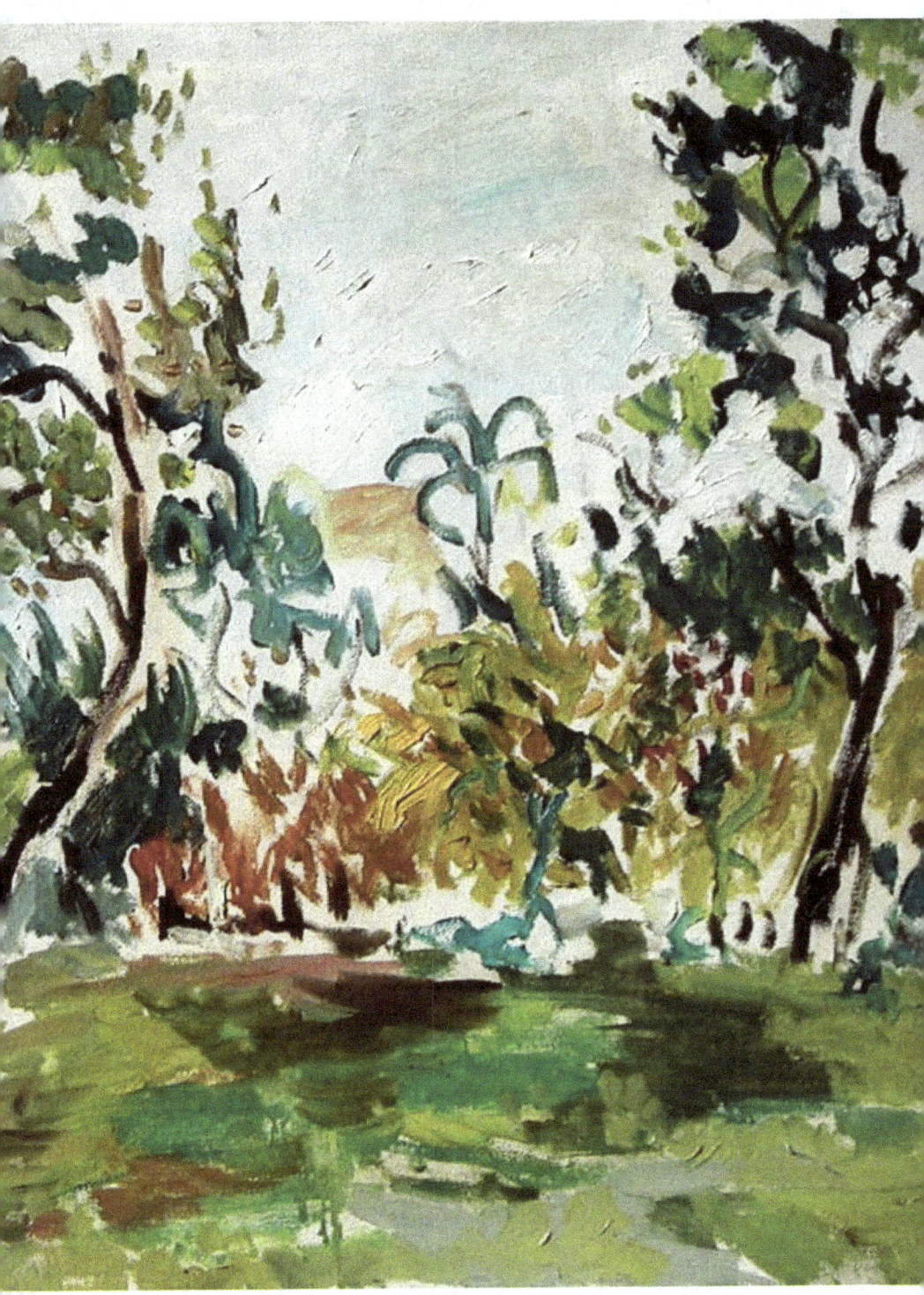

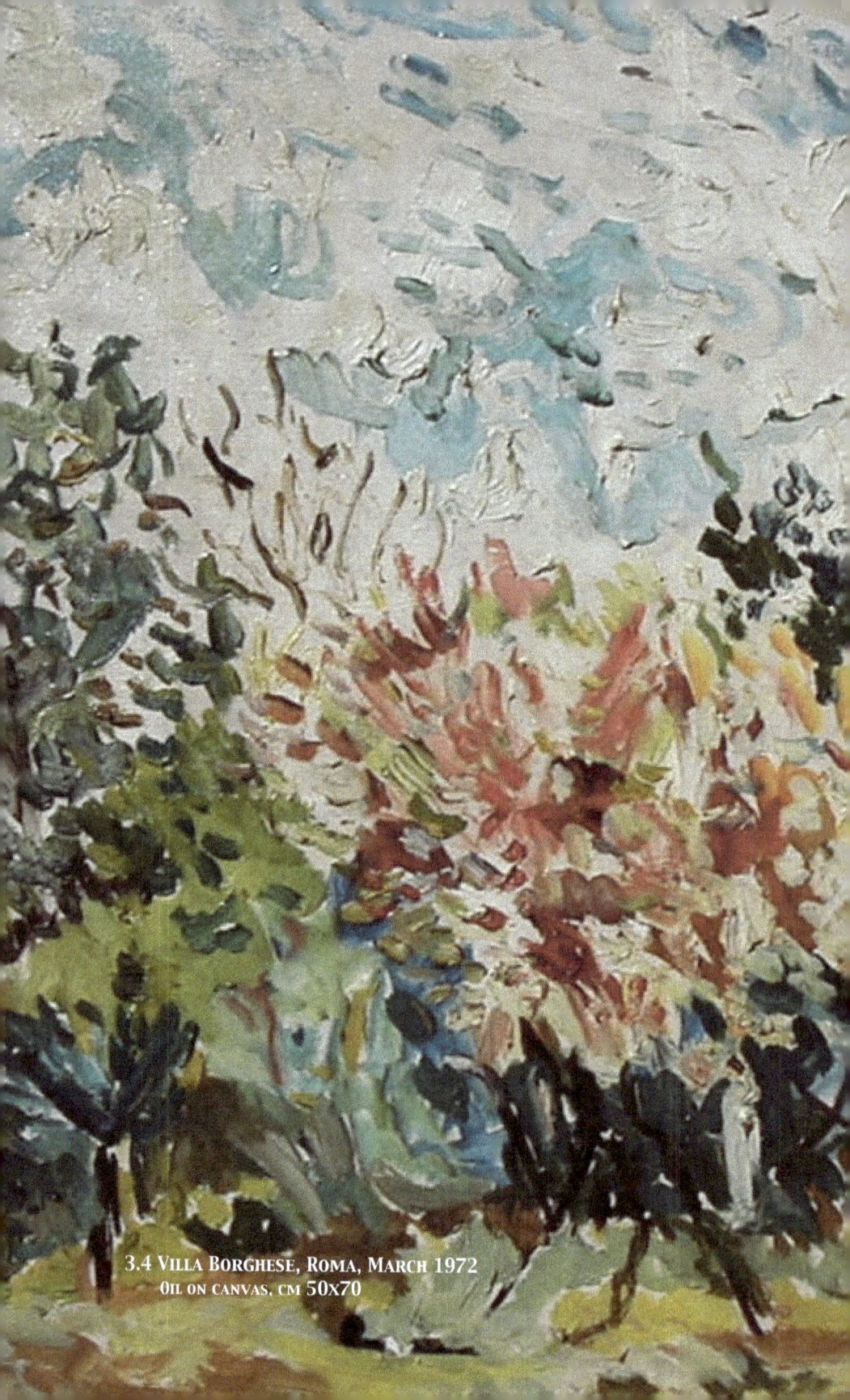

3.4 Villa Borghese, Roma, March 1972
Oil on canvas, cm 50x70

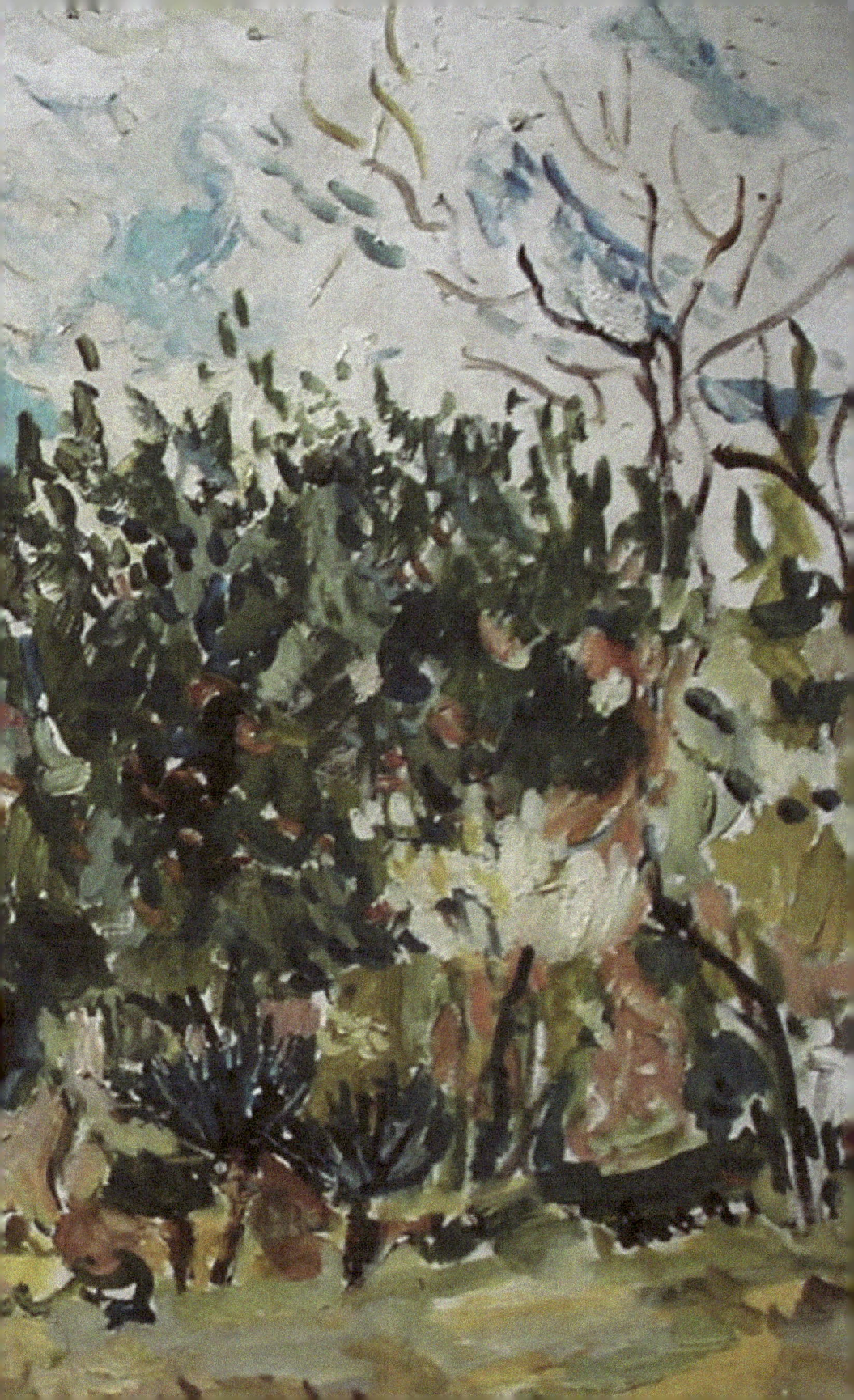

WHITE CITY

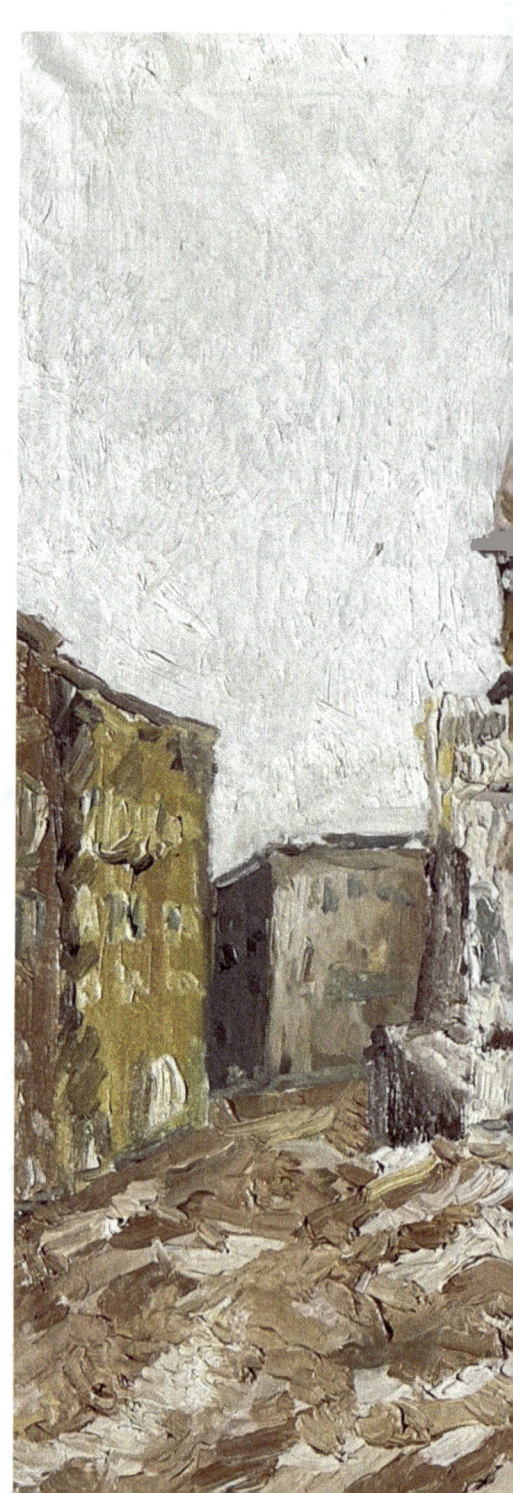

4.1 Santa Maria Maggiore, Roma, May 1971 Oil on canvas, cm 60x70

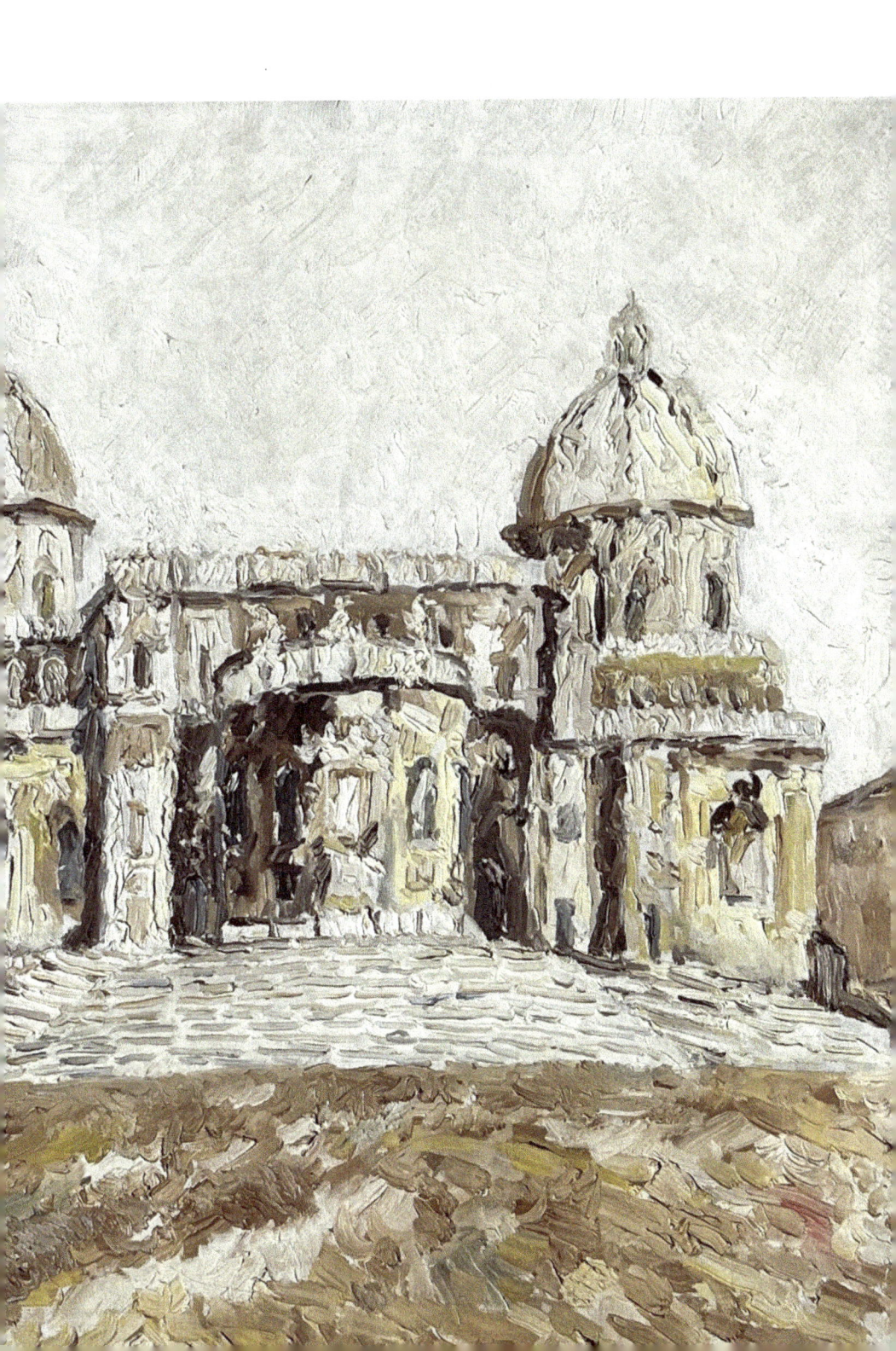

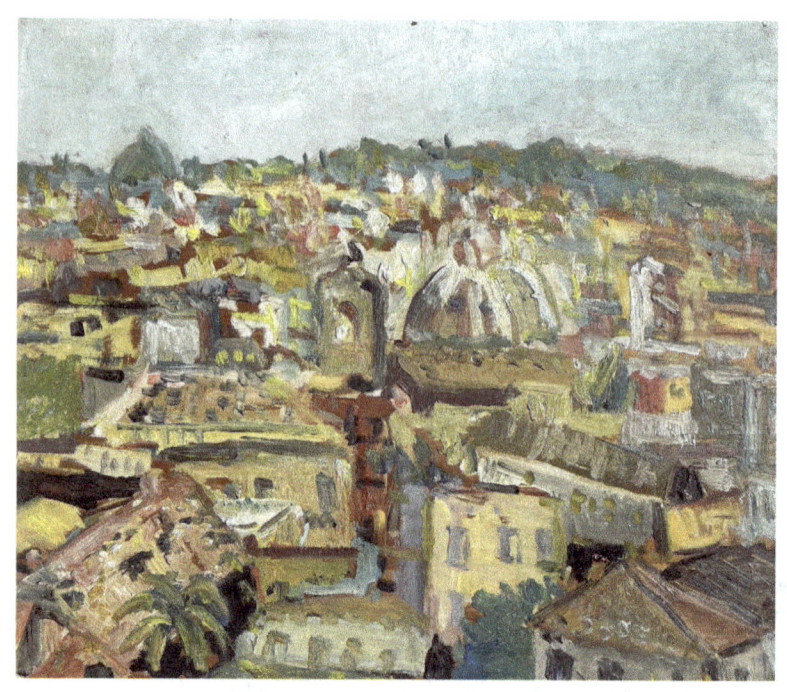

4.2 VIEW FROM PINCIO, ROMA, 1973
OIL ON CARDBOARD, 35X40

4.3 VILLA SCIARRA, ROMA, JUNE 1971
OIL ON CANVAS, CM 40X50

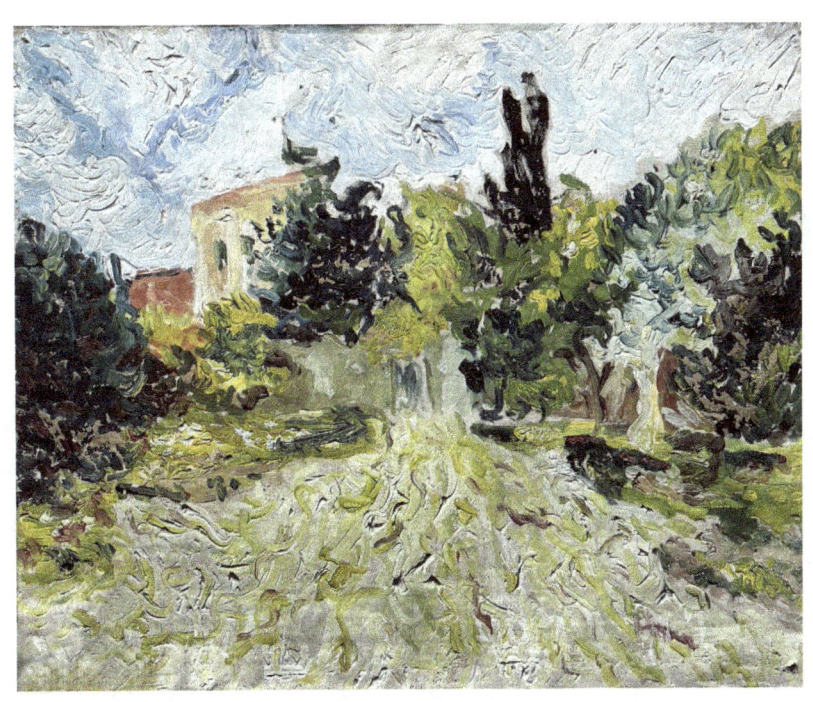

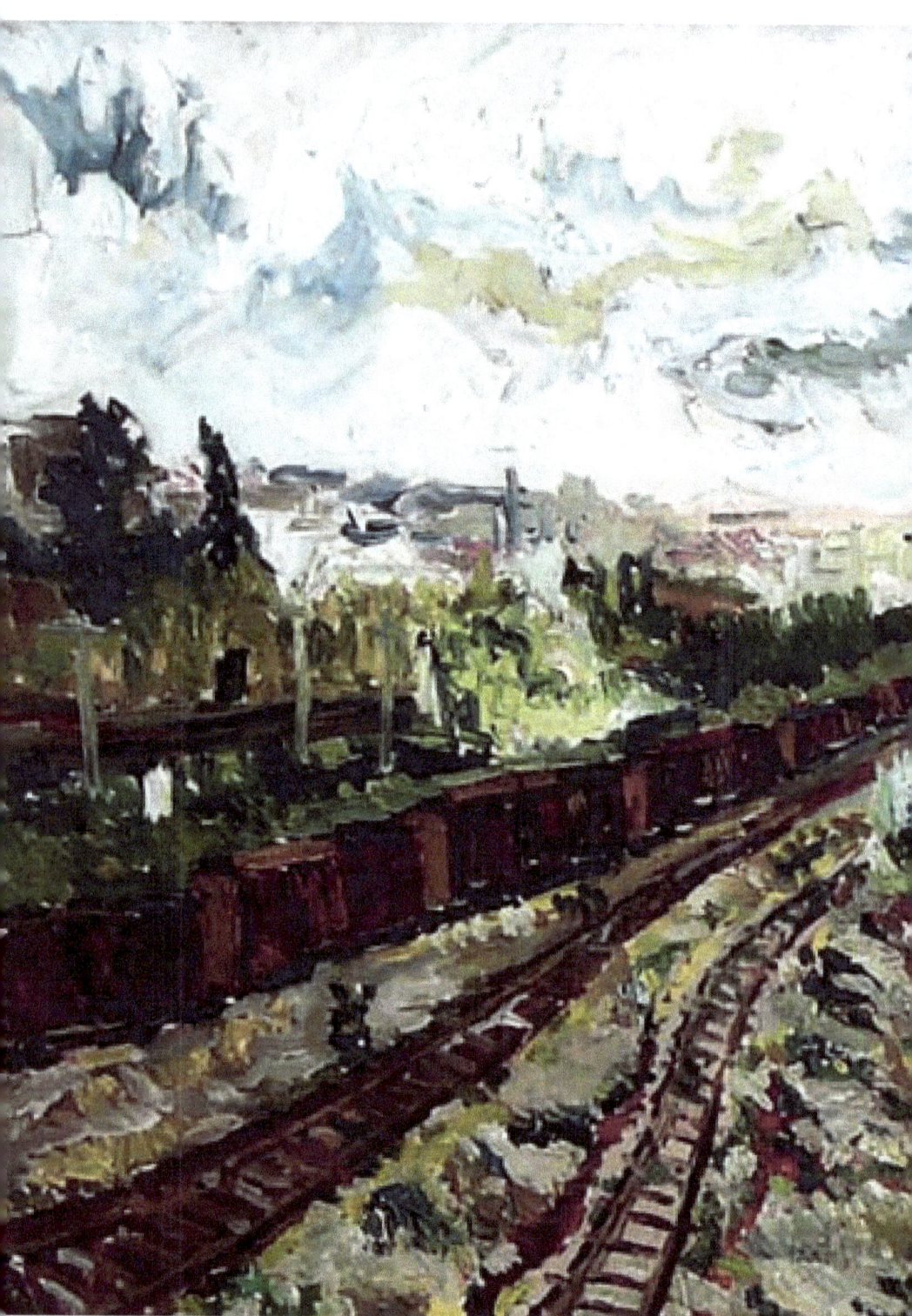

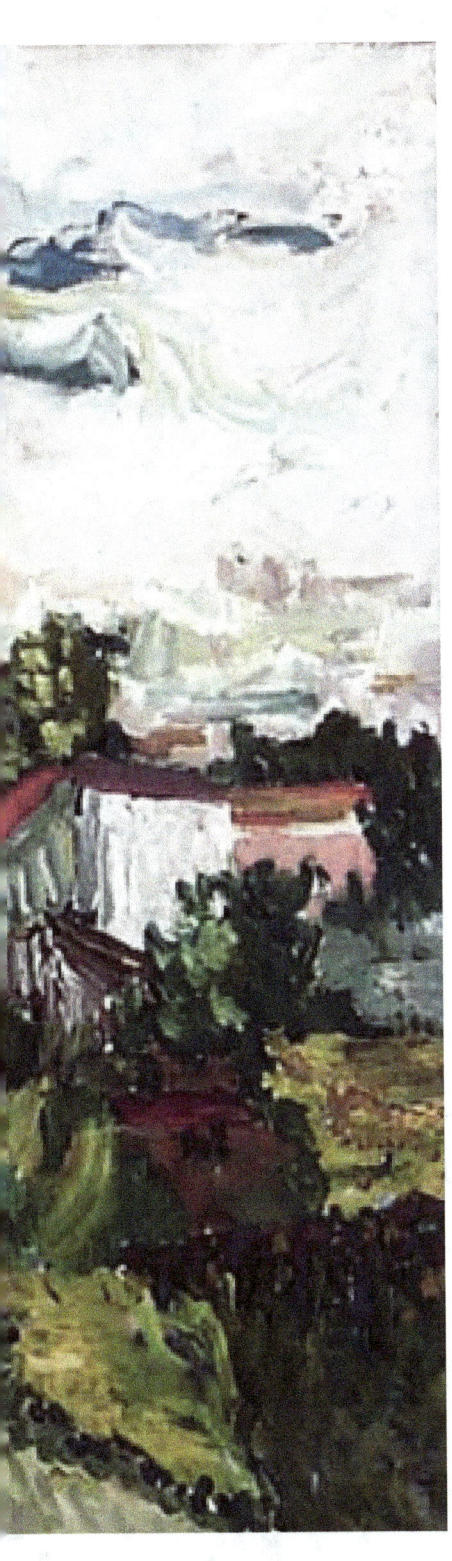

4.4 Railway from Colombo street, Roma, July 1972
Oil on canvas, cm 50x60

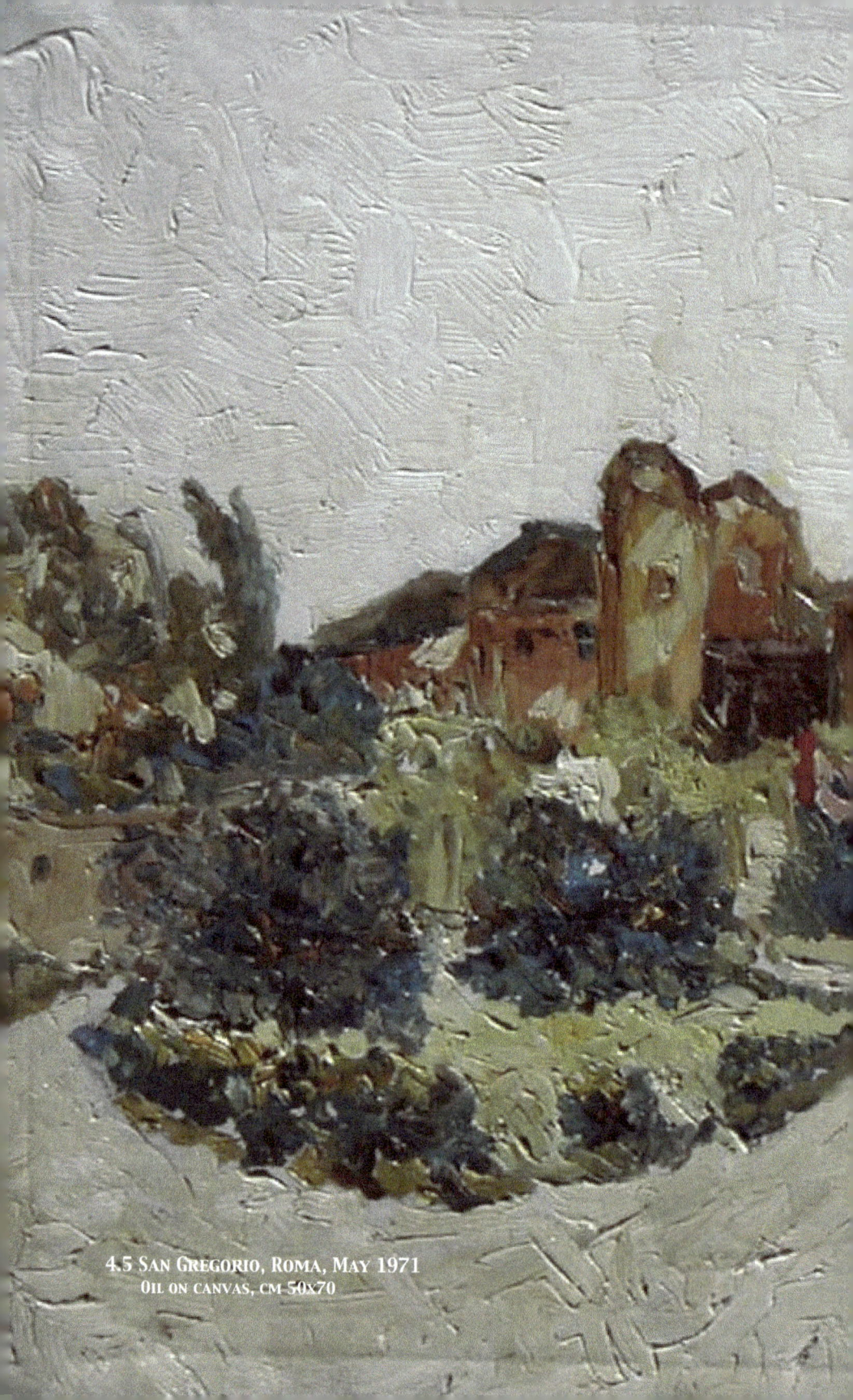

4.5 San Gregorio, Roma, May 1971
Oil on canvas, cm 50x70

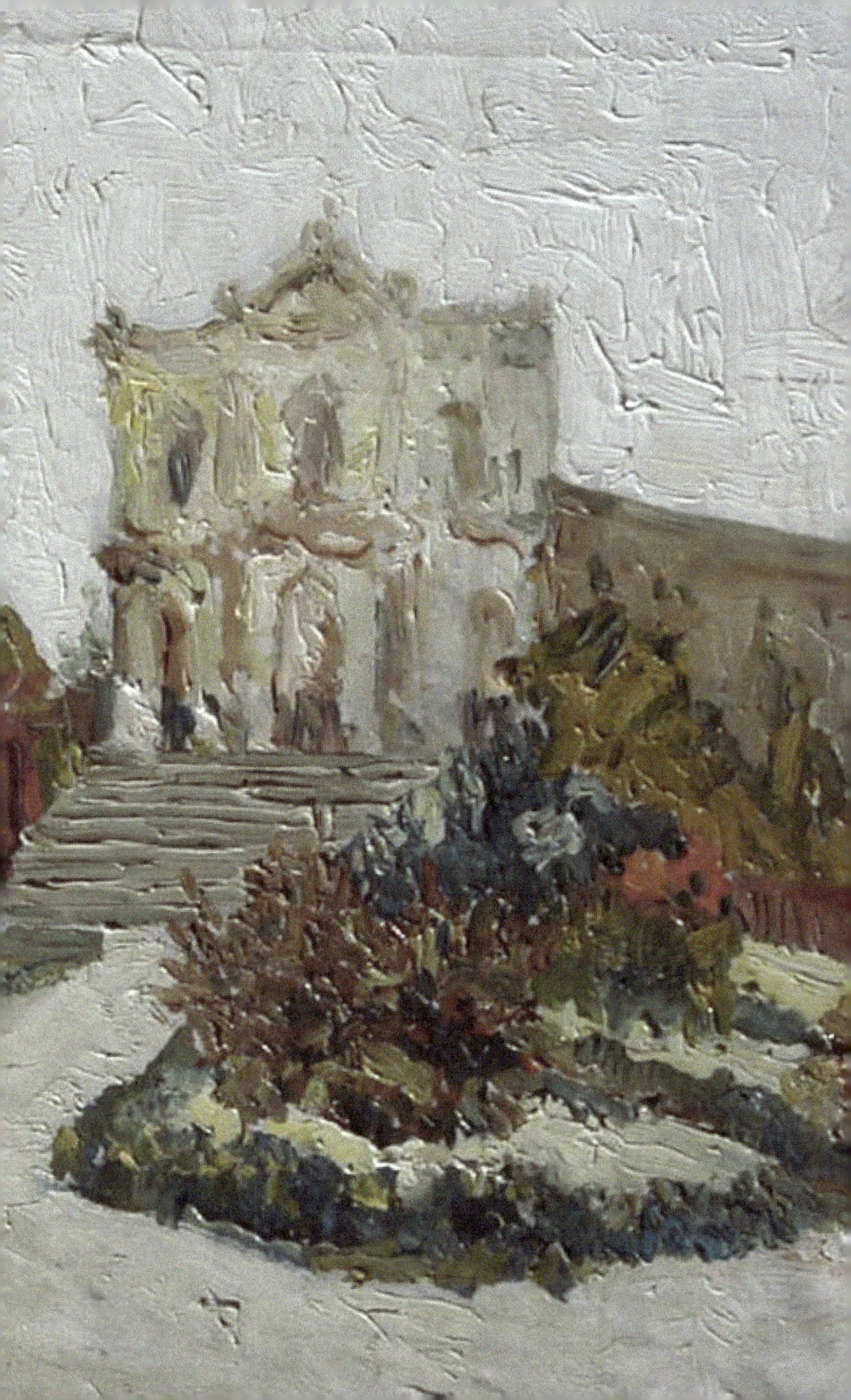

BACK IN SICILY

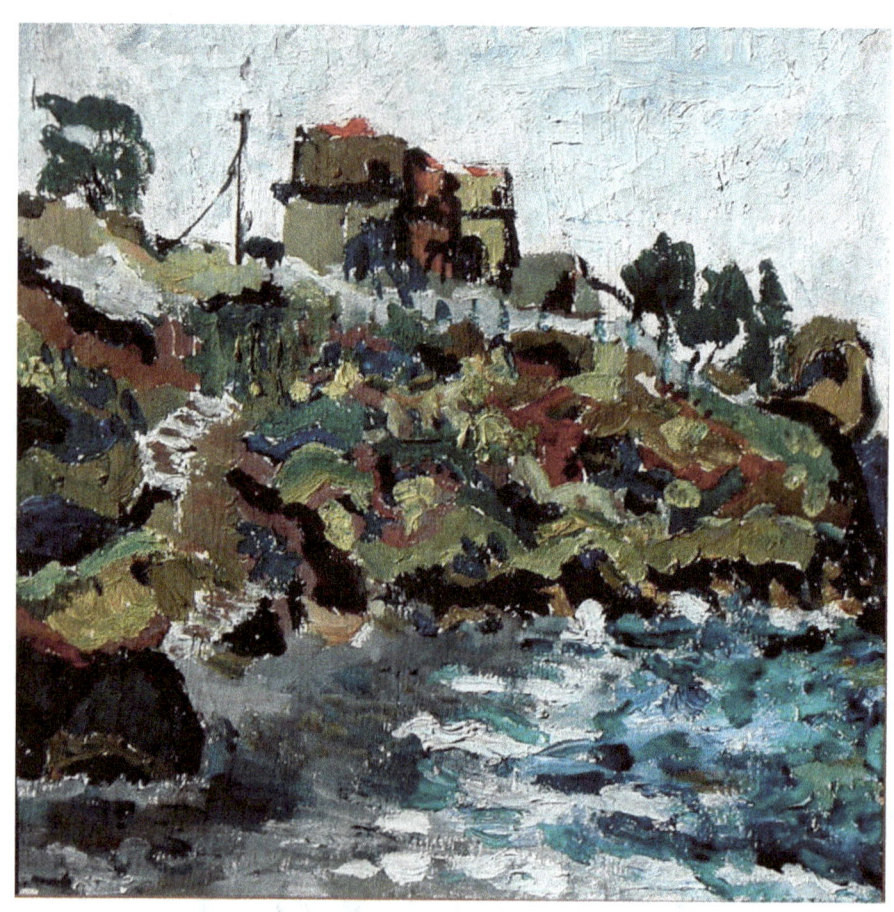

5.1 Scafa a Testa di Monaco, Sicilia, June 1971
   Oil on canvas, cm 30x30
5.2 Scafa con vista Capo d'Orlando, Sicilia, June 1971
   Oil on canvas, cm 50x70

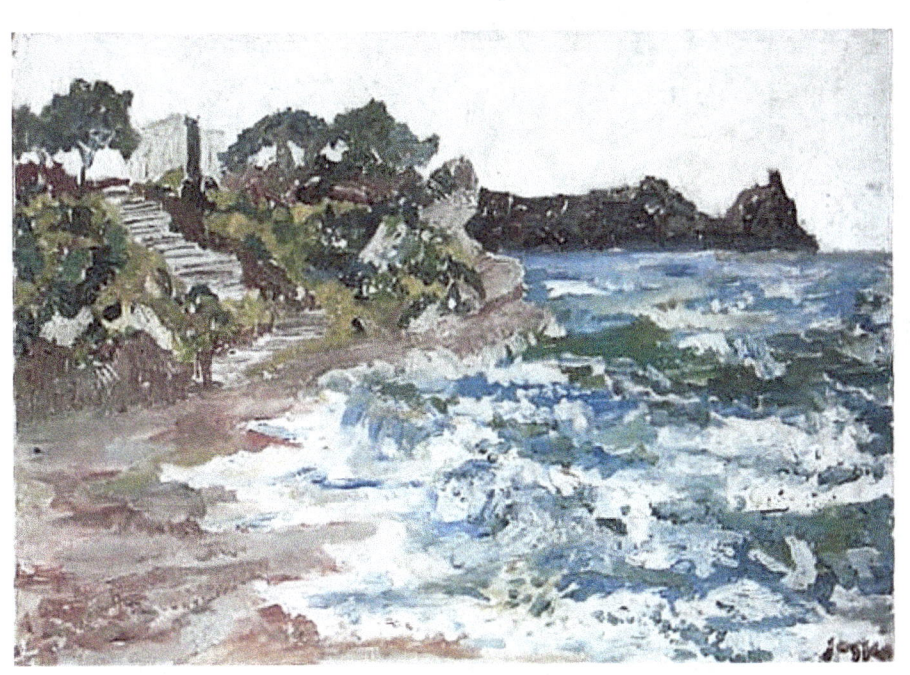

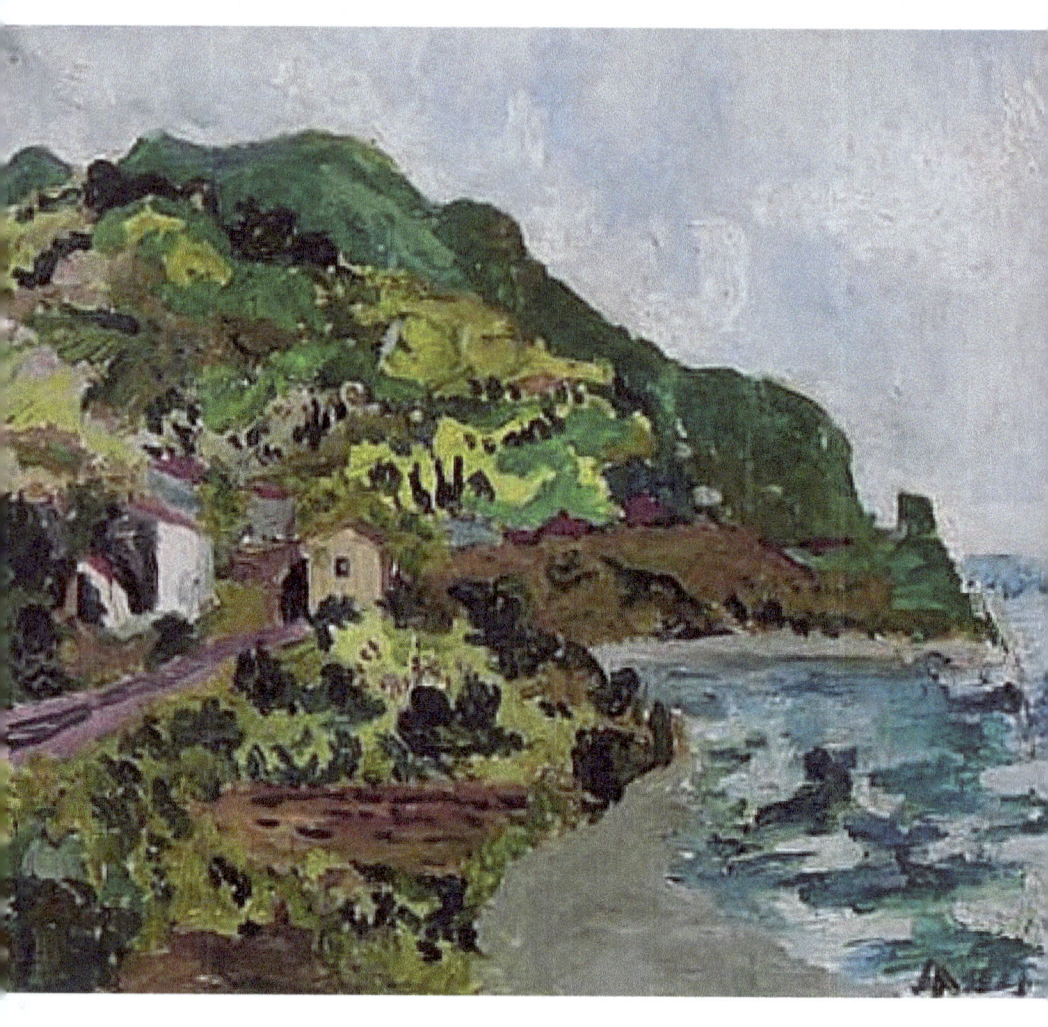

5.3 Villa Ridente, Sicilia June 1972
   Oil on canvas, cm 60x70
5.4 La Fiumara di Brolo, Sicilia June 1972
   Oil on canvas, cm 50x70

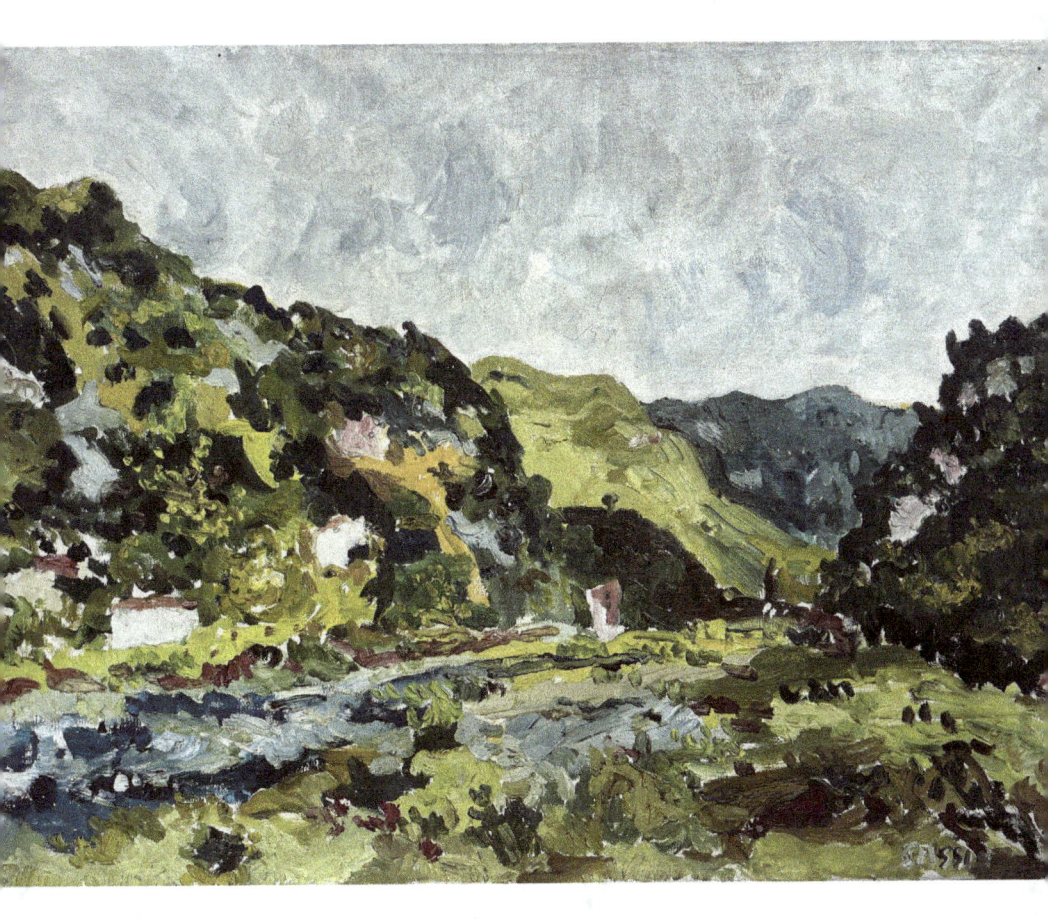

VINCENT AND PAUL

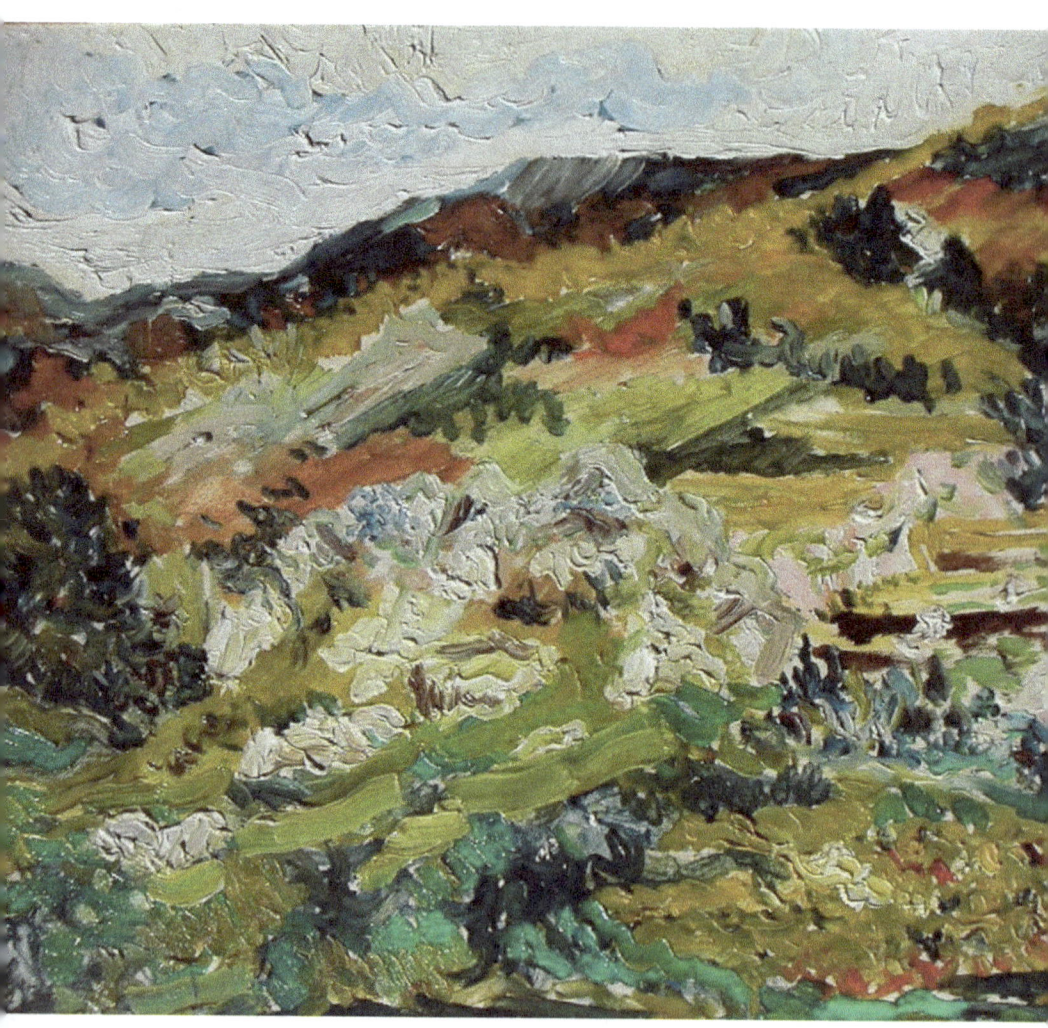

6.1 Prati di Tivoli, Roma, July 1971
   Oil on canvas, cm 40x50

6.2 Prati di Tivoli, Roma, July 1971
   Oil on canvas, cm 40x50

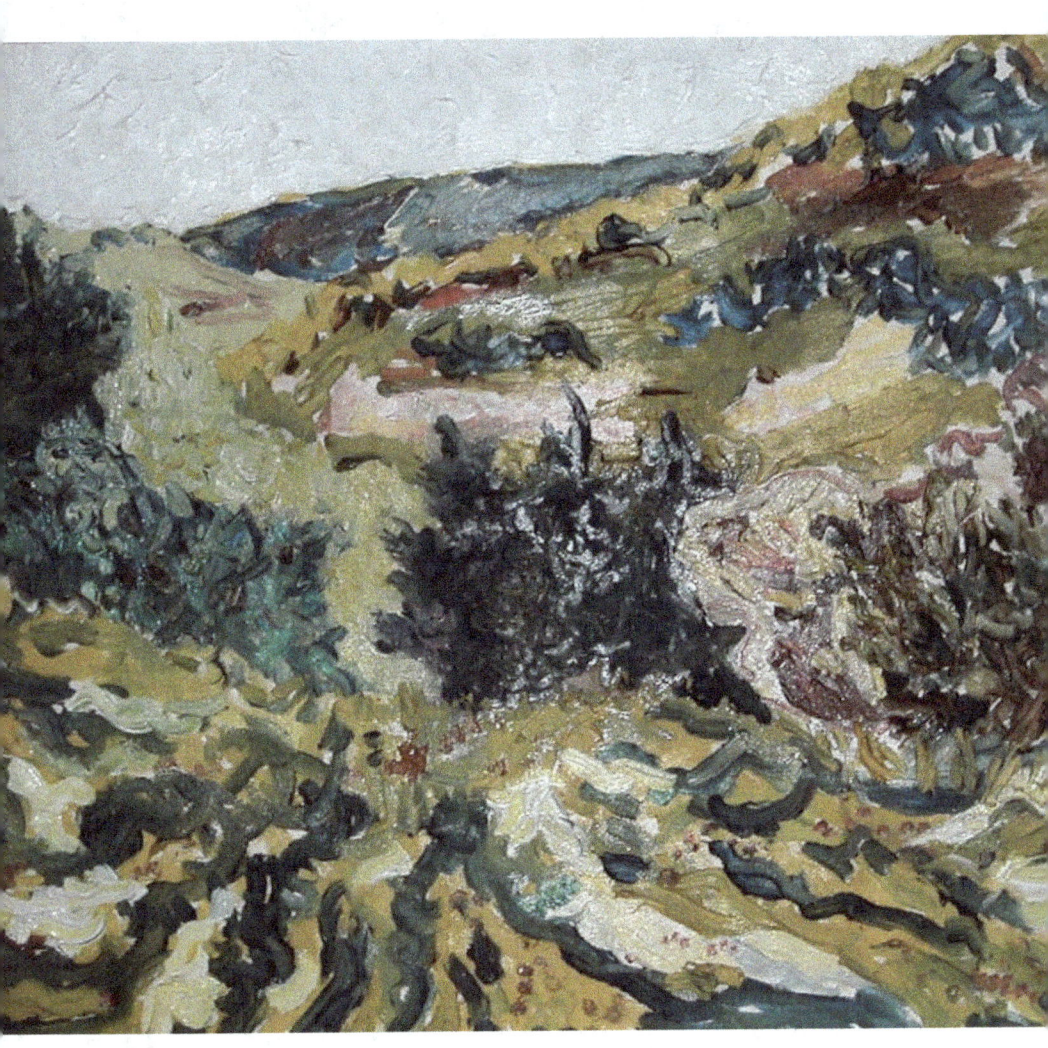

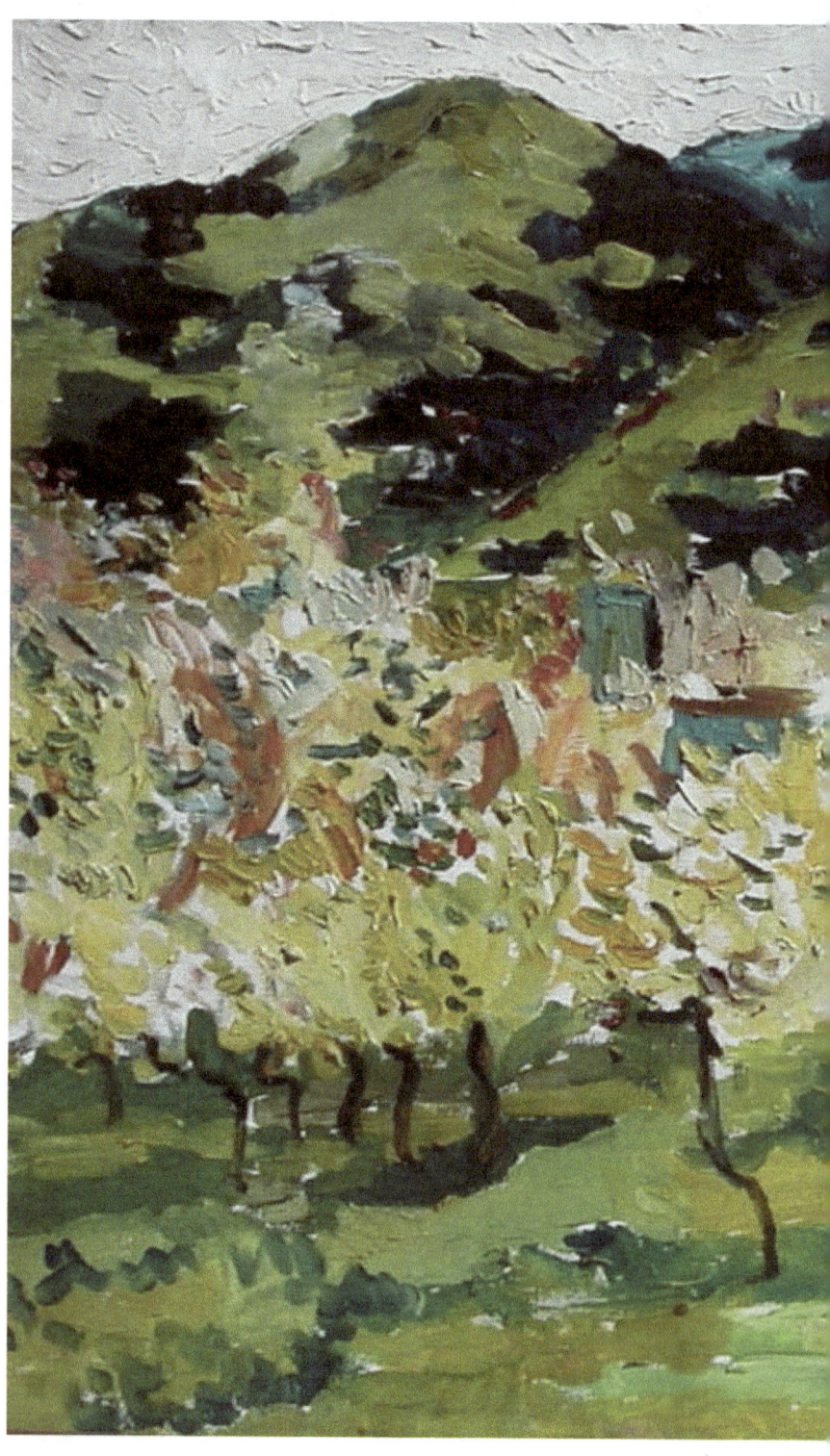

6.3 PRIMAVERA A SEZZE, LATINA APRIL 1972
OIL ON CANVAS, CM 50X70

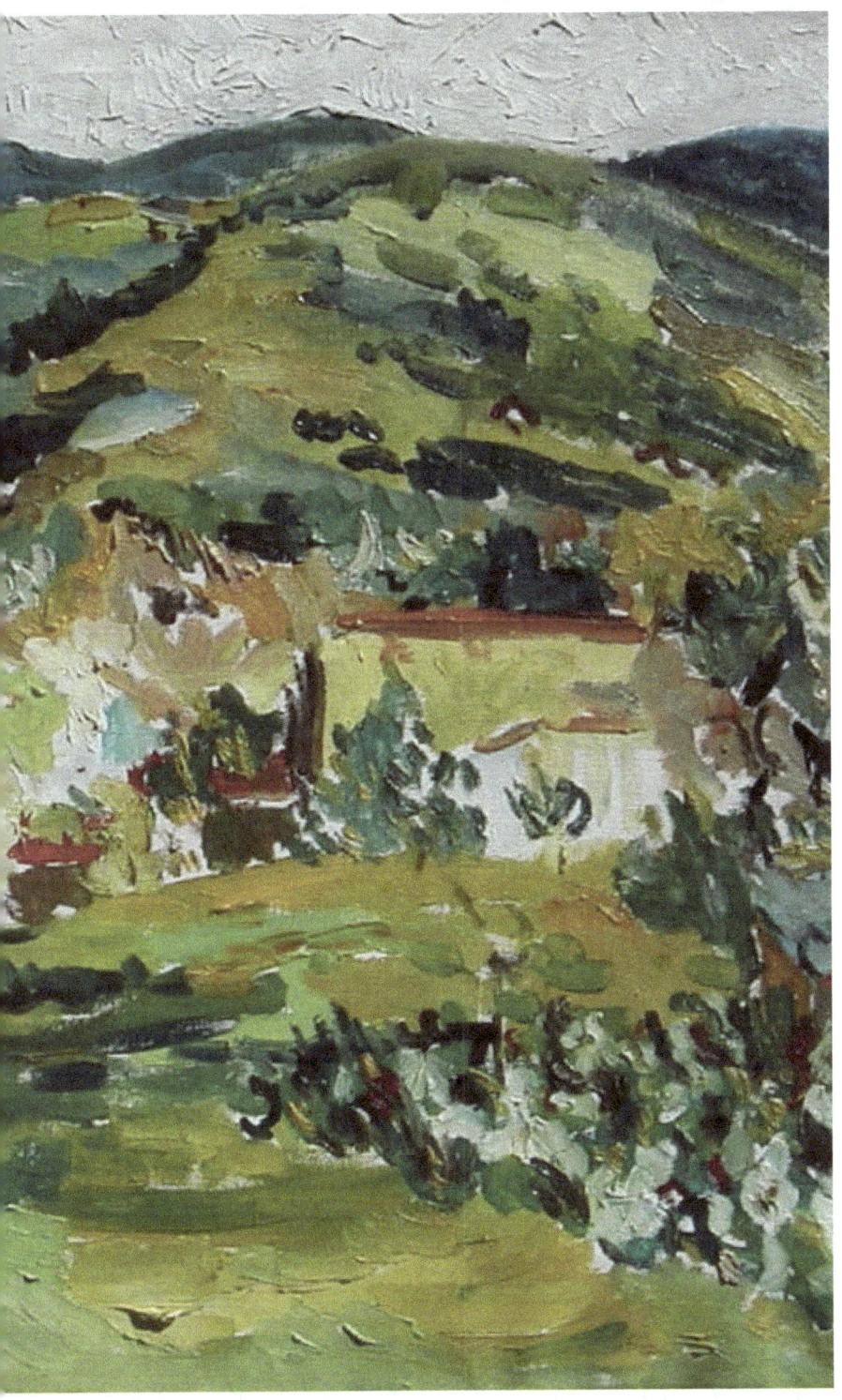

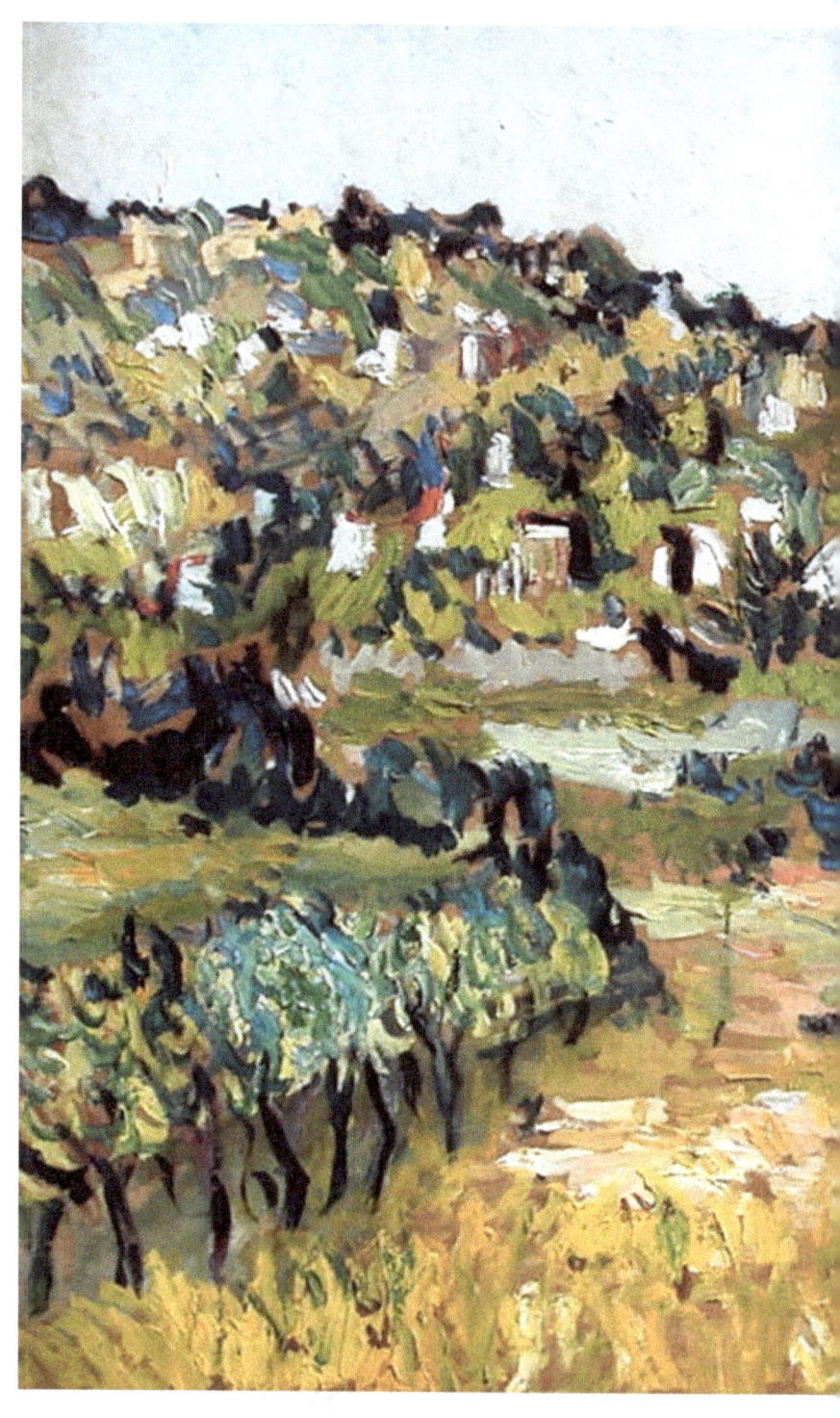

6.4 MIETITURA A SEZZE, LATINA JUNE 1973
OIL ON CARDBOARD, CM 50x70

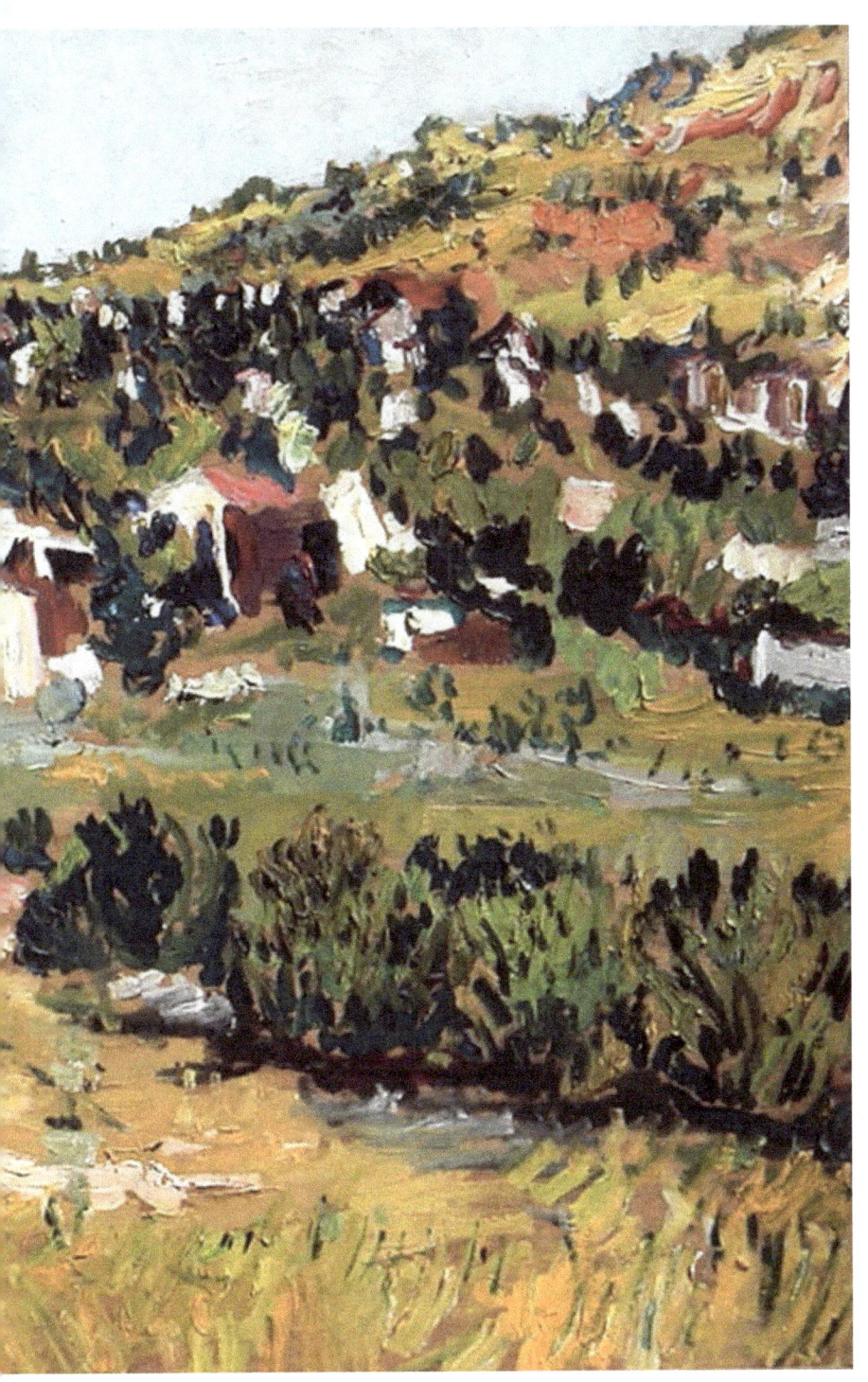

Wandering Magic

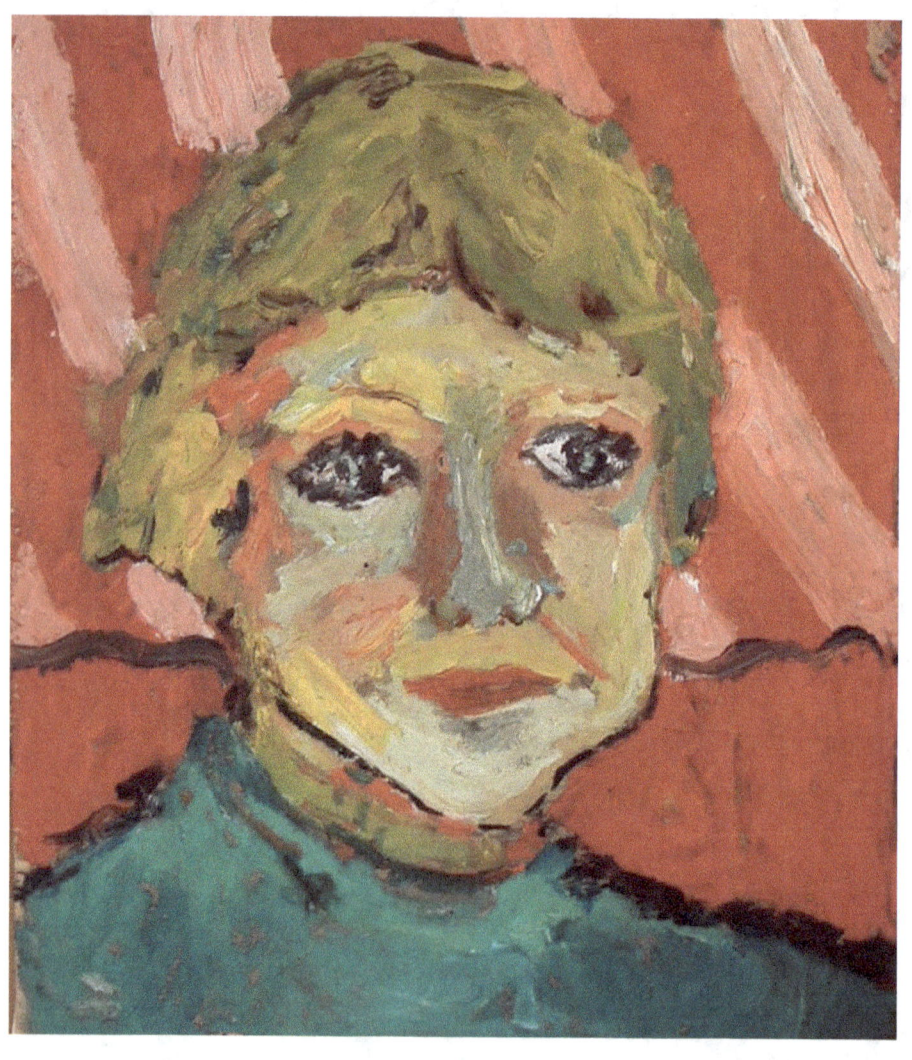

7.1 Caruso, Circo siciliano a v. Taranto, Roma, November 1974
oil on cardboard, cm 25x35

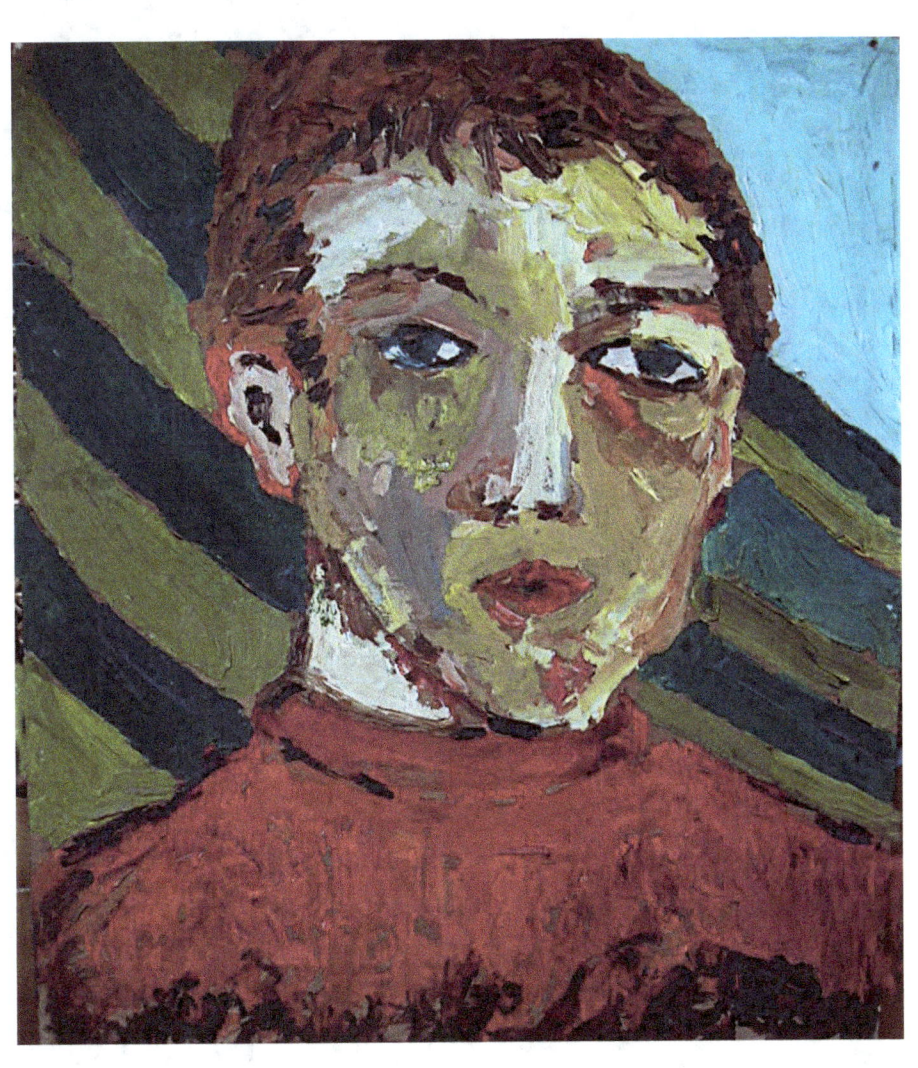

7.2 Caruso, Circo siciliano a v. Taranto, Roma, November 1974
  oil on cardboard, cm 25x35

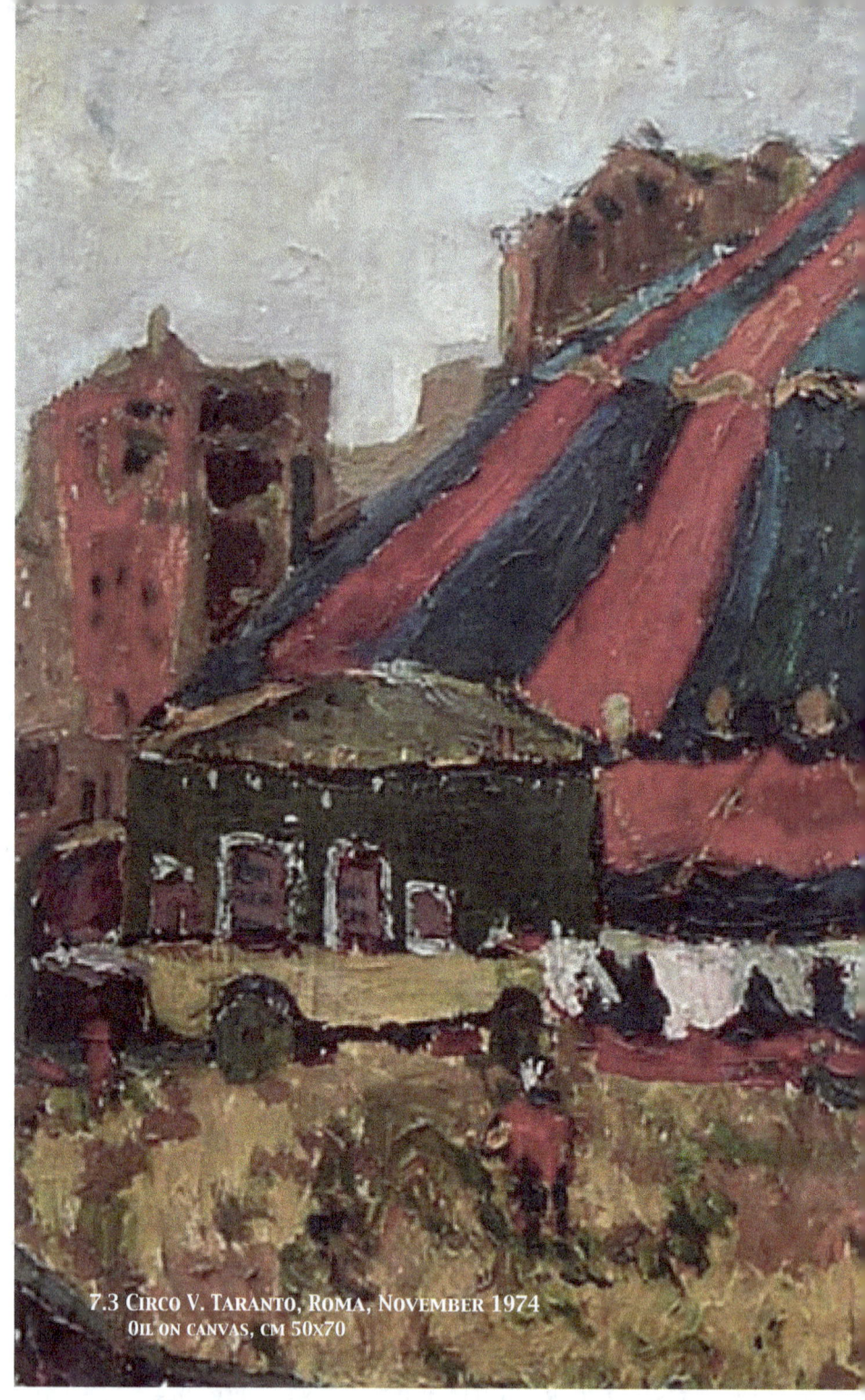

7.3 Circo V. Taranto, Roma, November 1974
Oil on canvas, cm 50x70

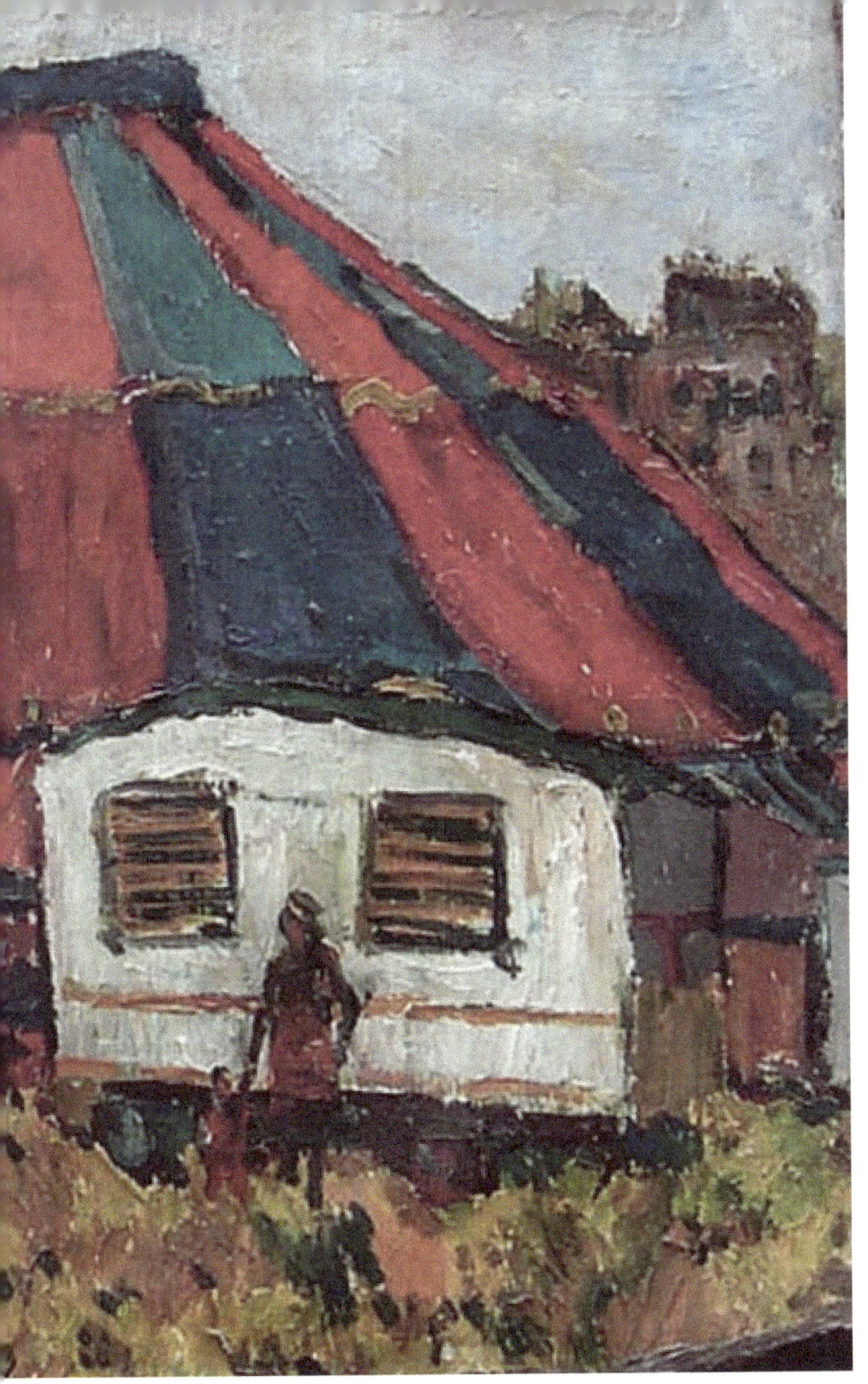

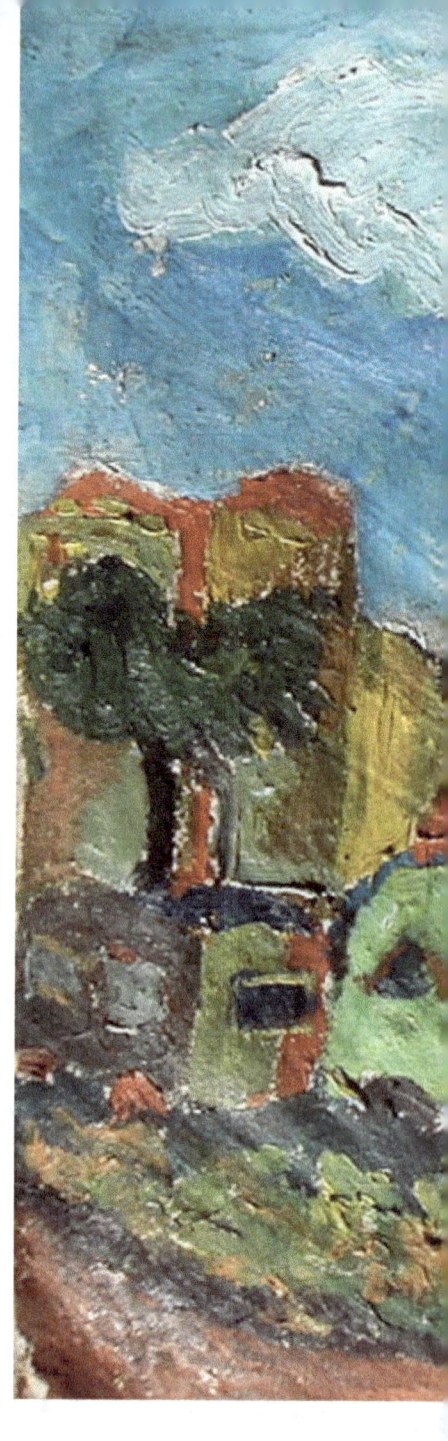

7.3 Circo V. Taranto, Roma, November 1974
Oil on canvas, cm 50x60

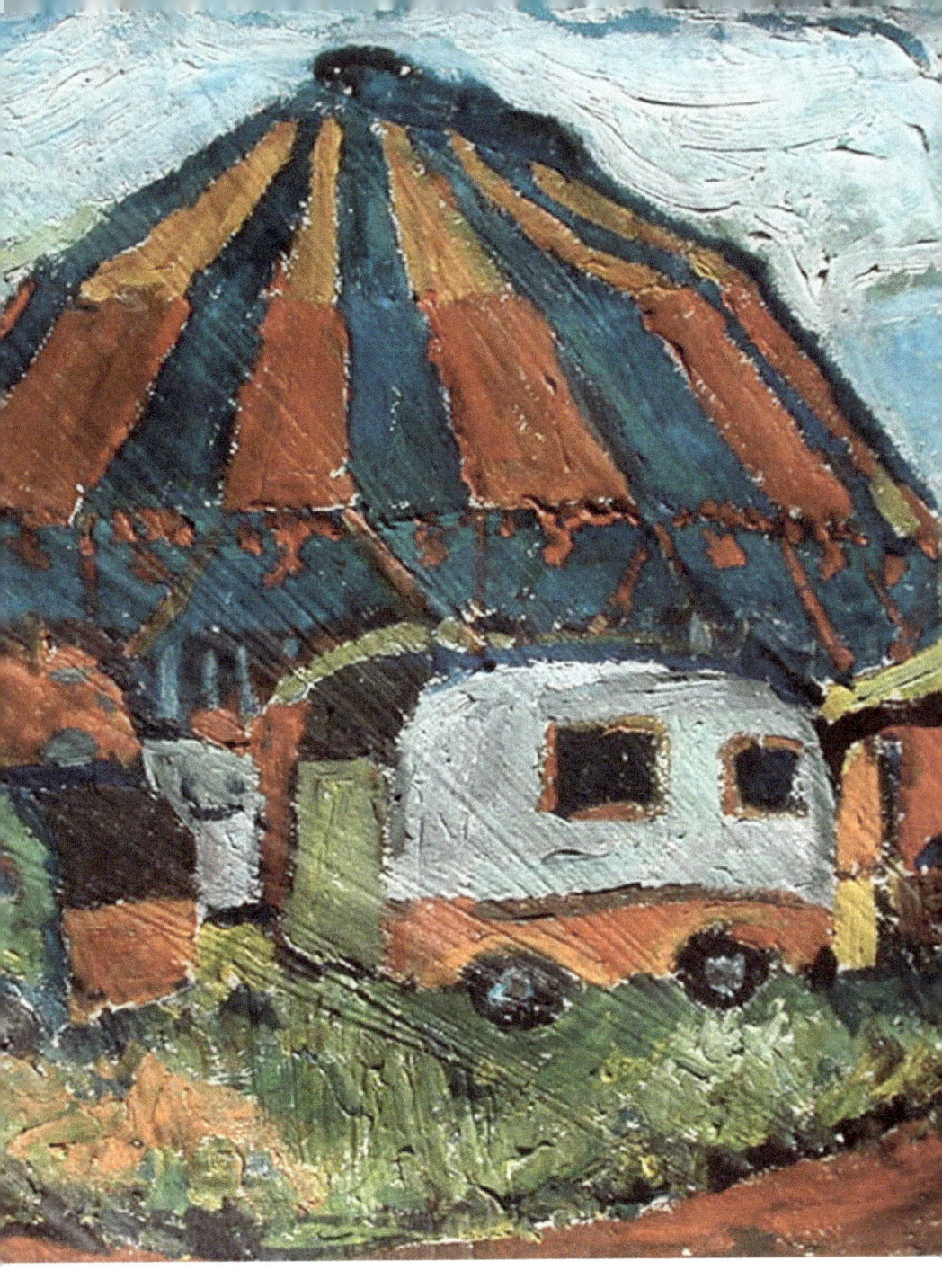

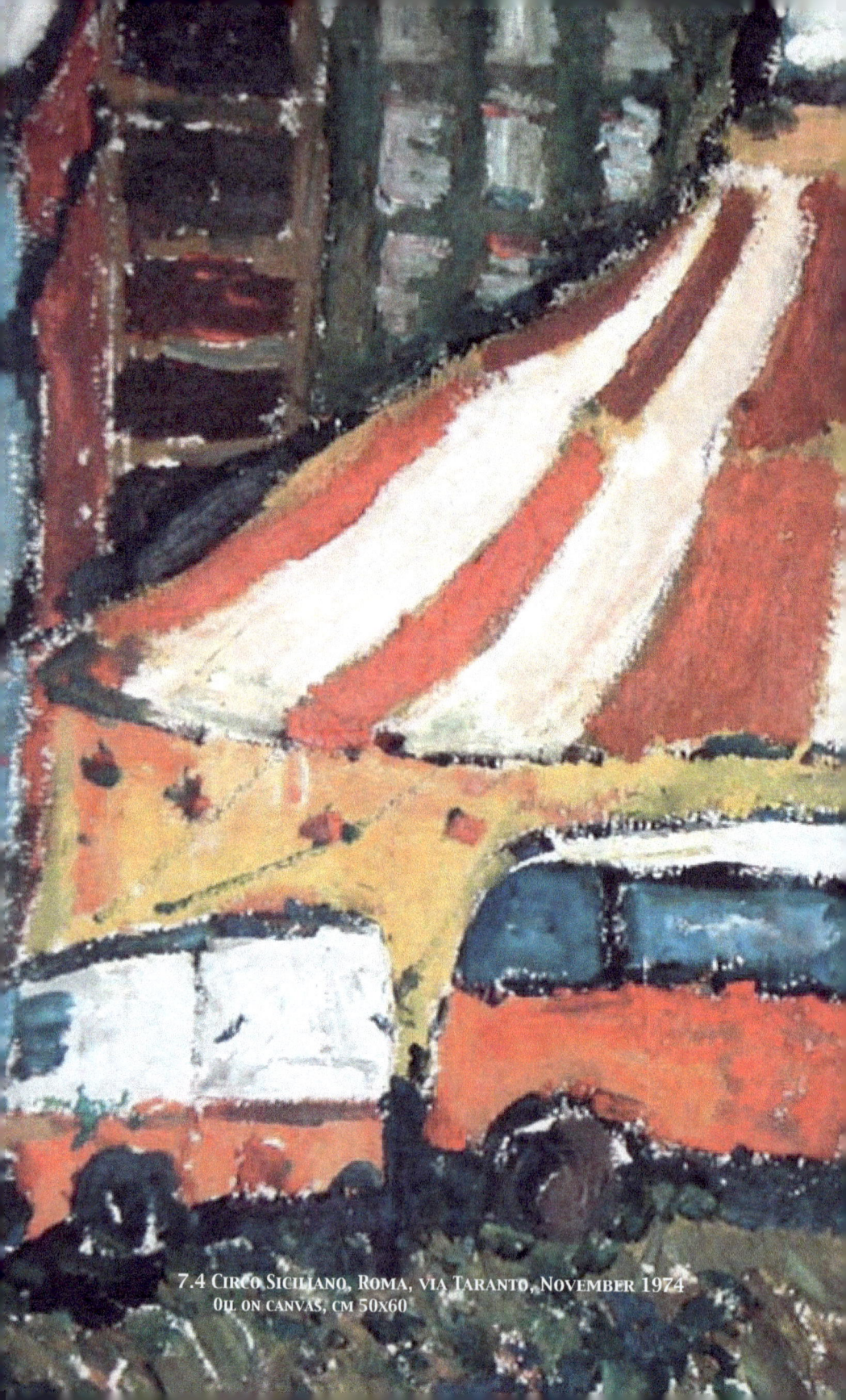

7.4 Circo Siciliano, Roma, via Taranto, November 1974
Oil on canvas, cm 50x60

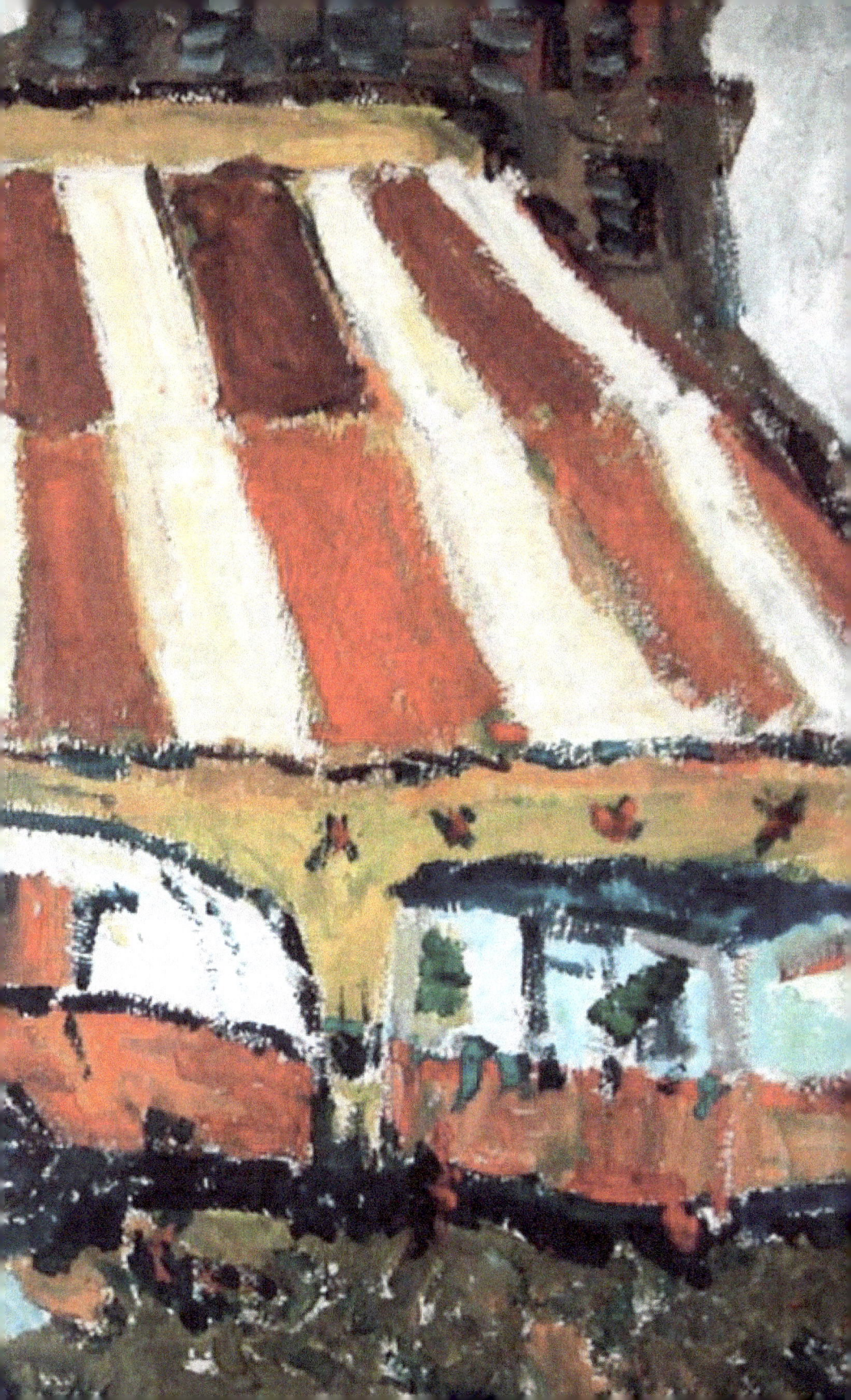

Abbey of the Tre Fontane

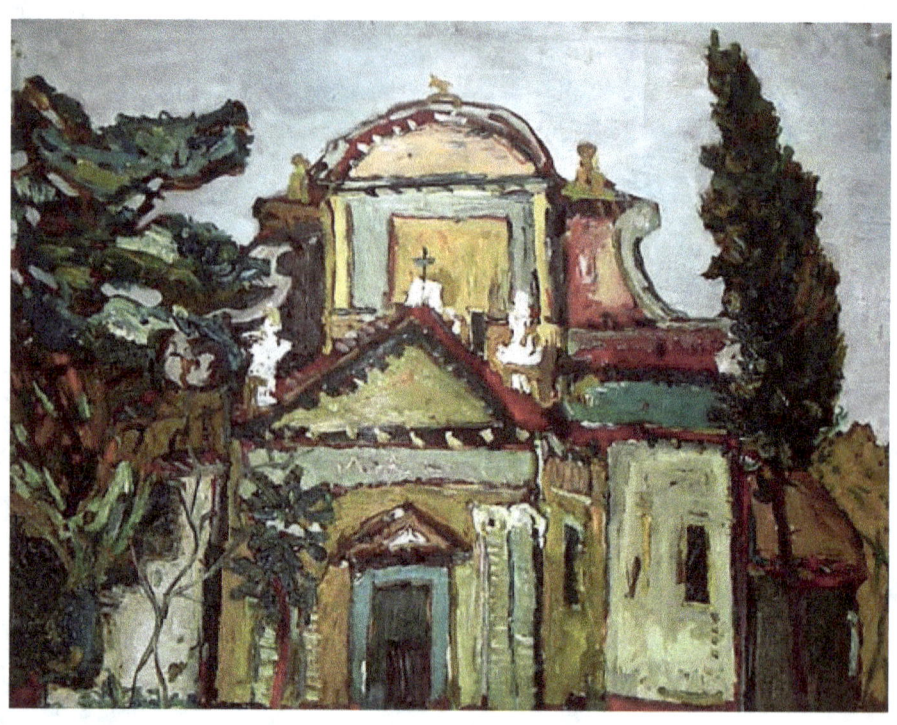

8.1 Tre Fontane, Roma, October 1974
Oil on cardboard, cm 60x80

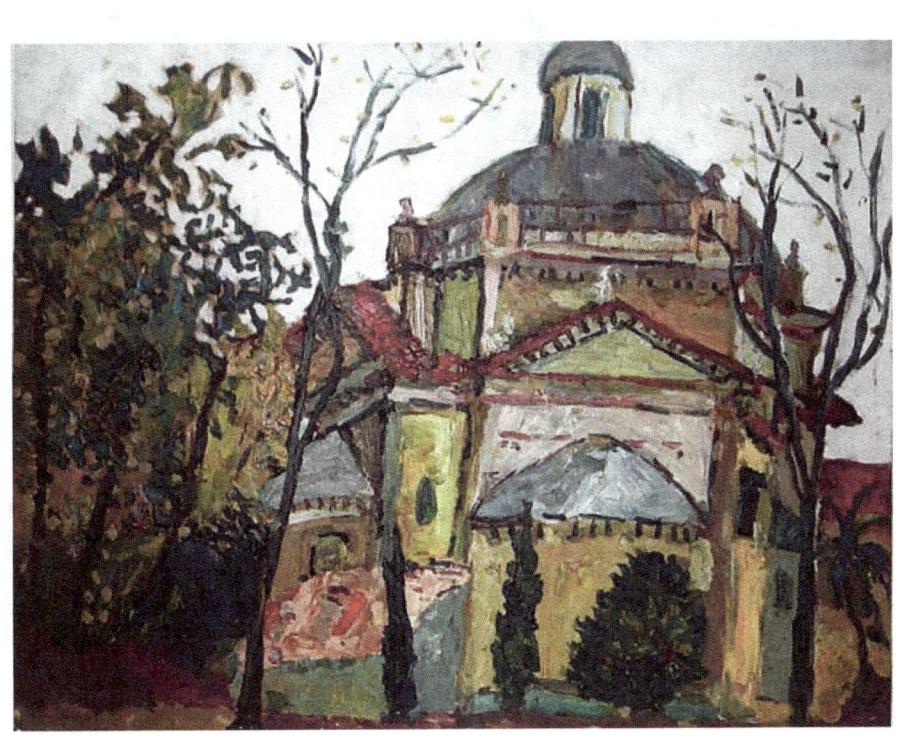

8.2 TRE FONTANE SANTA MARIA IN COELI ROMA, OCTOBER 1974
  OIL ON CARDBOARD, CM 60X80

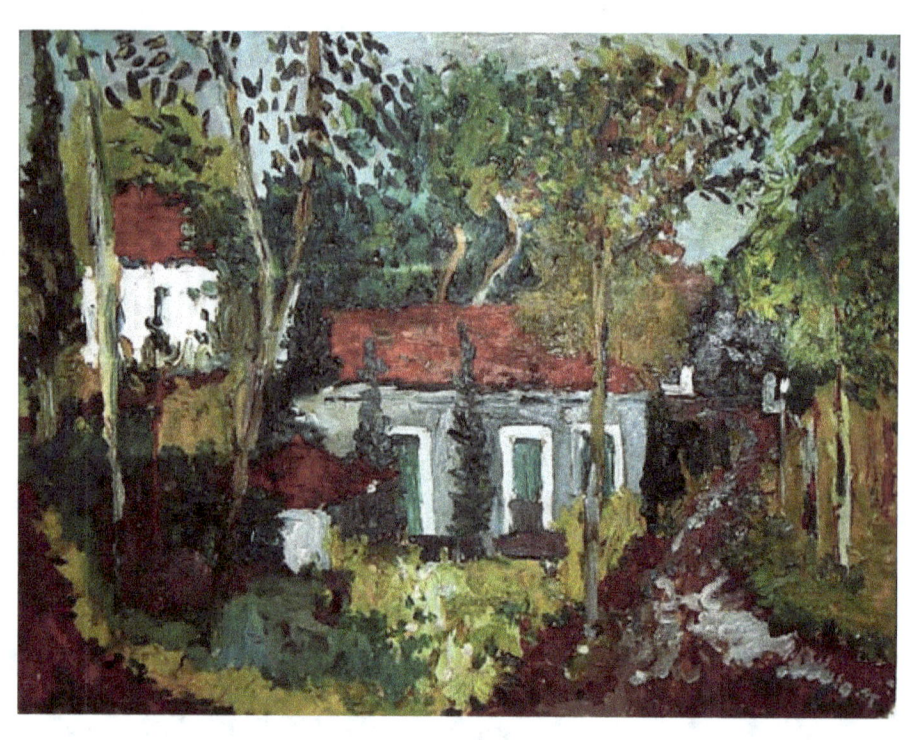

8.3 TRE FONTANE: THE WOOD, ROMA, OCTOBER 1974
OIL ON CARDBOARD, CM 60X80

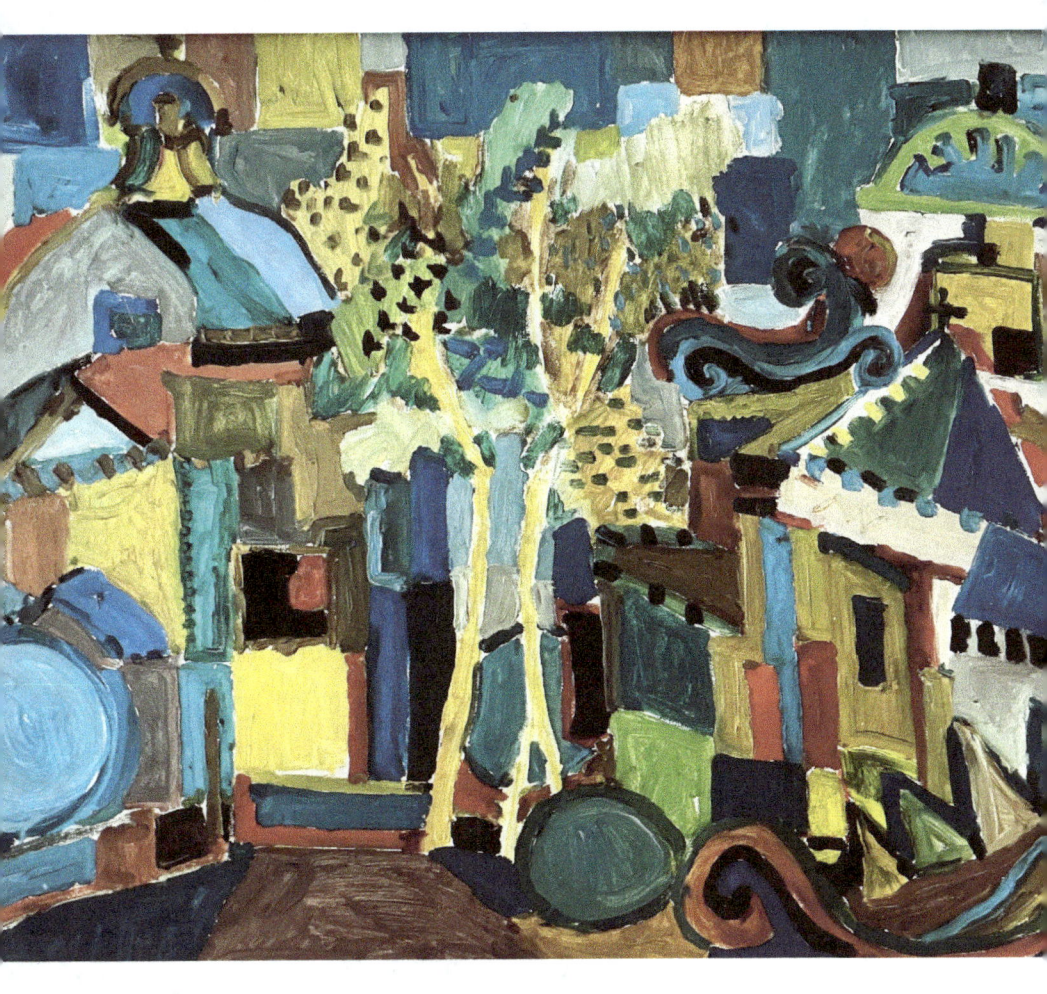

8.4 Tre Fontane Santa: Maria in Coeli, on the right: San Paolo, Roma, October 1982
Oil on canvas, cm 60x80

HILLS

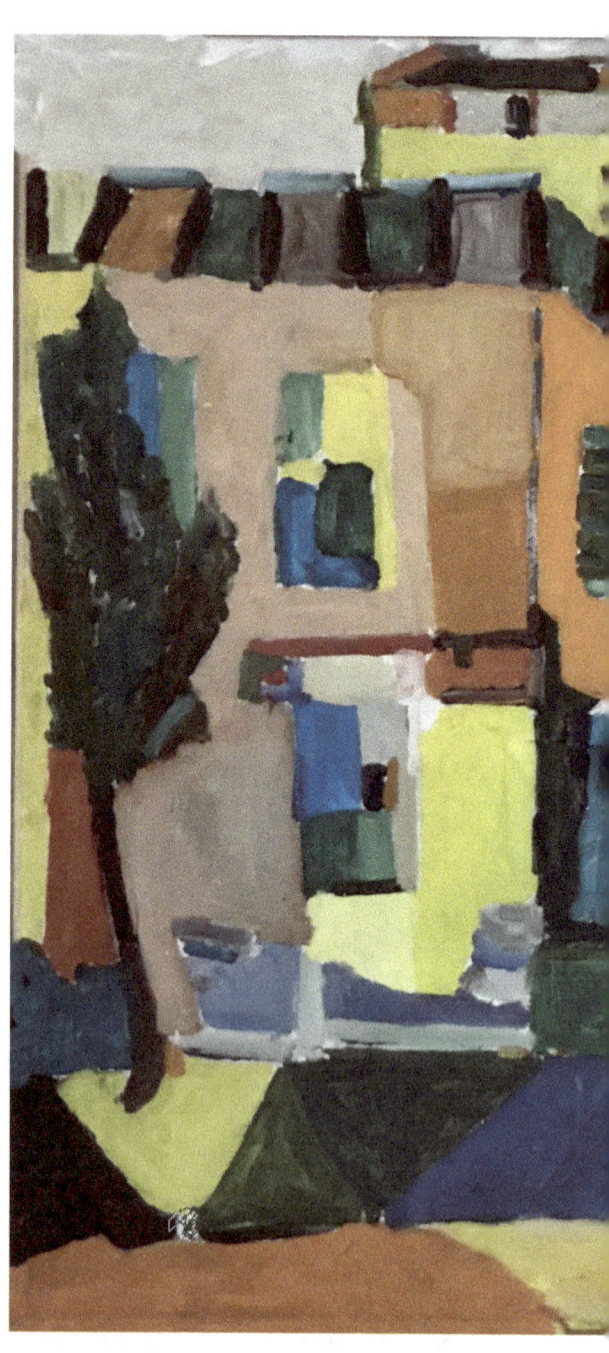

9.1 SAN SABA ROMA, JULY 1978
OIL ON CANVAS, CM 60X80

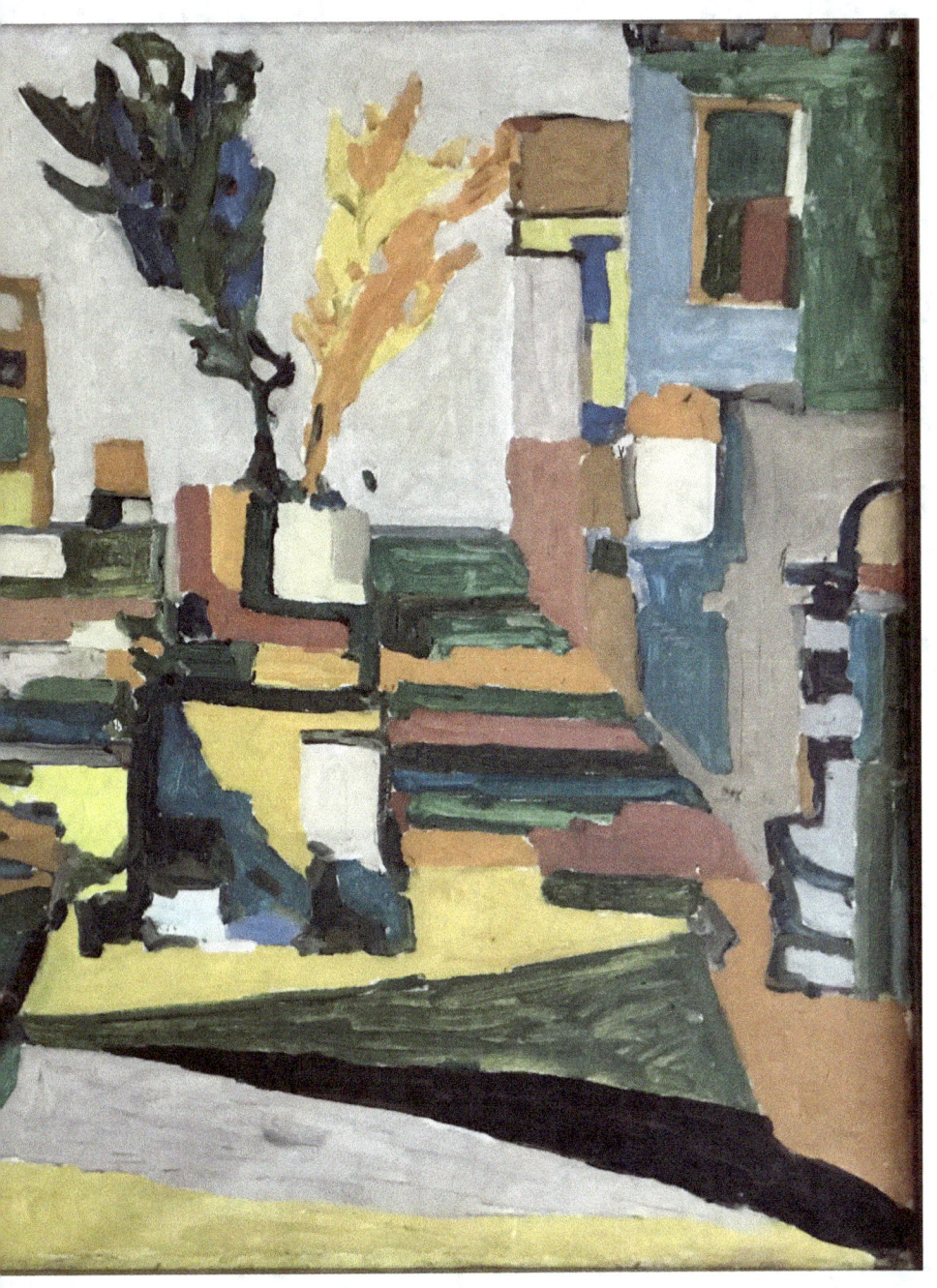

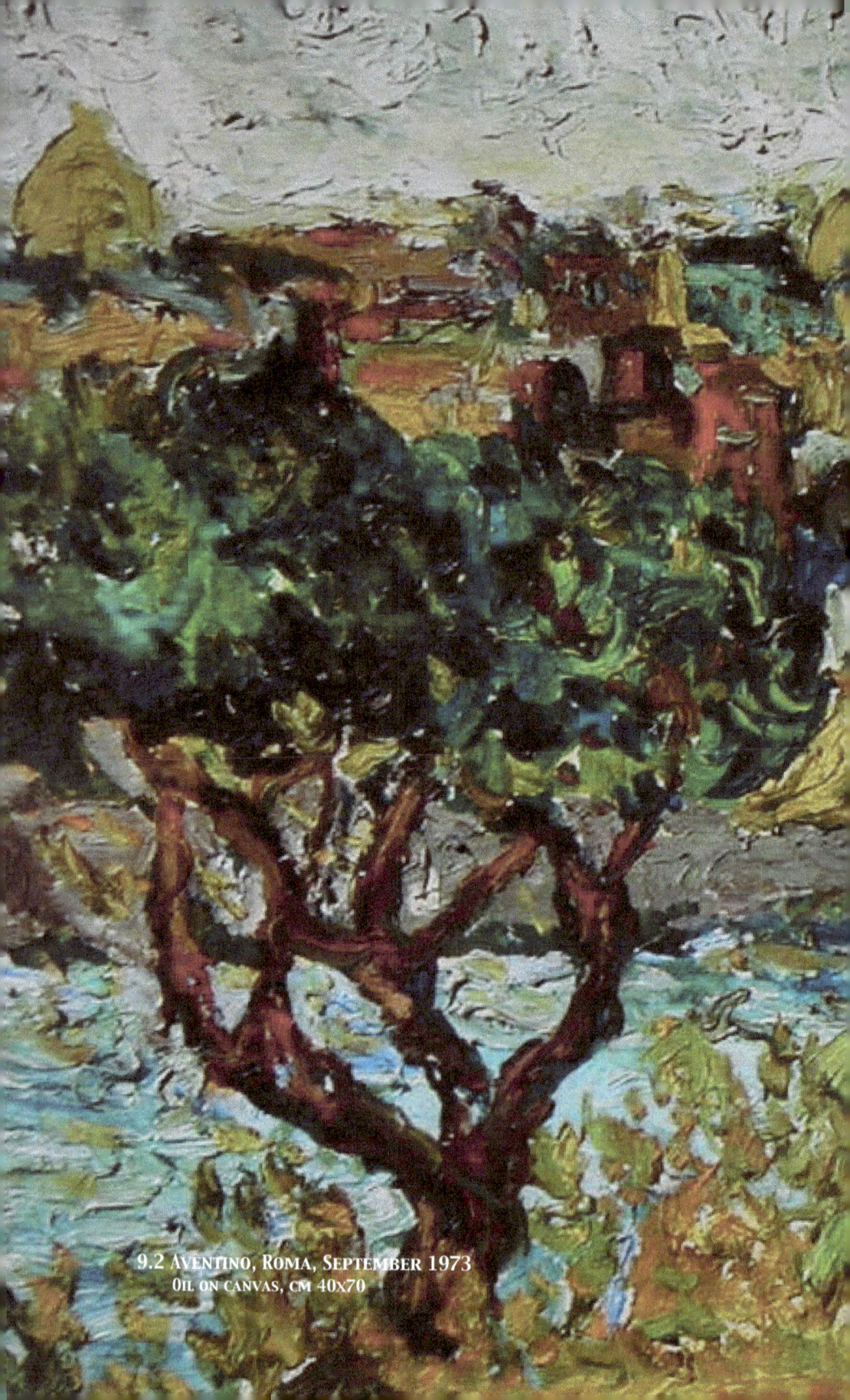

9.2 Aventino, Roma, September 1973
Oil on canvas, cm 40x70

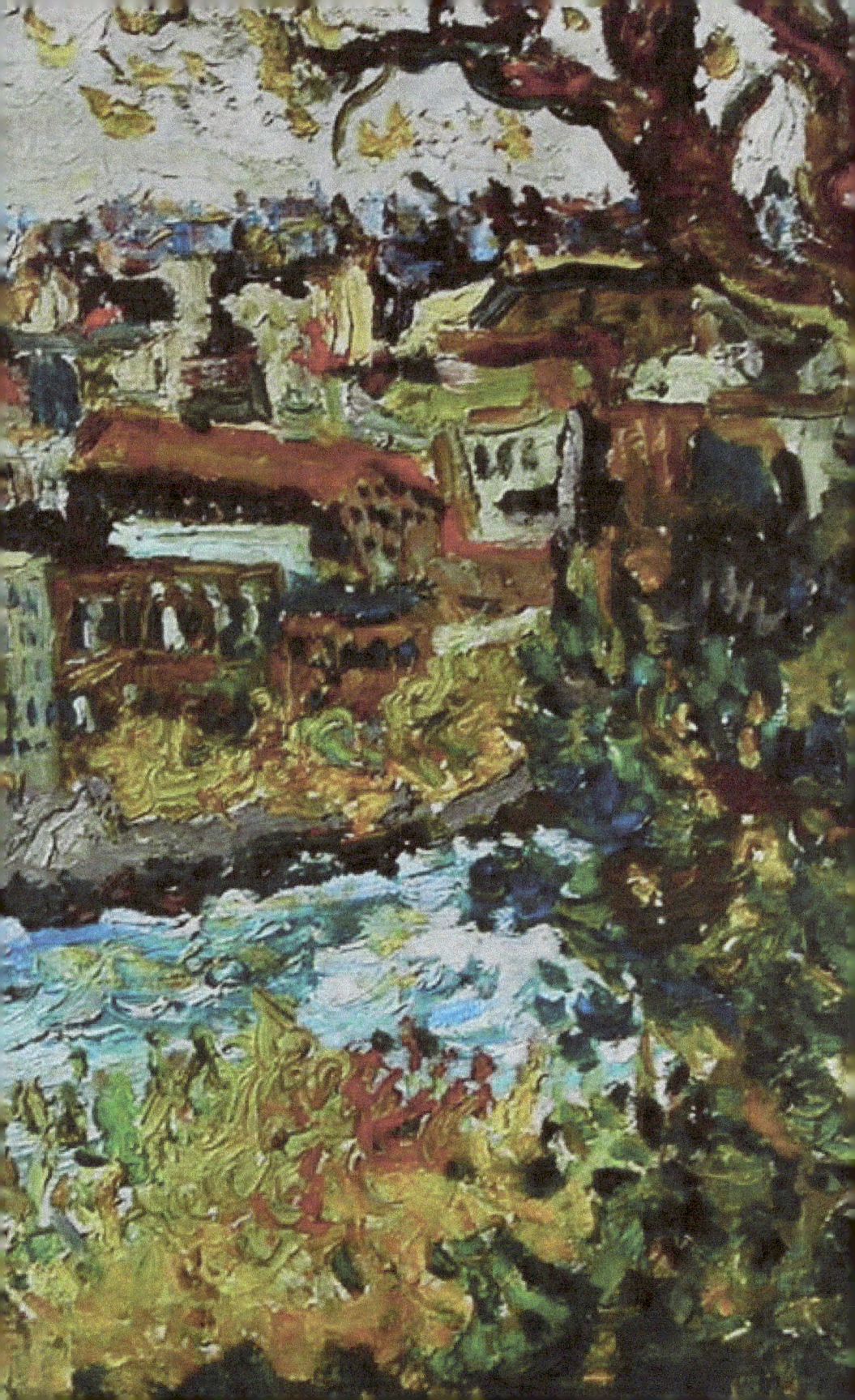

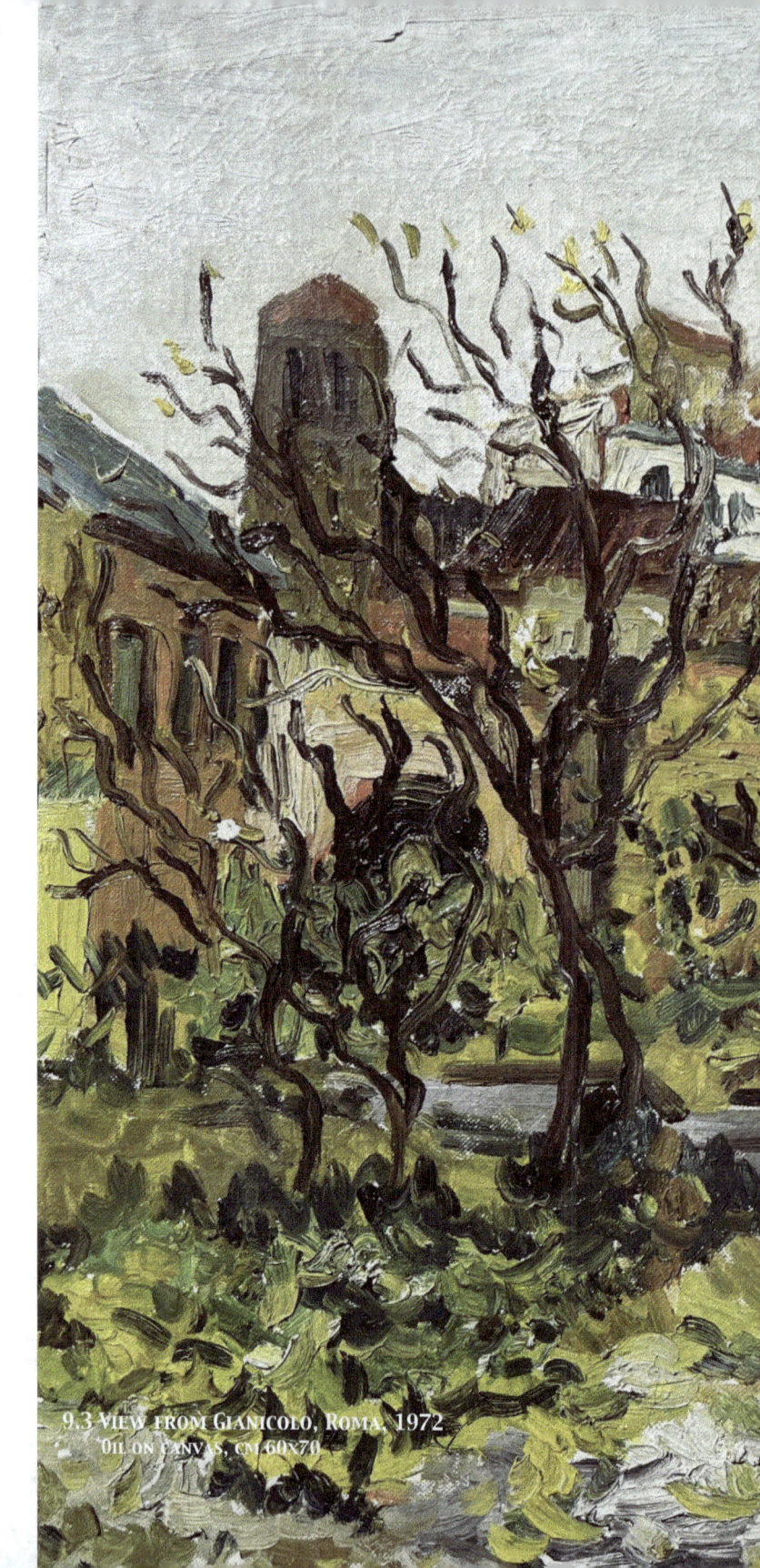

9.3 View from Gianicolo, Roma, 1972
Oil on canvas, cm 60x70

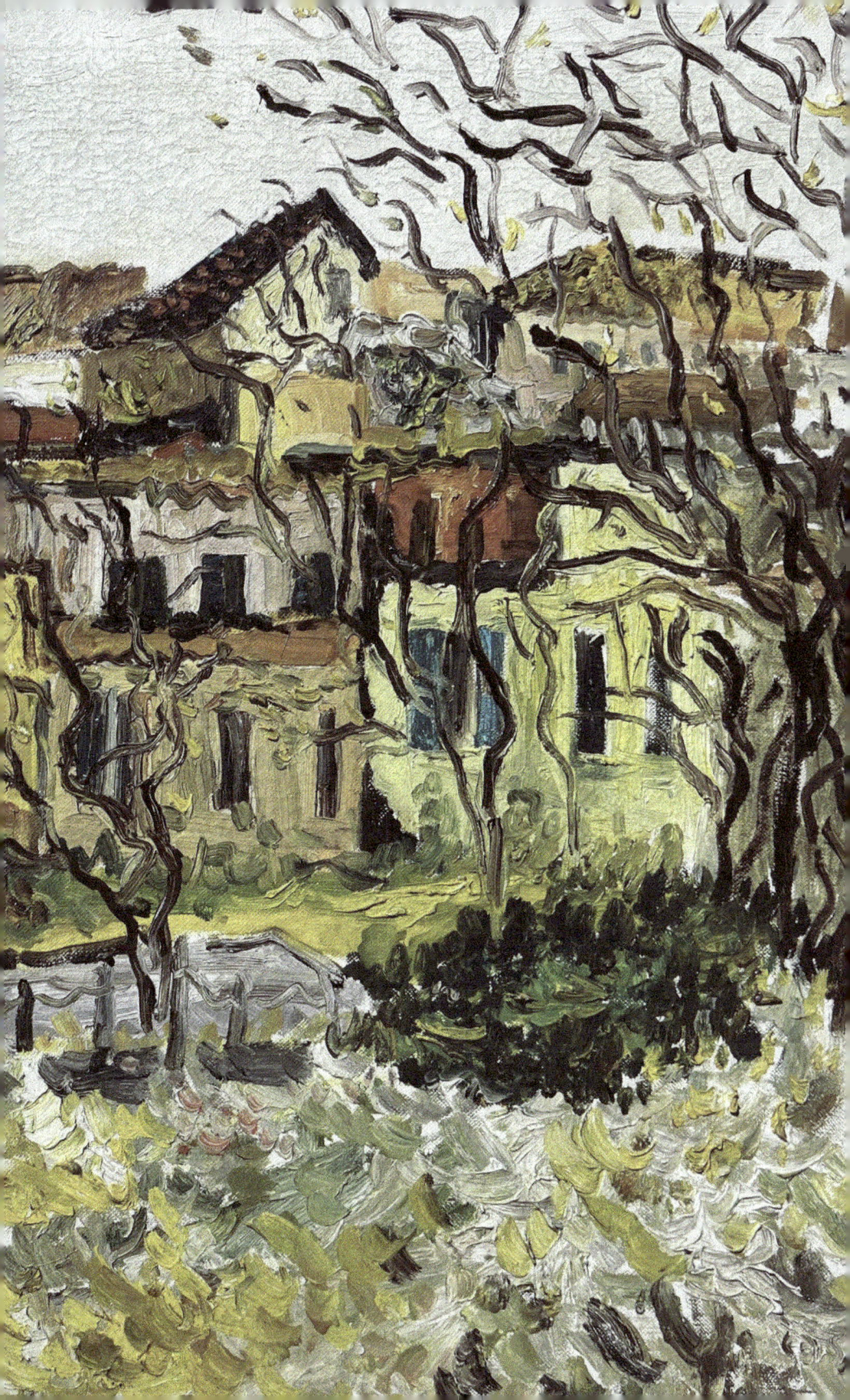

NEW CITY

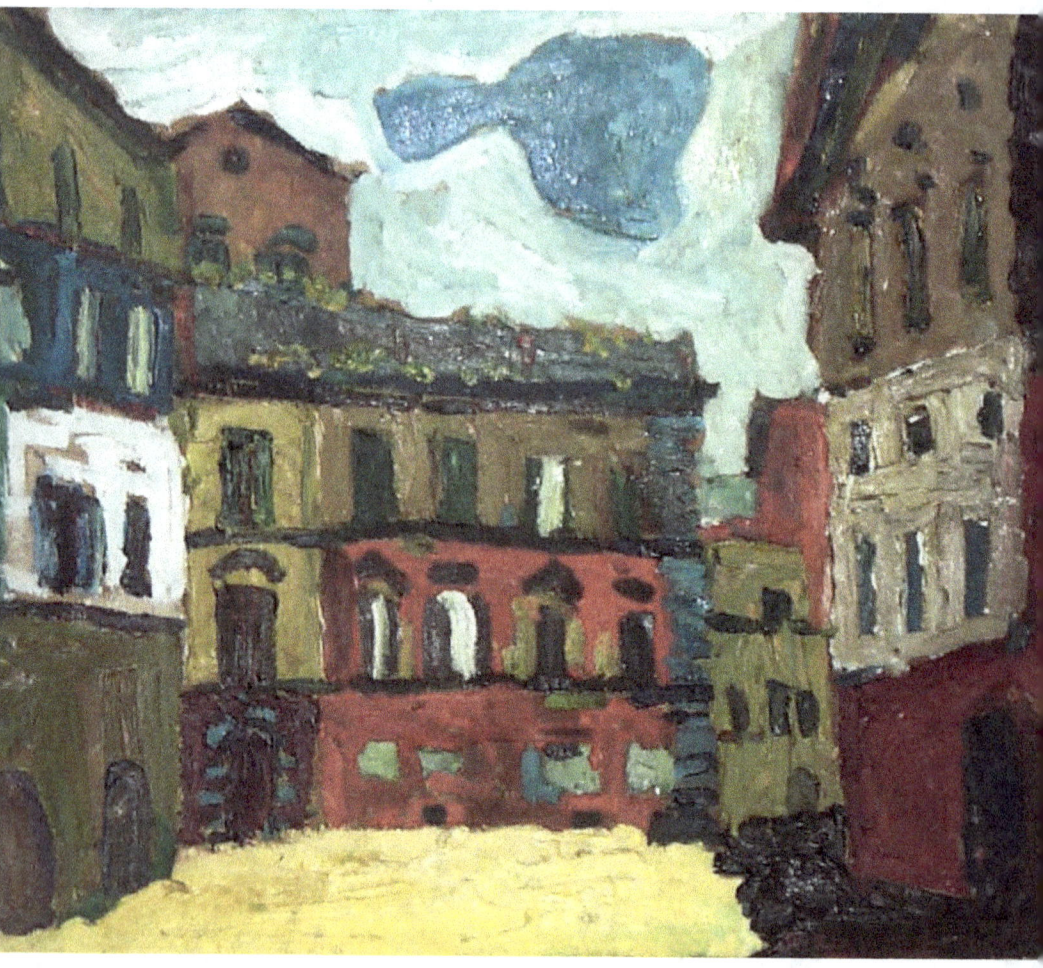

10.1 GHETTO, ROMA, SEPTEMBER 1975
OIL ON CANVAS, CM 40x50

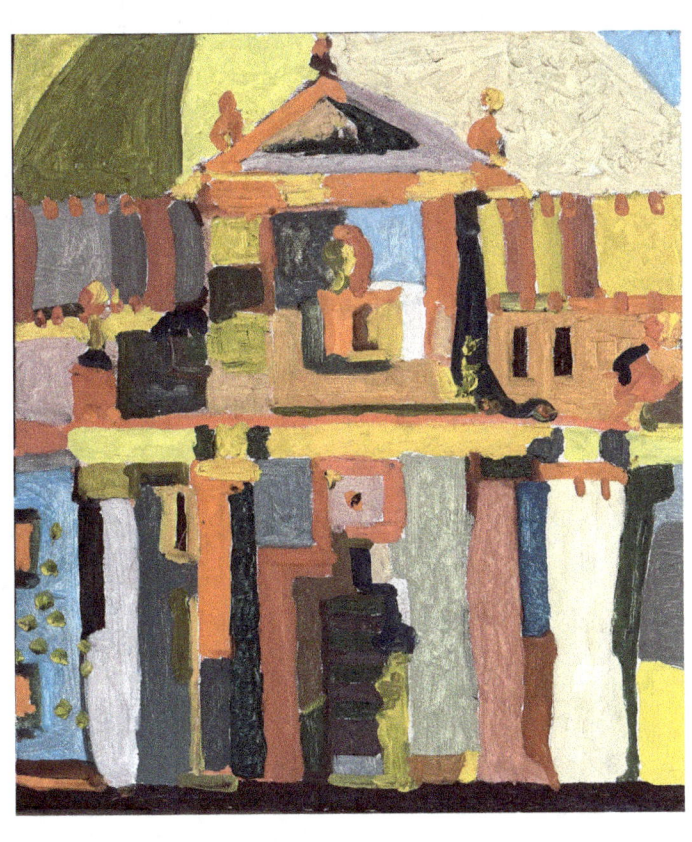

10.2 Roman church, Roma, September 1985
Oil on canvas, cm 40x40

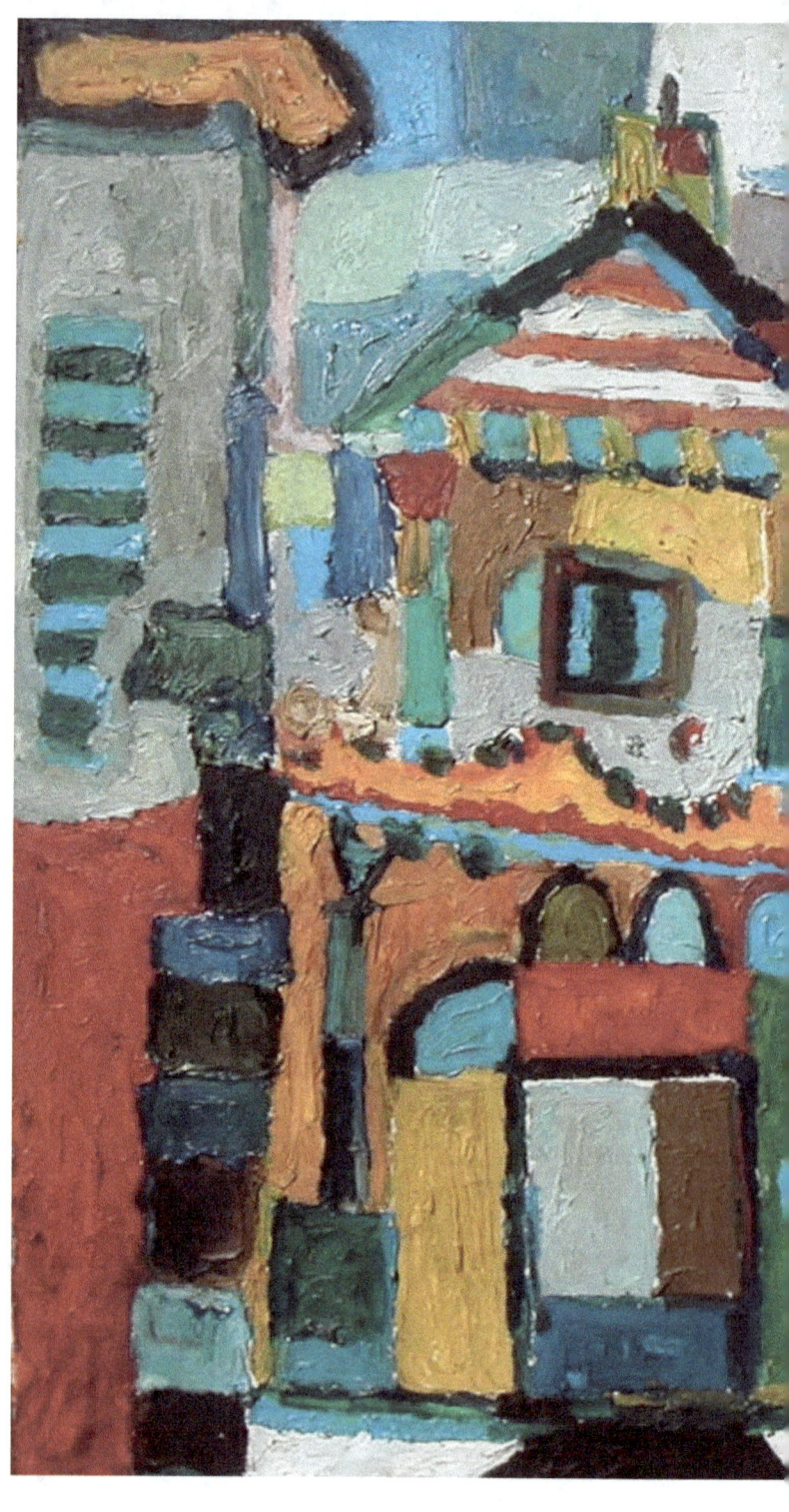

10.3 Santa Caterina dei Furnari, Roma, September 1975
Oil on canvas, cm 60x70

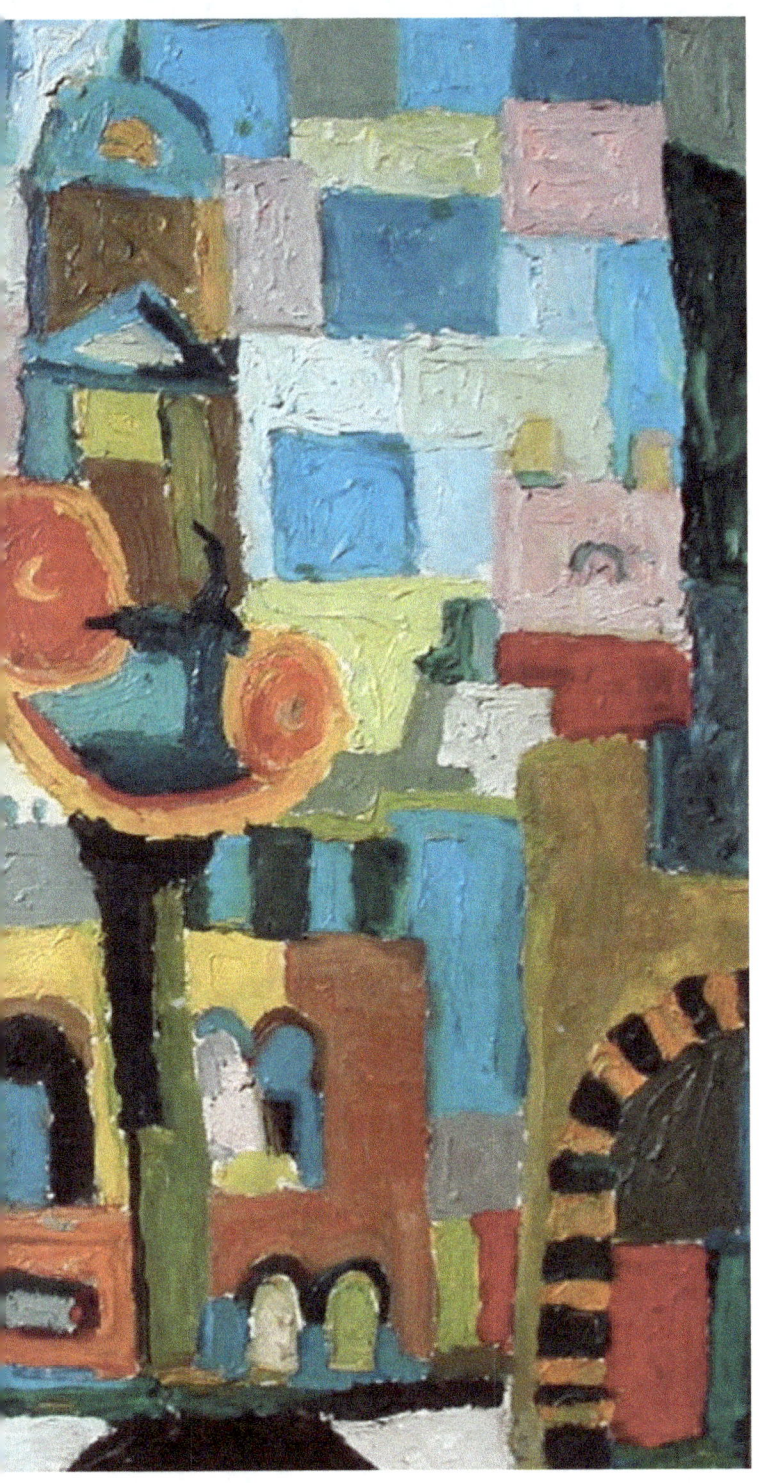

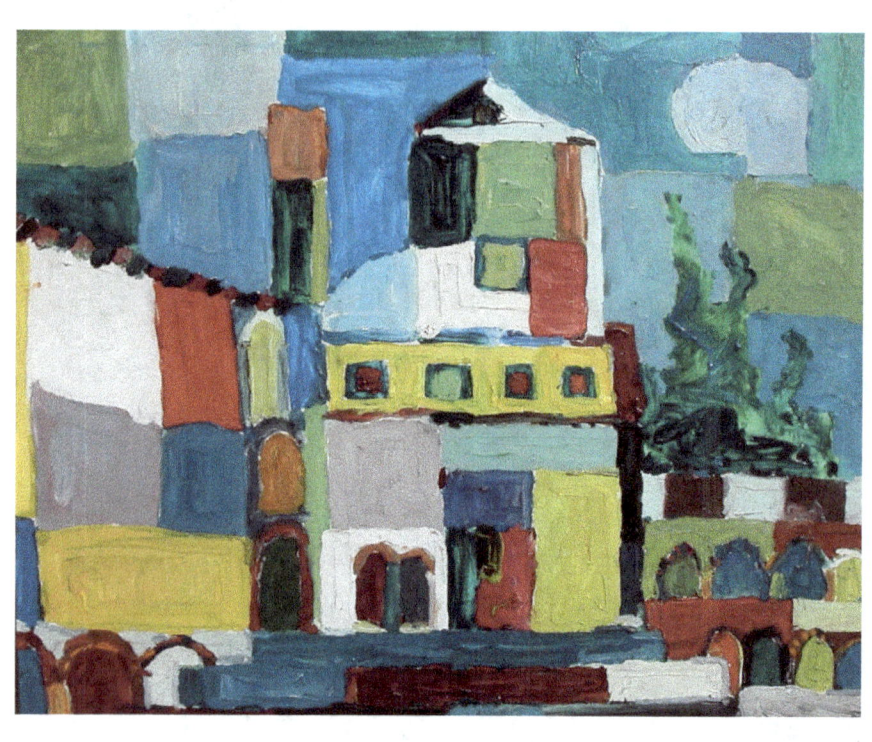

10.4 SANTA MARIA NOVELLA, FIRENZE OCTOBER 1975
ACRYLIC ON CANVAS CM 40X50

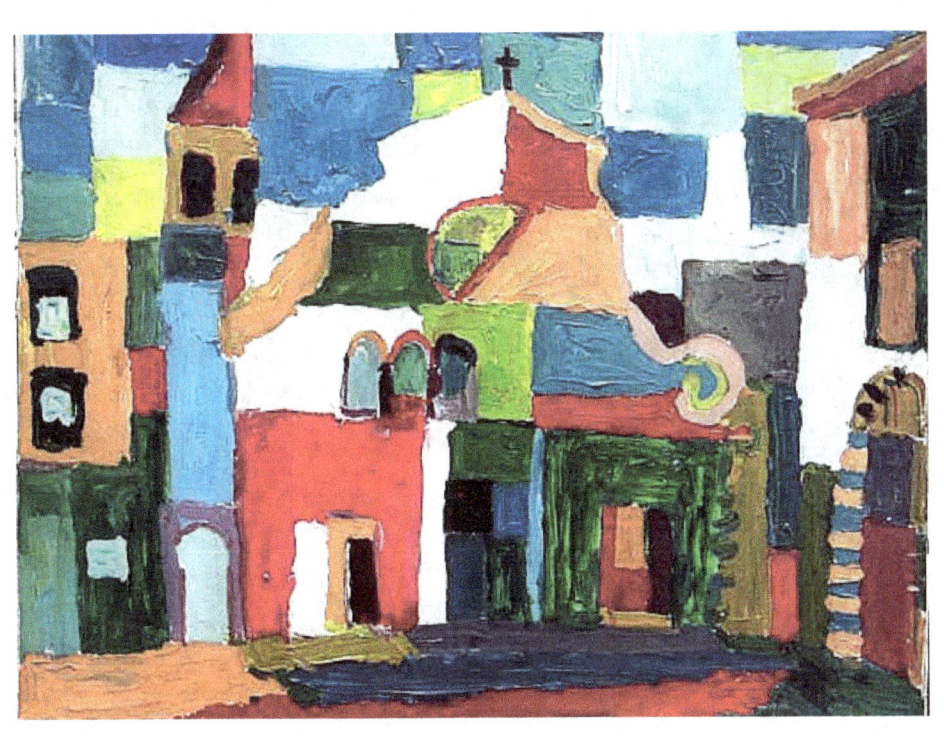

10.5 Santo Spirito, Firenze October 1975
Acrylic, on canvas, cm 40x50

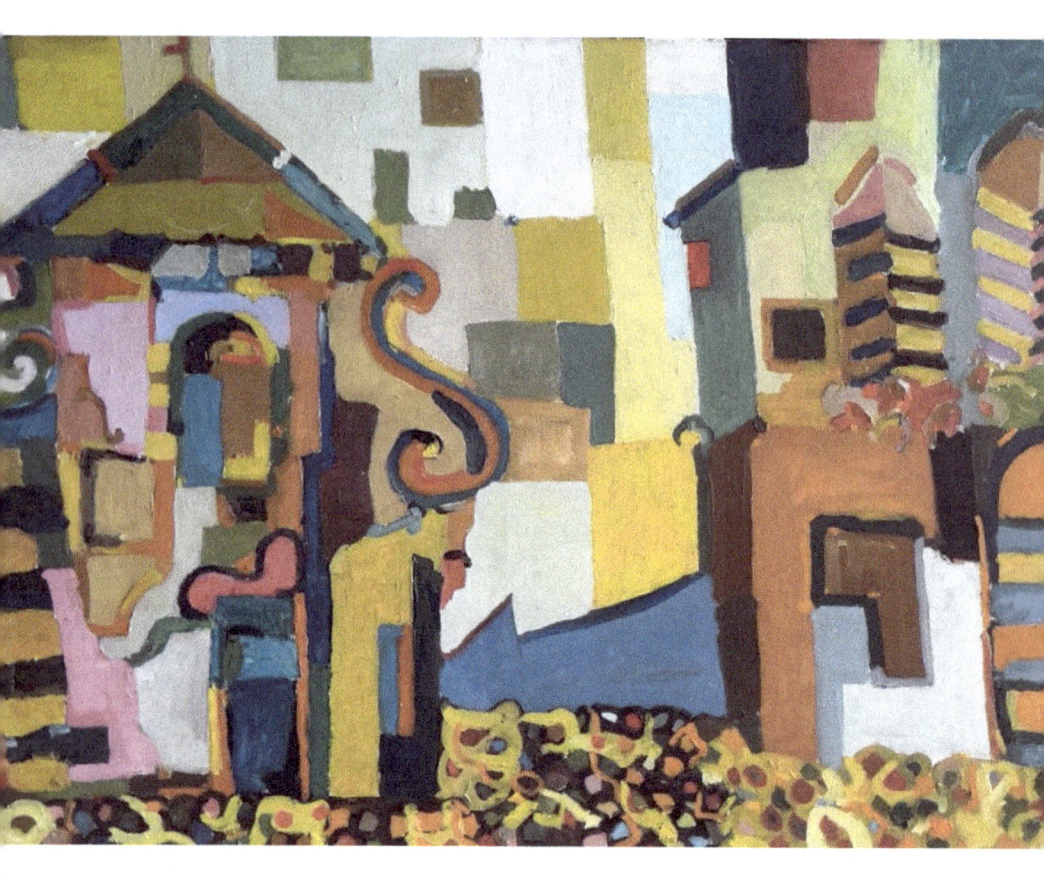

10.6 Piazza Santa Caterina, Roma, October 1987
Oil on canvas, cm 70x100

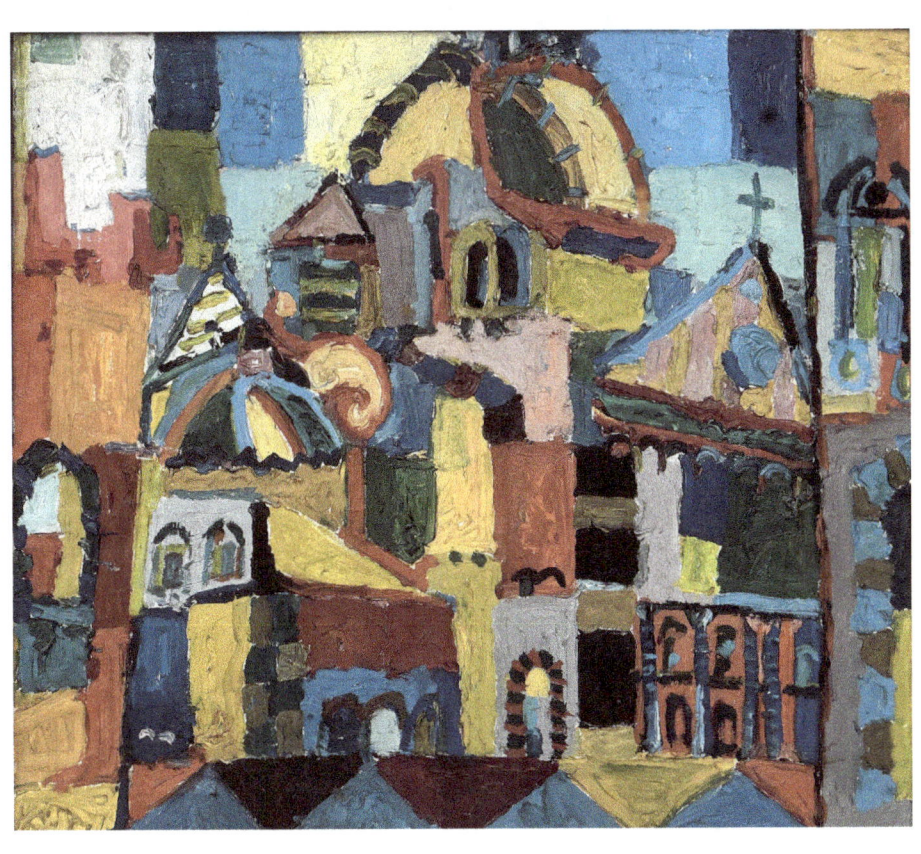

10.7 Roman church, Roma, October 1975
   Oil on canvas, cm 60x70

PAST LIVES

11.1 SELFPORTRAIT, ROMA, 1976
OIL ON CANVAS, CM 60X50

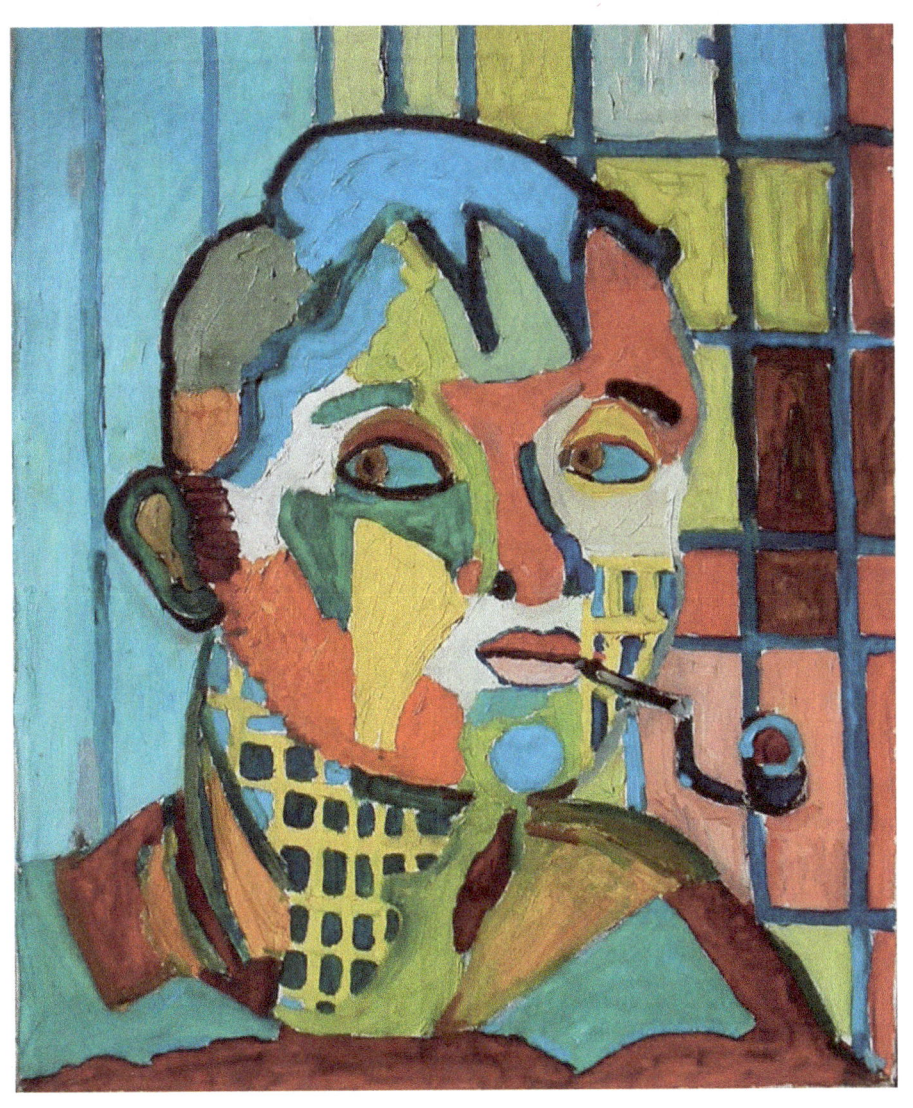

11.2 GISA, ROMA, SEPTEMBER 1975
OIL ON CANVAS, CM 40x50

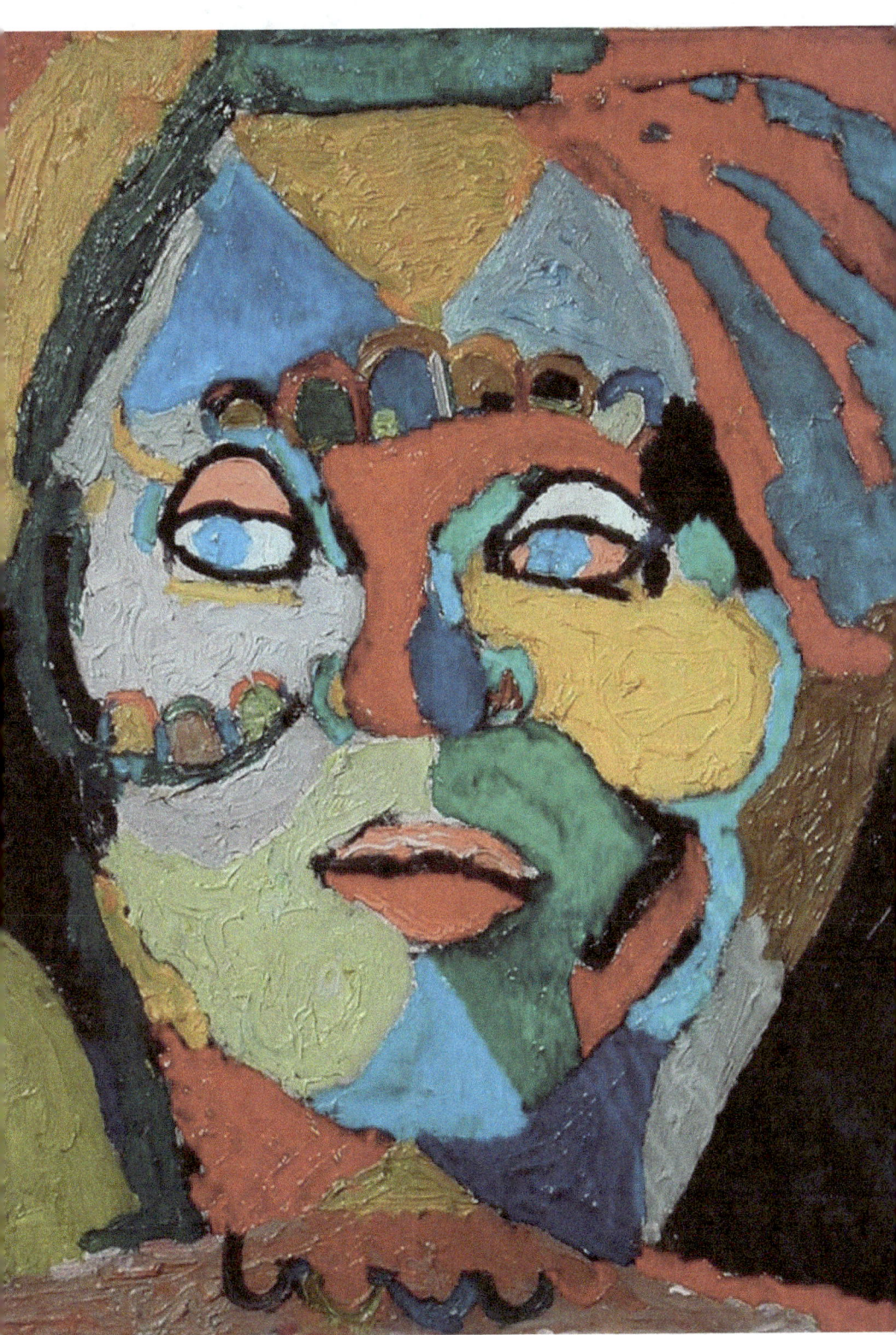

11.3 GISA, ROMA, 1978
OIL ON CANVAS, CM 50X60

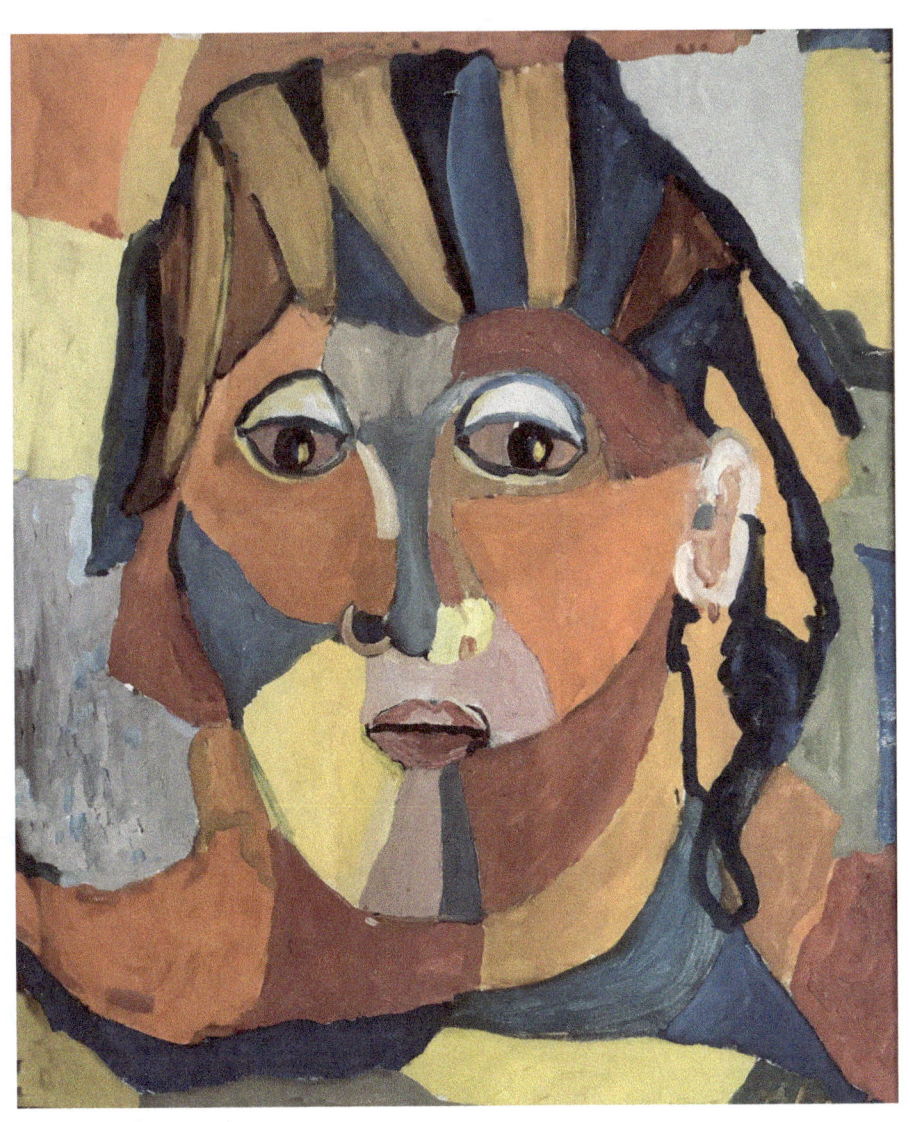

Tevere

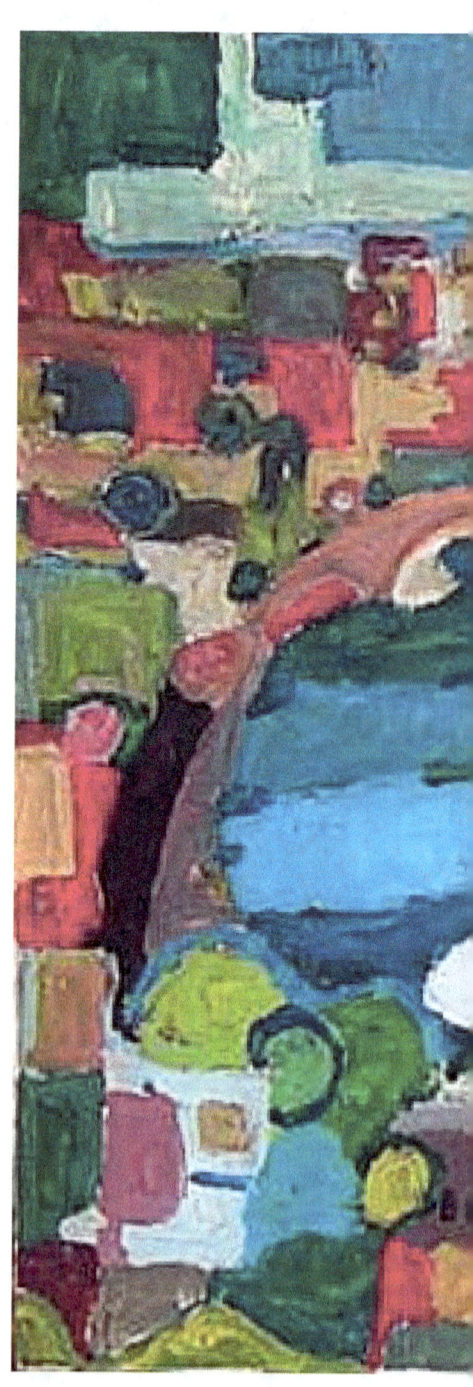

12.1 View from Montemario, Roma, September 1975 oil on canvas, cm 60x80

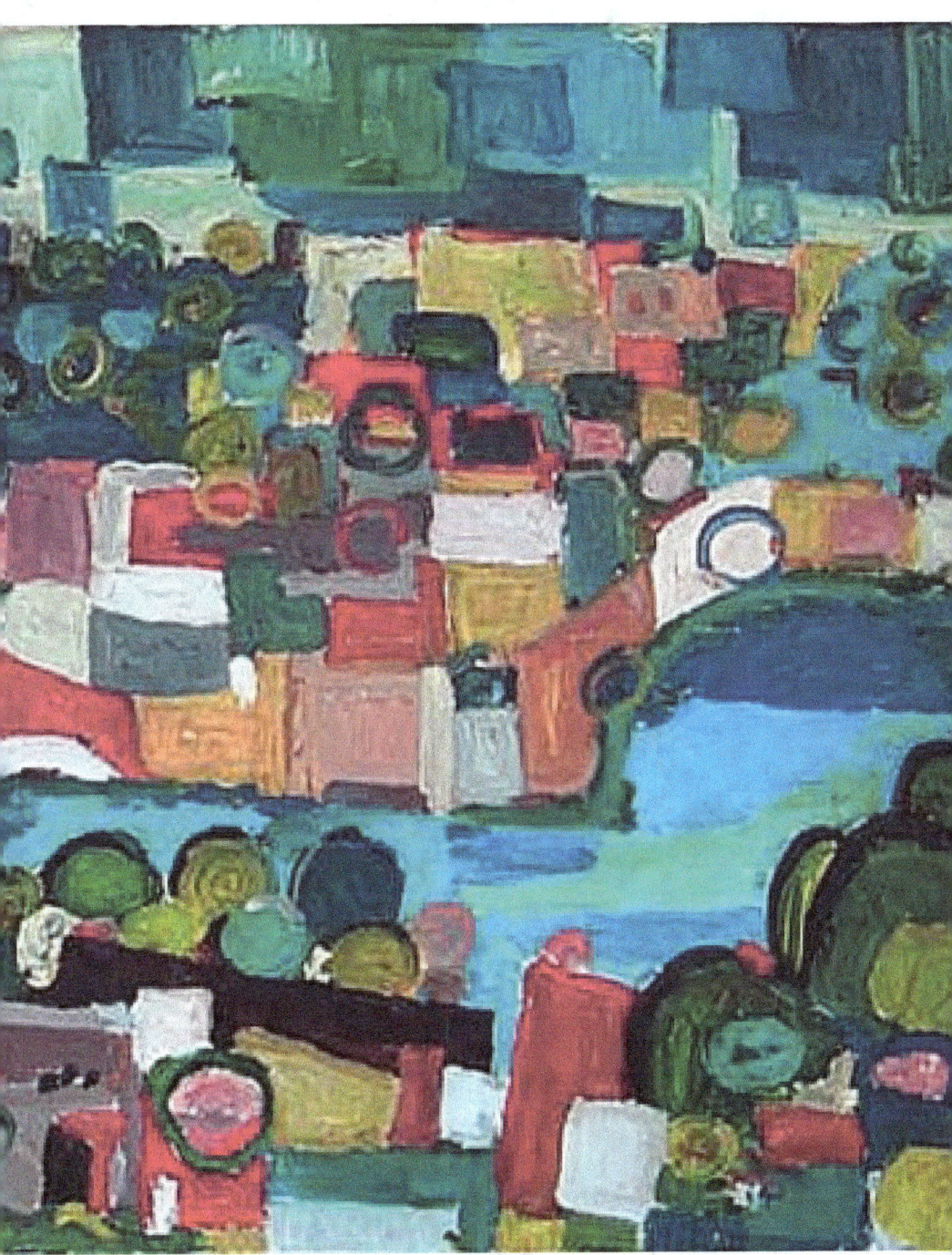

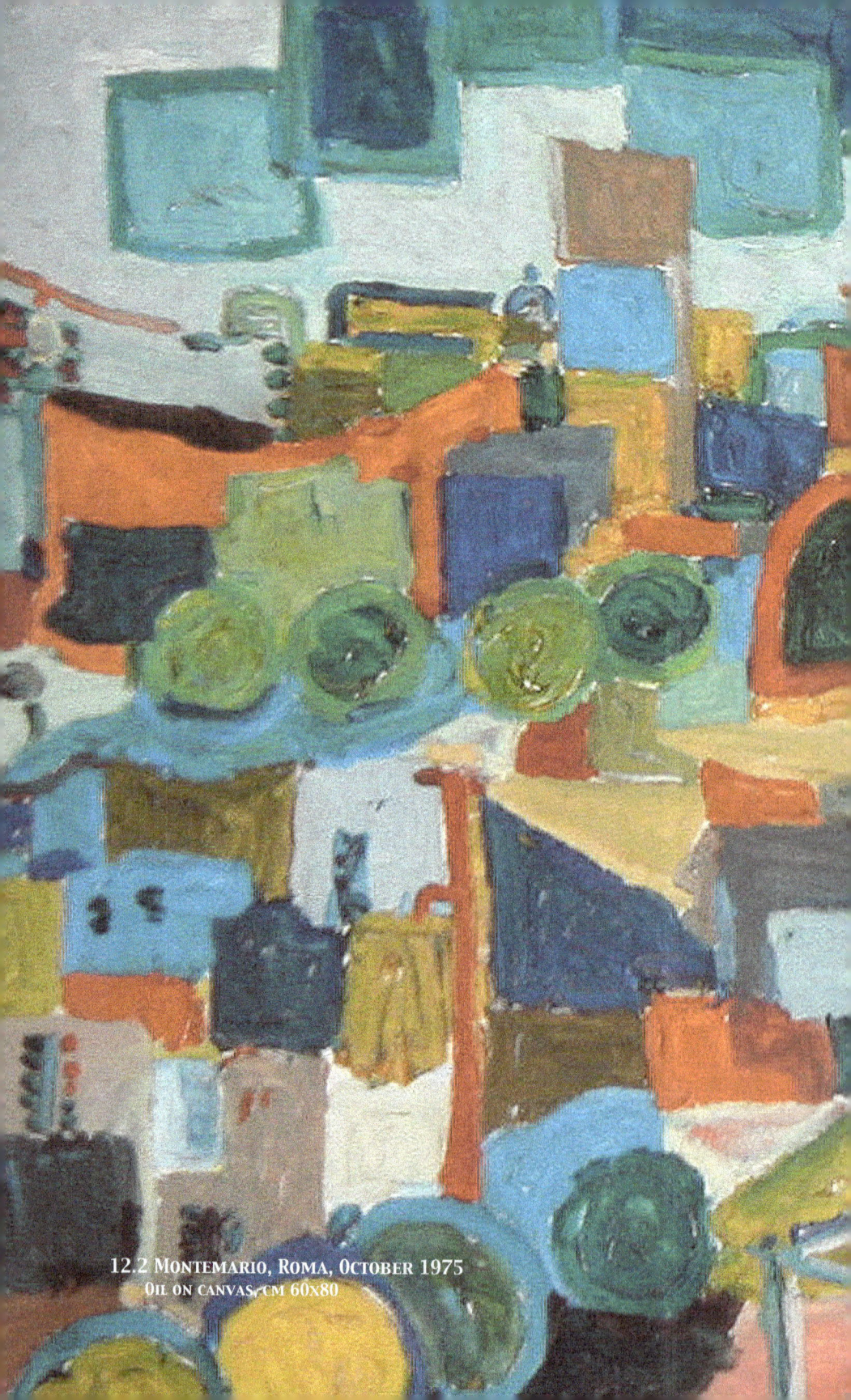

12.2 Montemario, Roma, October 1975
Oil on canvas, cm 60x80

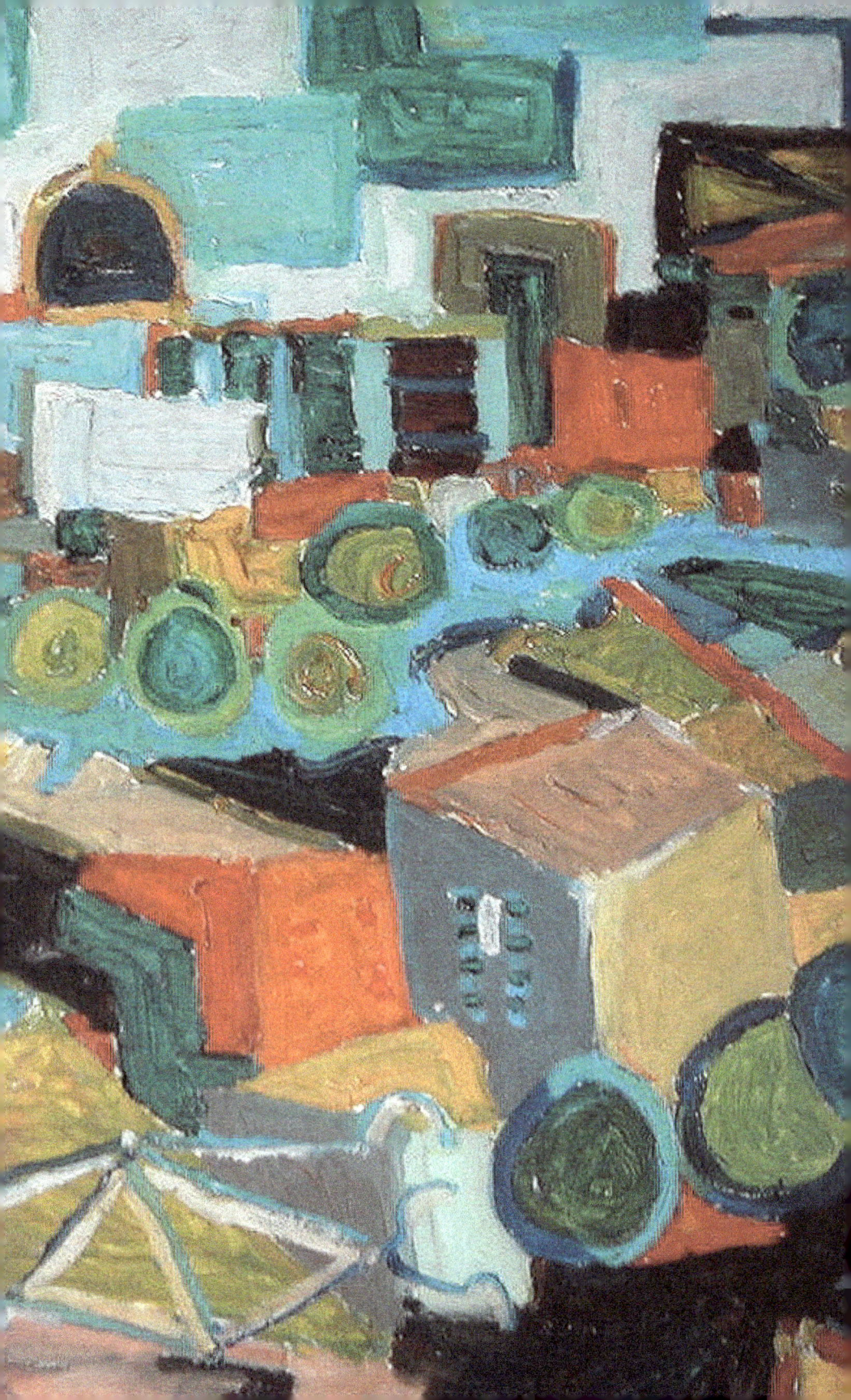

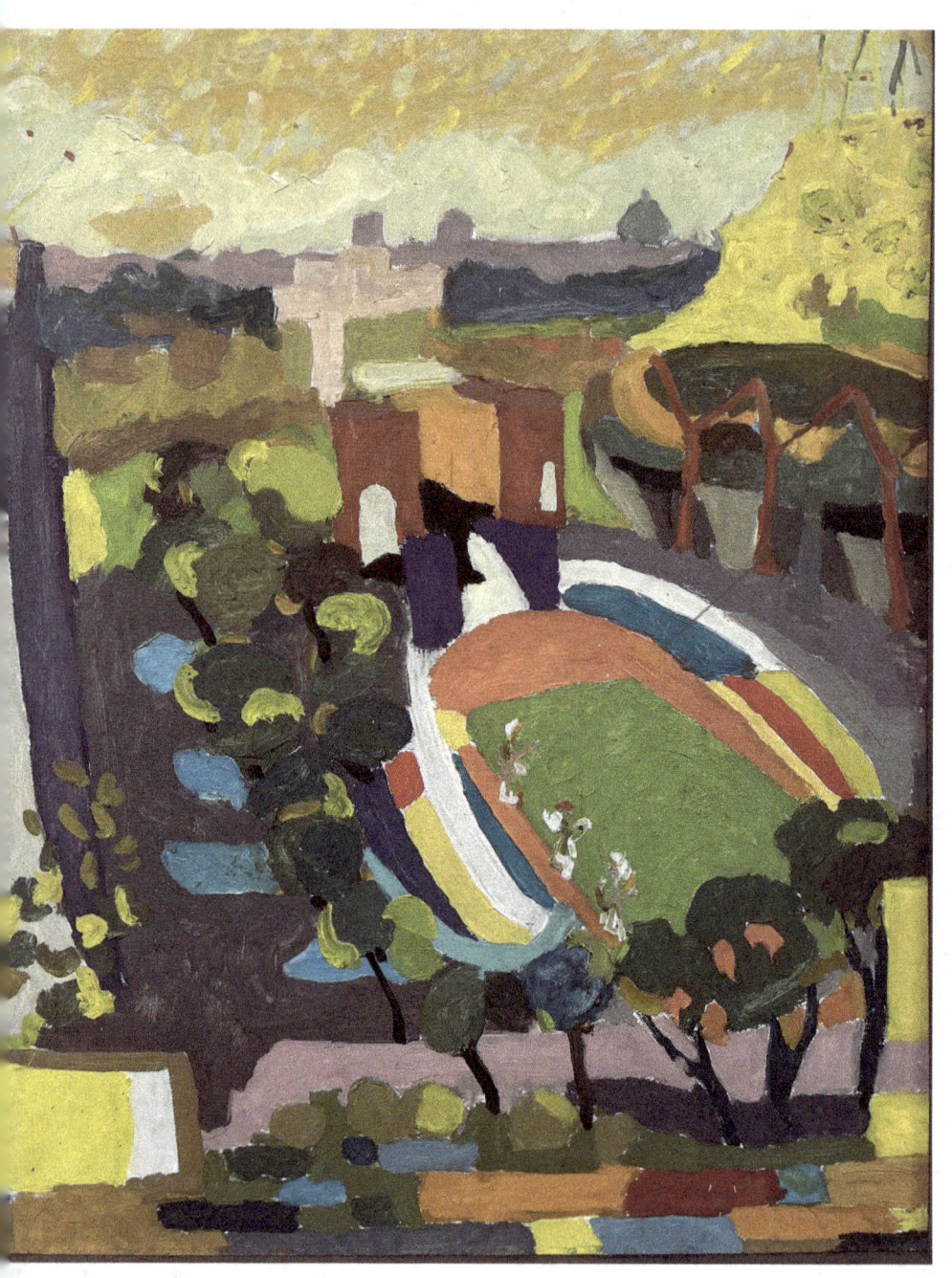

12.3. VIEW OF FORO ITALICO FROM MOTE MARIO, ROMA, OCTOBER 17, 1999
OIL ON CANVAS, CM 60X70

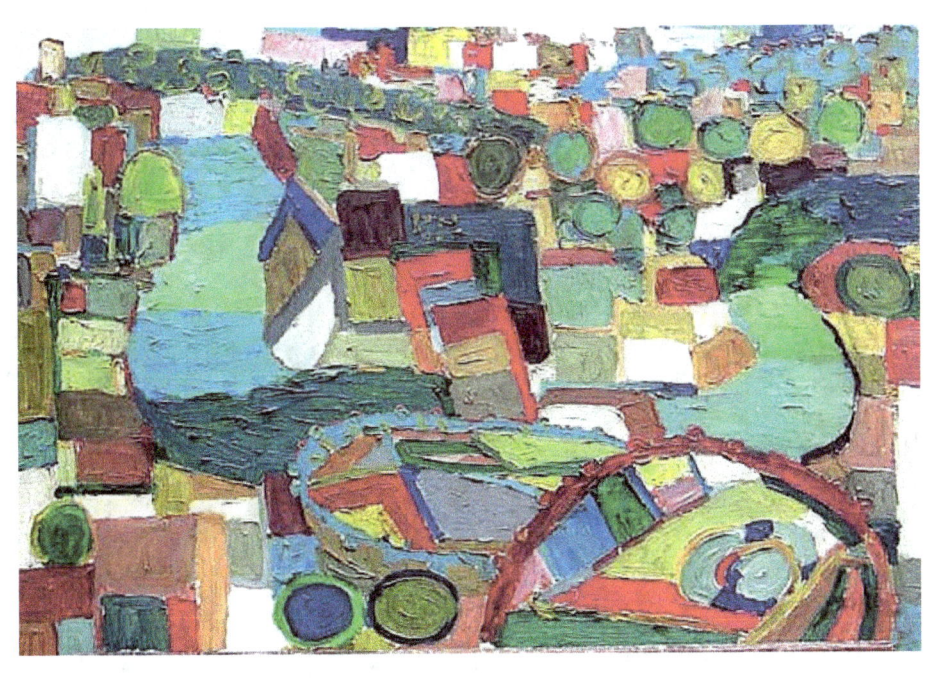

124. View of the Olympic Bend, Roma, September 1975
Oil on canvas, cm 60x80

Urban Glimpses

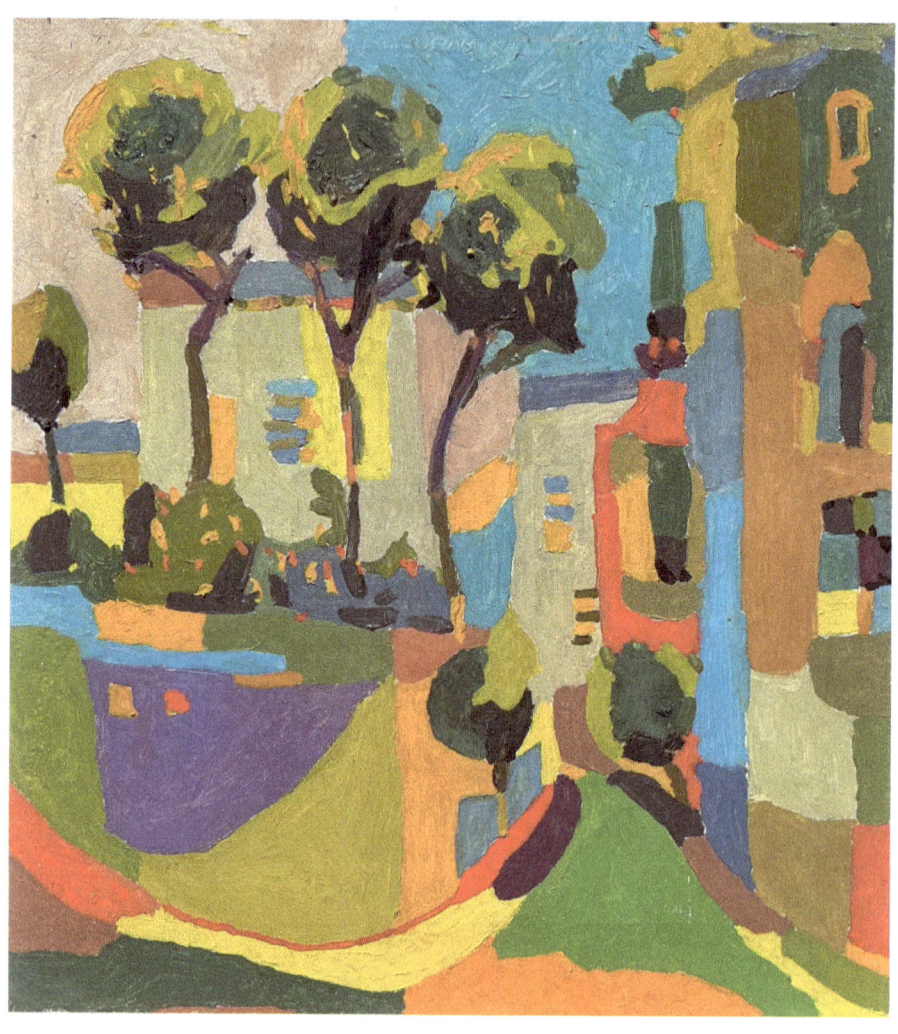

13.1 Ascent in Parioli, September 1992
  Oil on canvas, cm, 45x55

13.2 San Crescenzio, Roma, March 1990 1979
  Oil on canvas, cm, 40x40

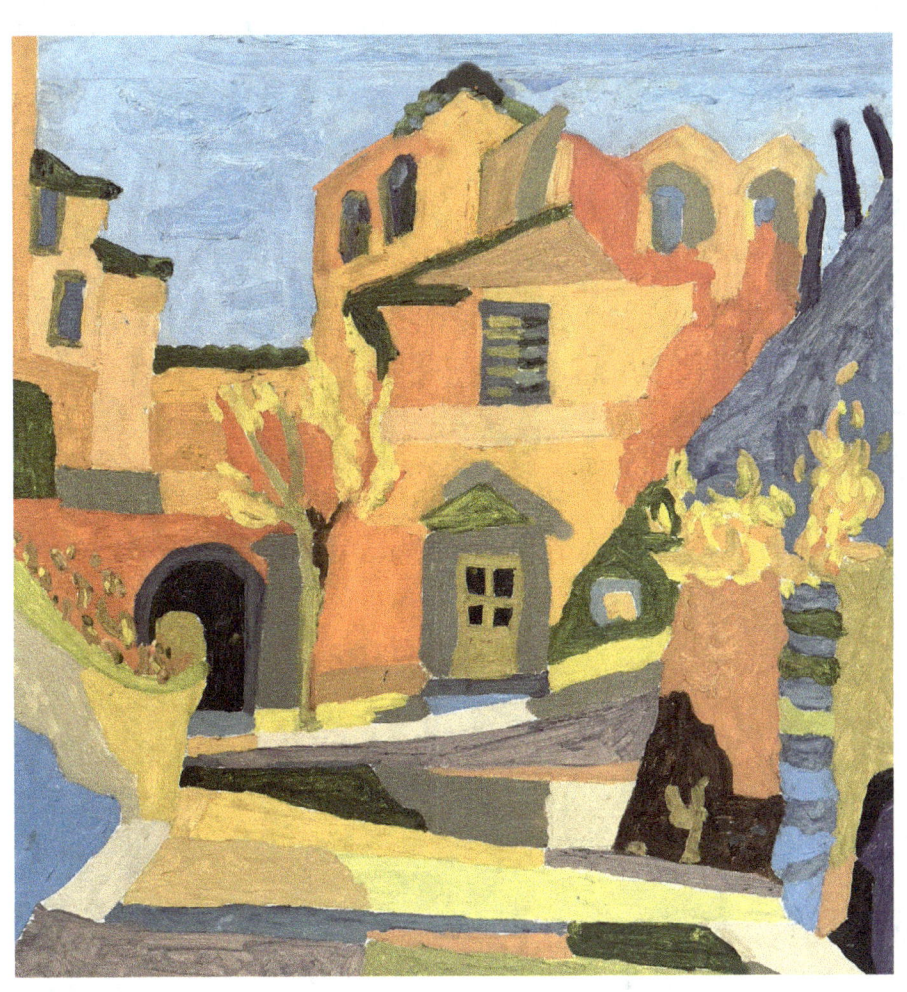

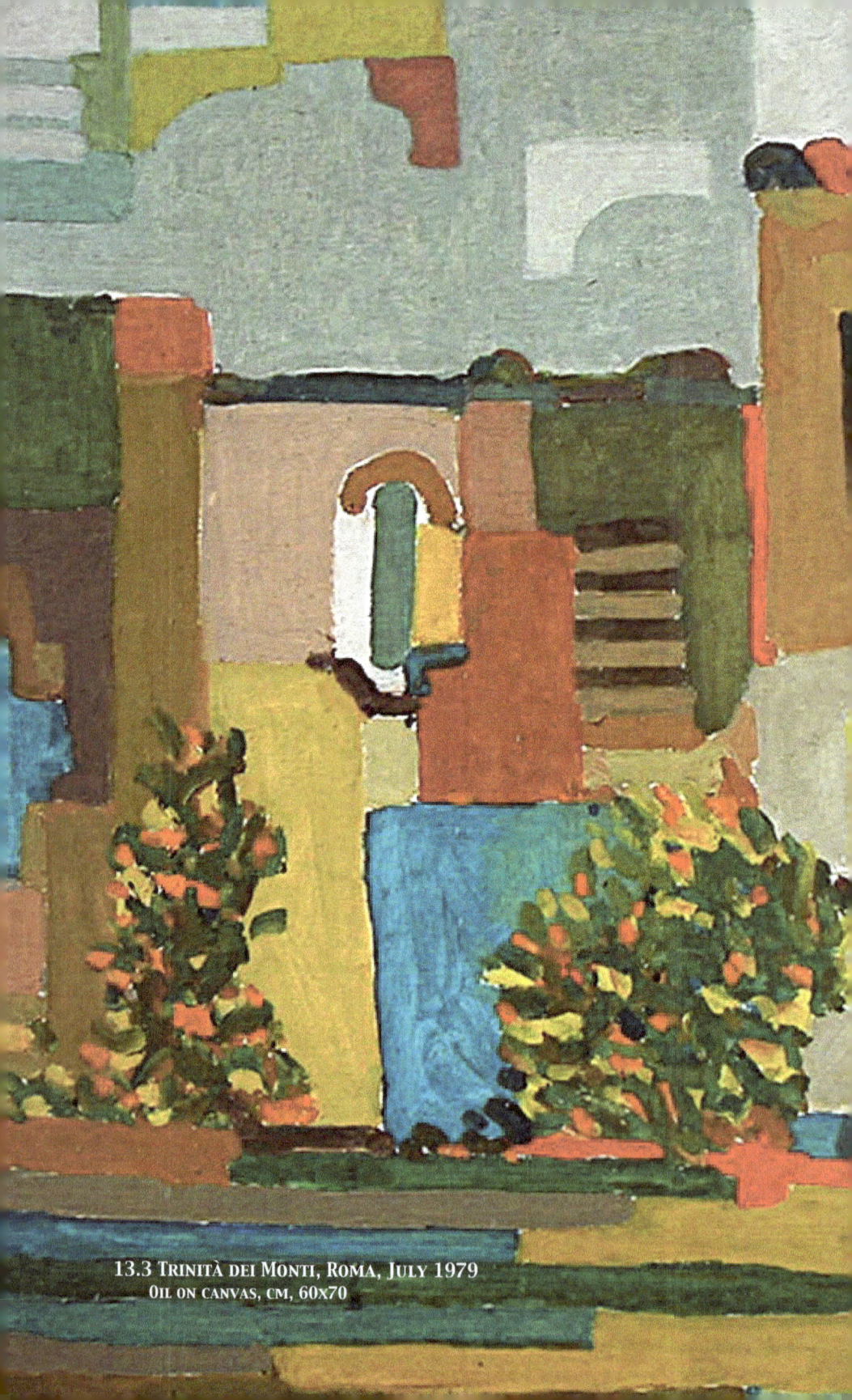

13.3 Trinità dei Monti, Roma, July 1979
Oil on canvas, cm, 60x70

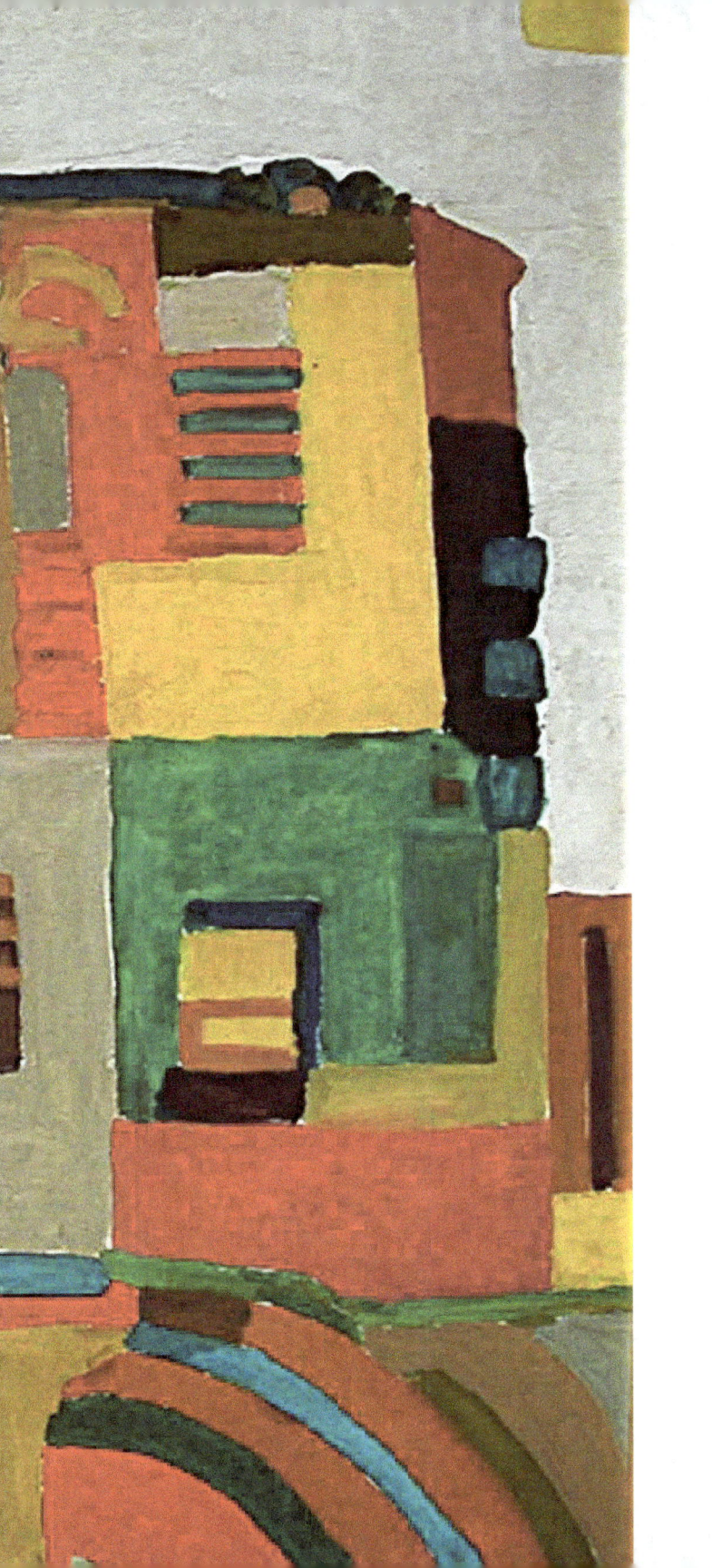

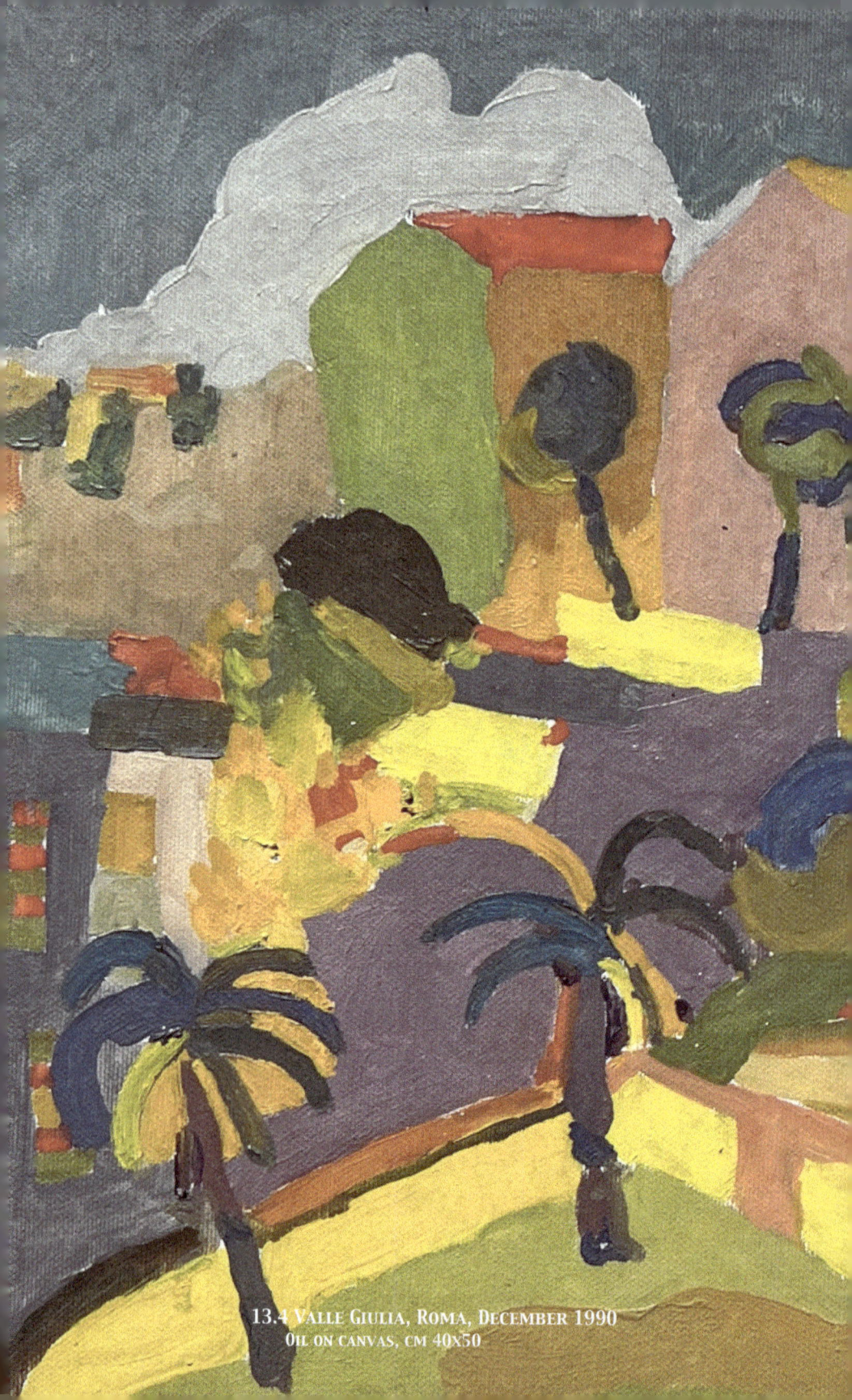

13.4 Valle Giulia, Roma, December 1990
Oil on canvas, cm 40x50

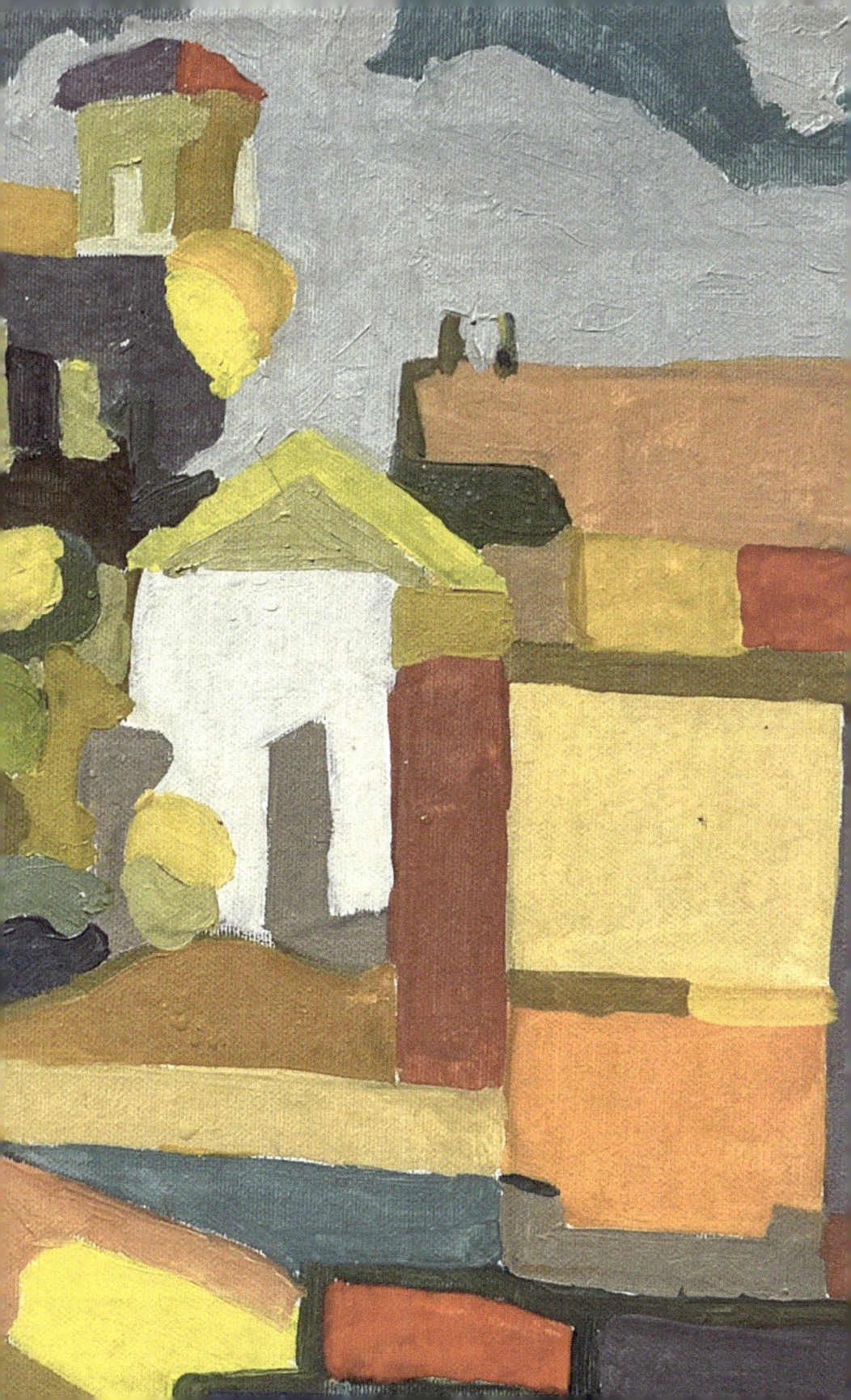

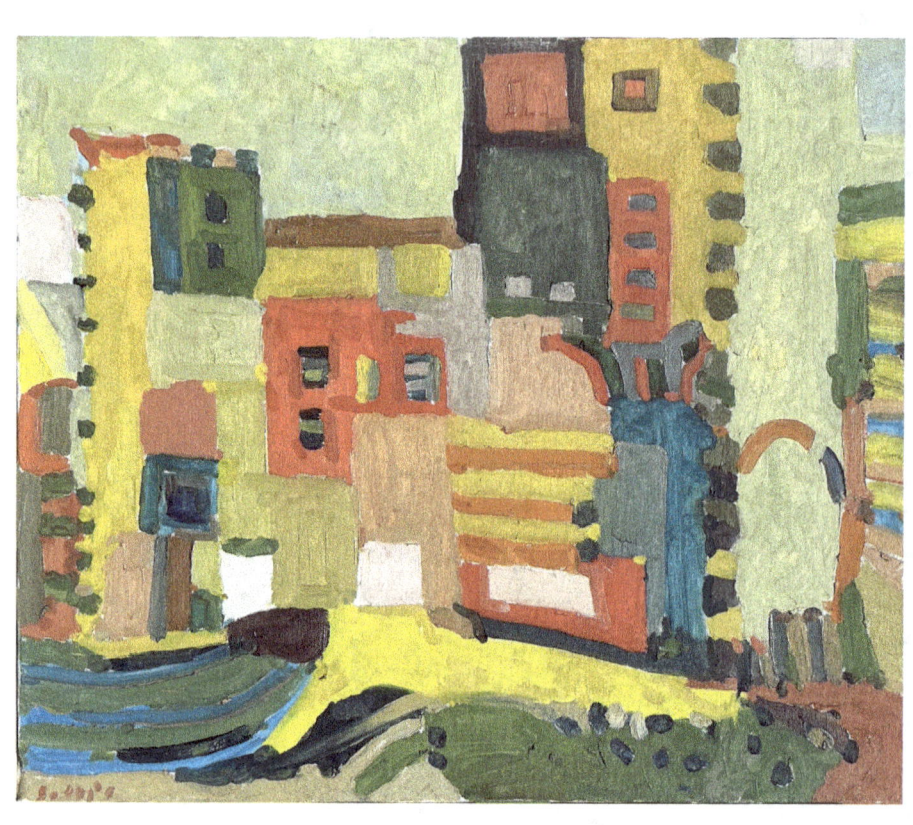

13.5 TRINITÀ DEI MONTI, ROMA, 1986
 OIL ON CANVAS, CM 50x60

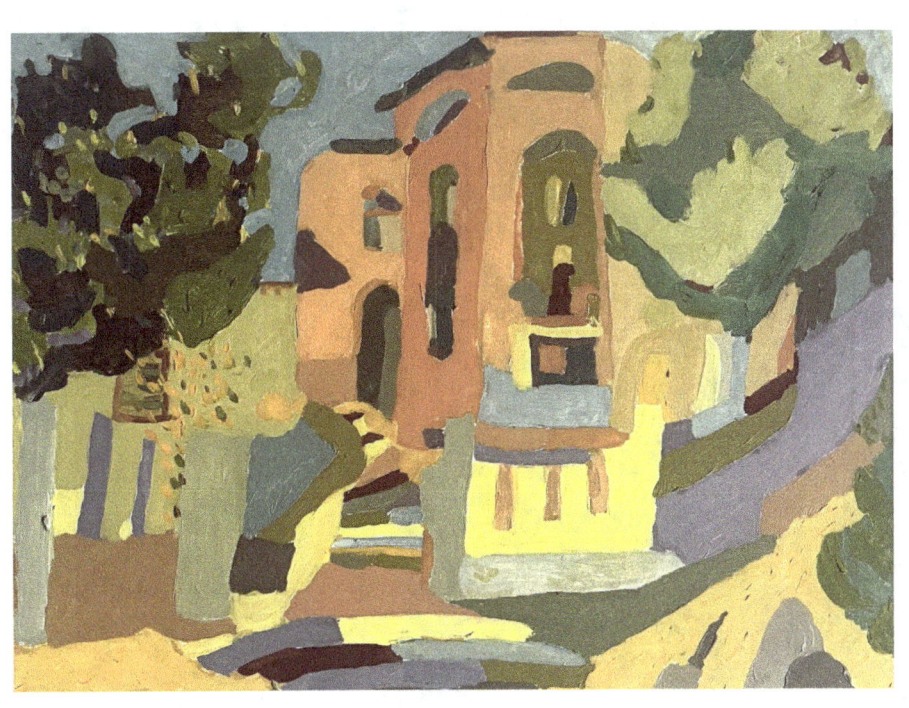

13,6 SCHOOL AT PARCO NEMORENSE ROMA, 1986
OIL ON CANVAS, CM 45X55

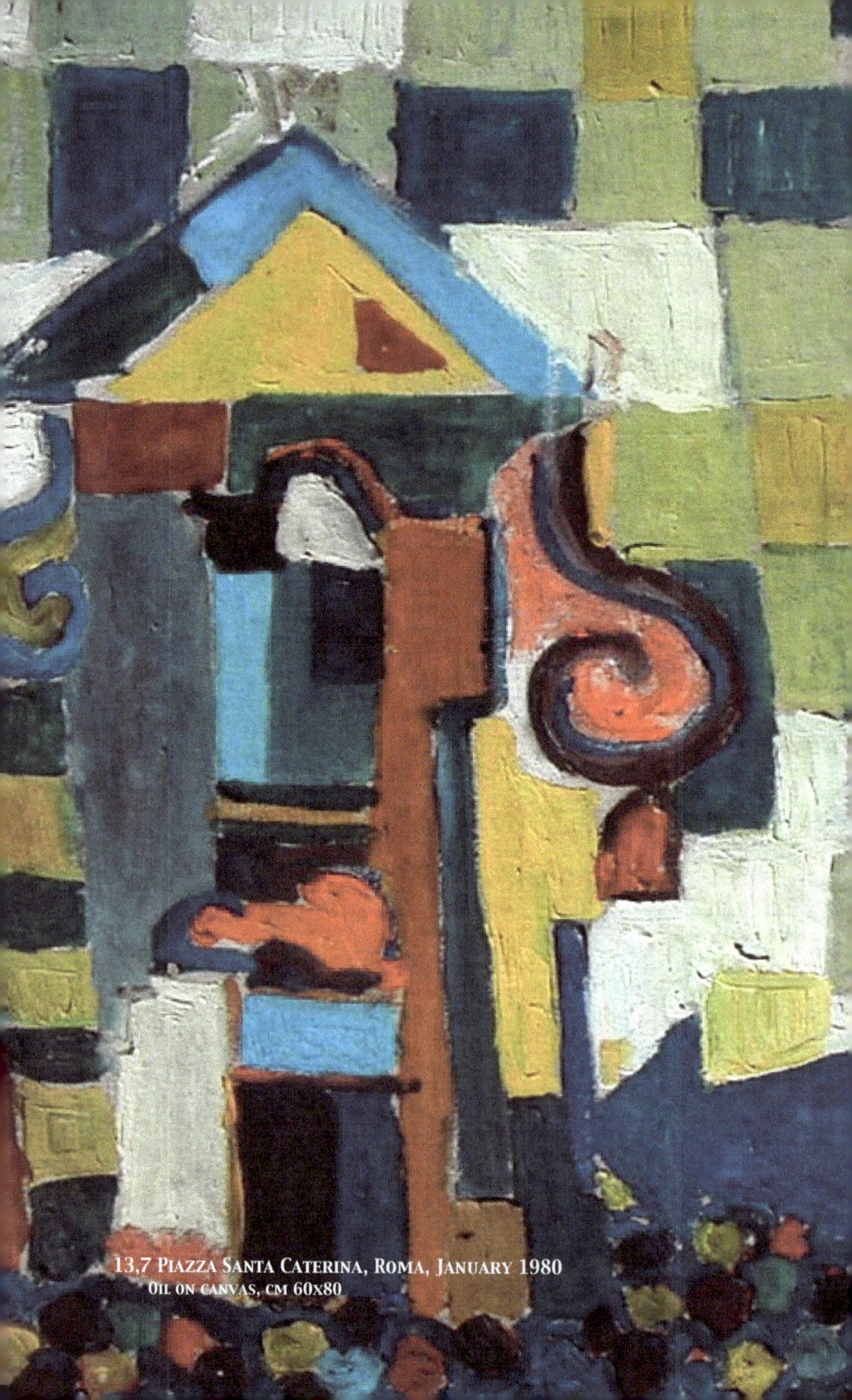

13,7 Piazza Santa Caterina, Roma, January 1980
Oil on canvas, cm 60x80

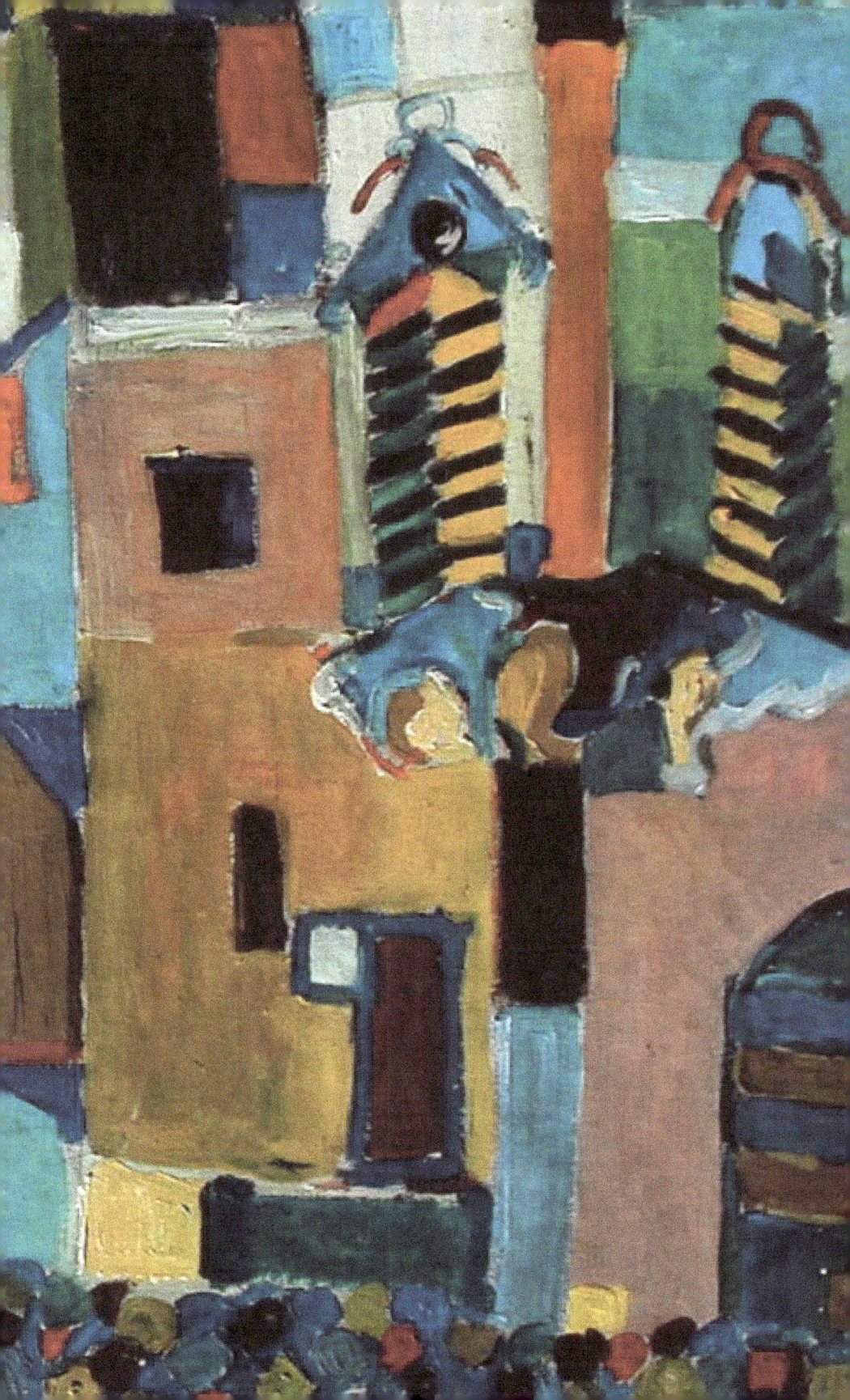

Landscape Glimpses

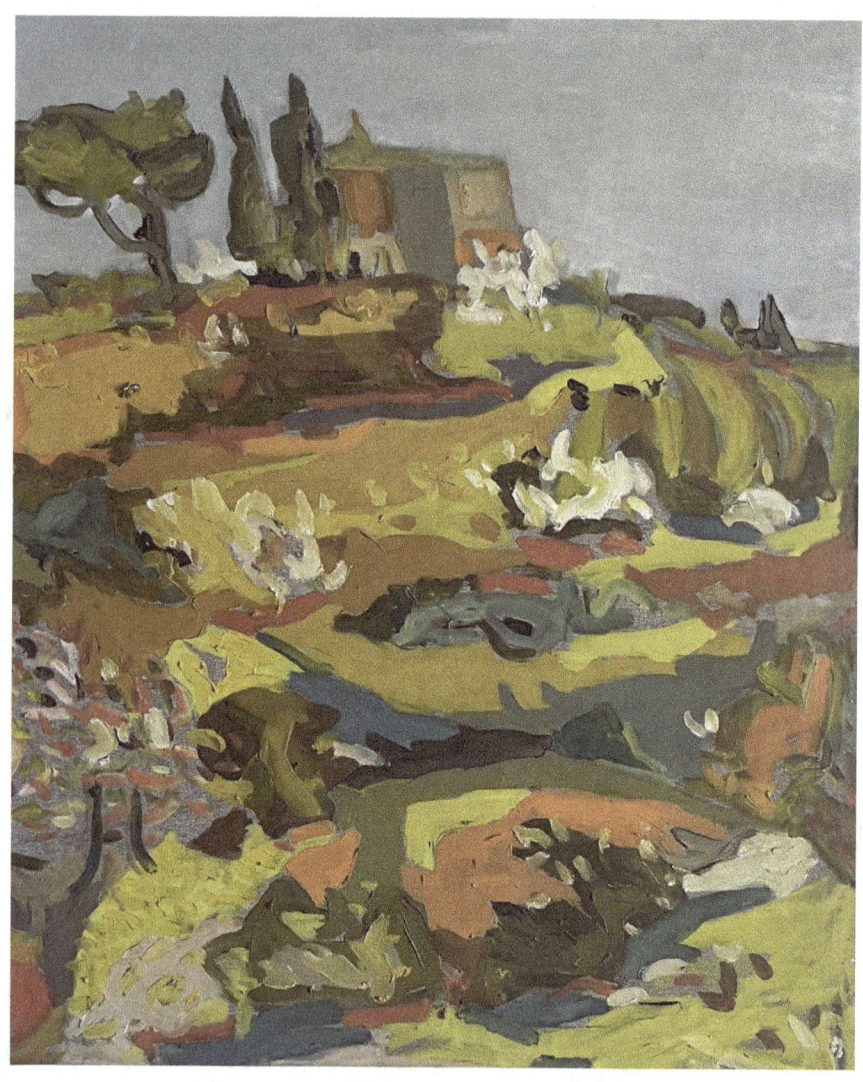

14.1 Italian landscape inspired by Giorgio Morandi, 1978
   Oil on canvas, cm 60x70

14.3 Italian landscape inspired by Franco Fontana, 1978
   Oil on canvas, cm 60x70

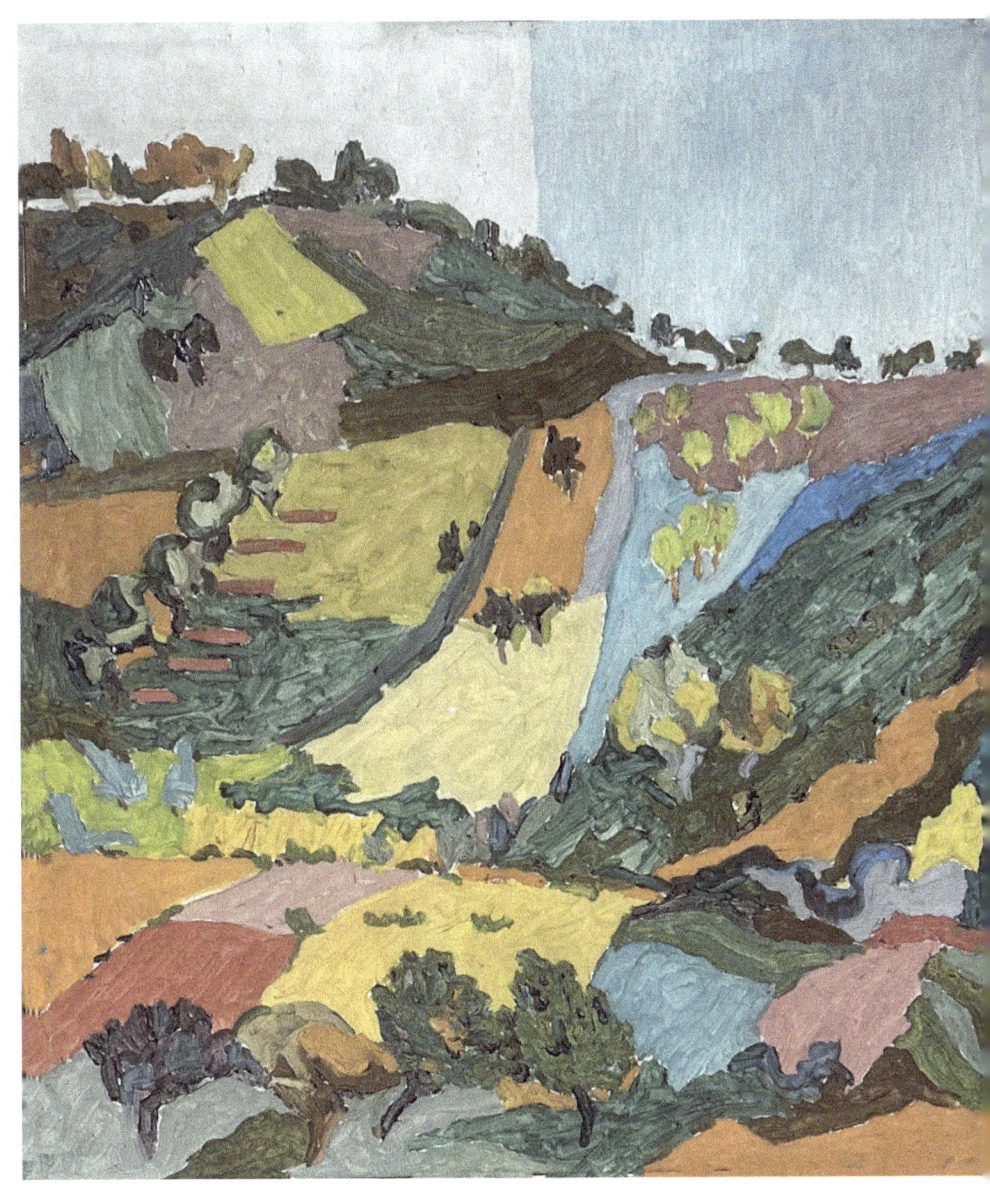

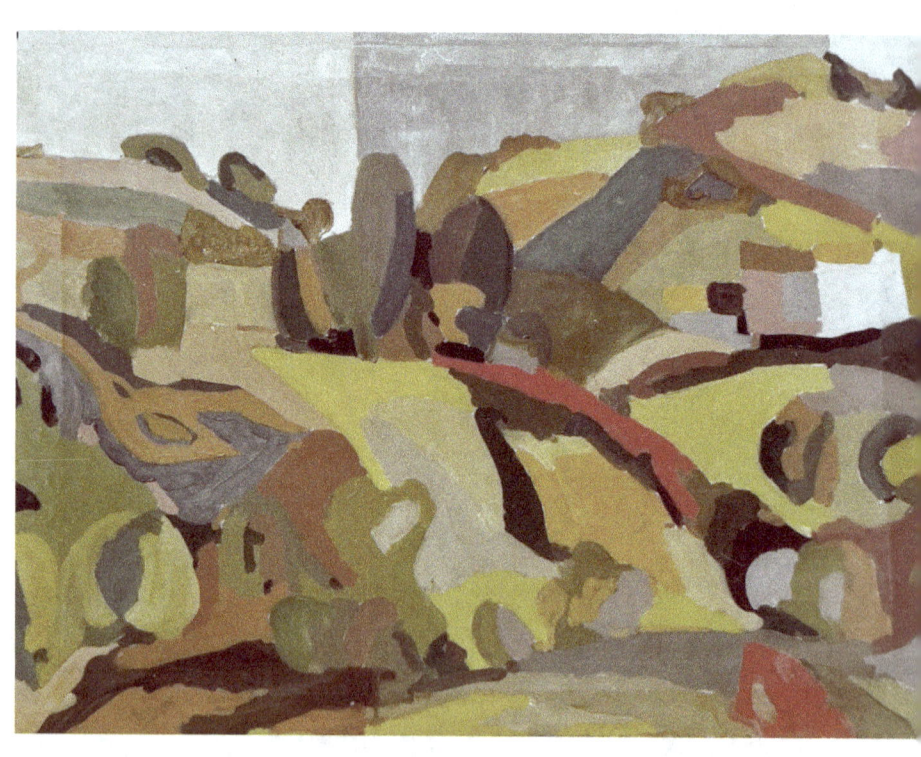

14.4 ITALIAN LANDSCAPE, ROMA, 1985
OIL ON CANVAS, CM 70X100

14.5 ITALIAN LAMDSCAE, ROMA, 1985
OIL ON CANVAS, CM 70X120

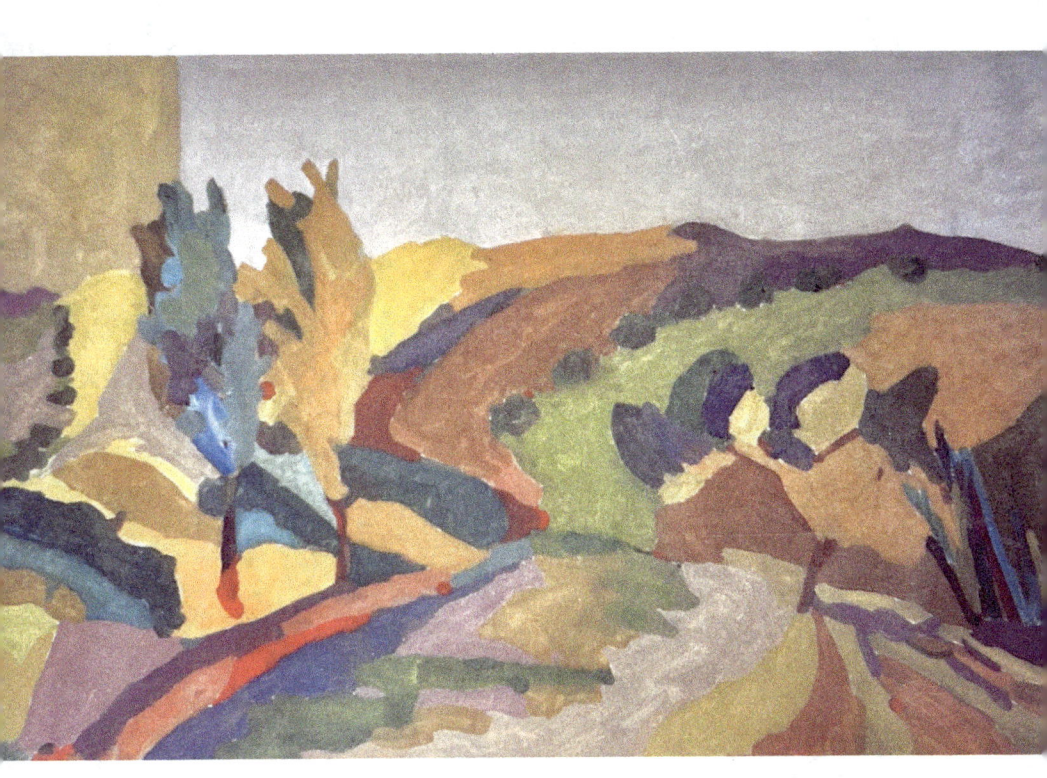

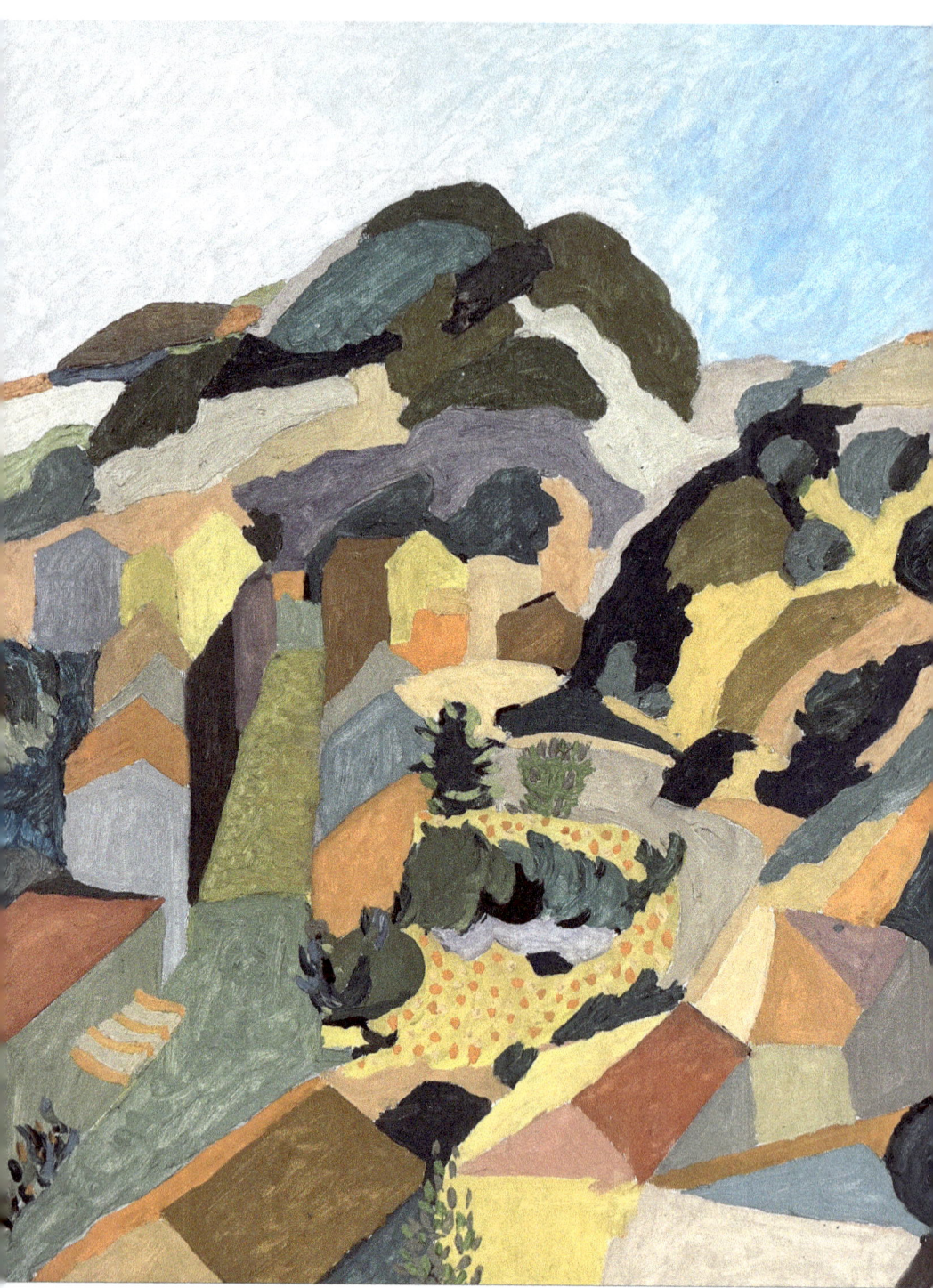

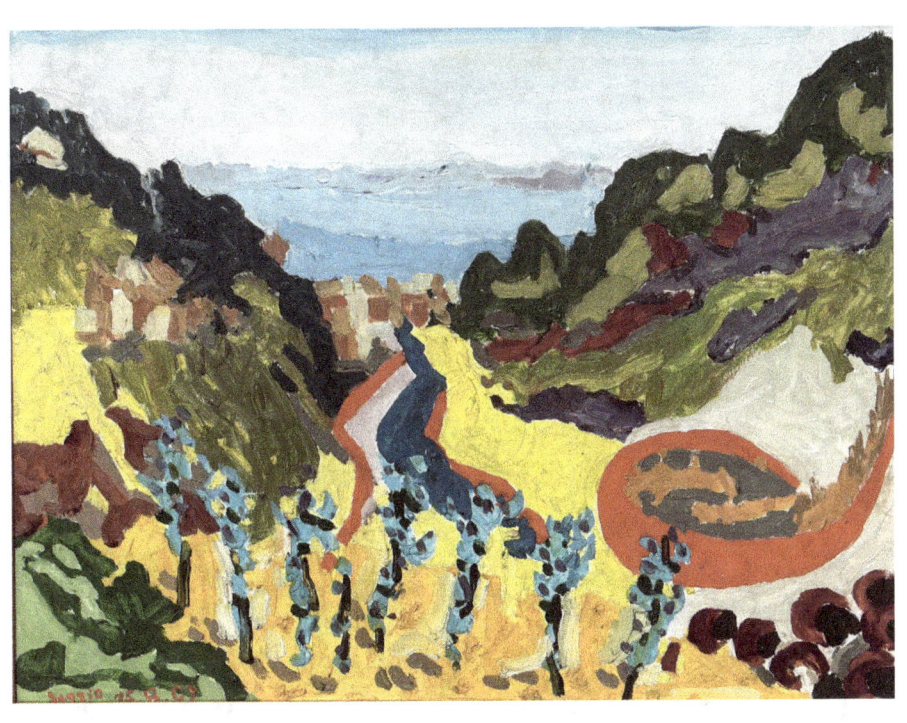

14.6 THE MOUNTAIN OF DREAMS, PATTI JULY 1990
   OIL ON CANVAS, CM 60X70

14.7 ZAPPARDINO STREAM, GIOIOSA MAREA, AUGUST 2010
   OIL ON CANVAS, CM 90X100

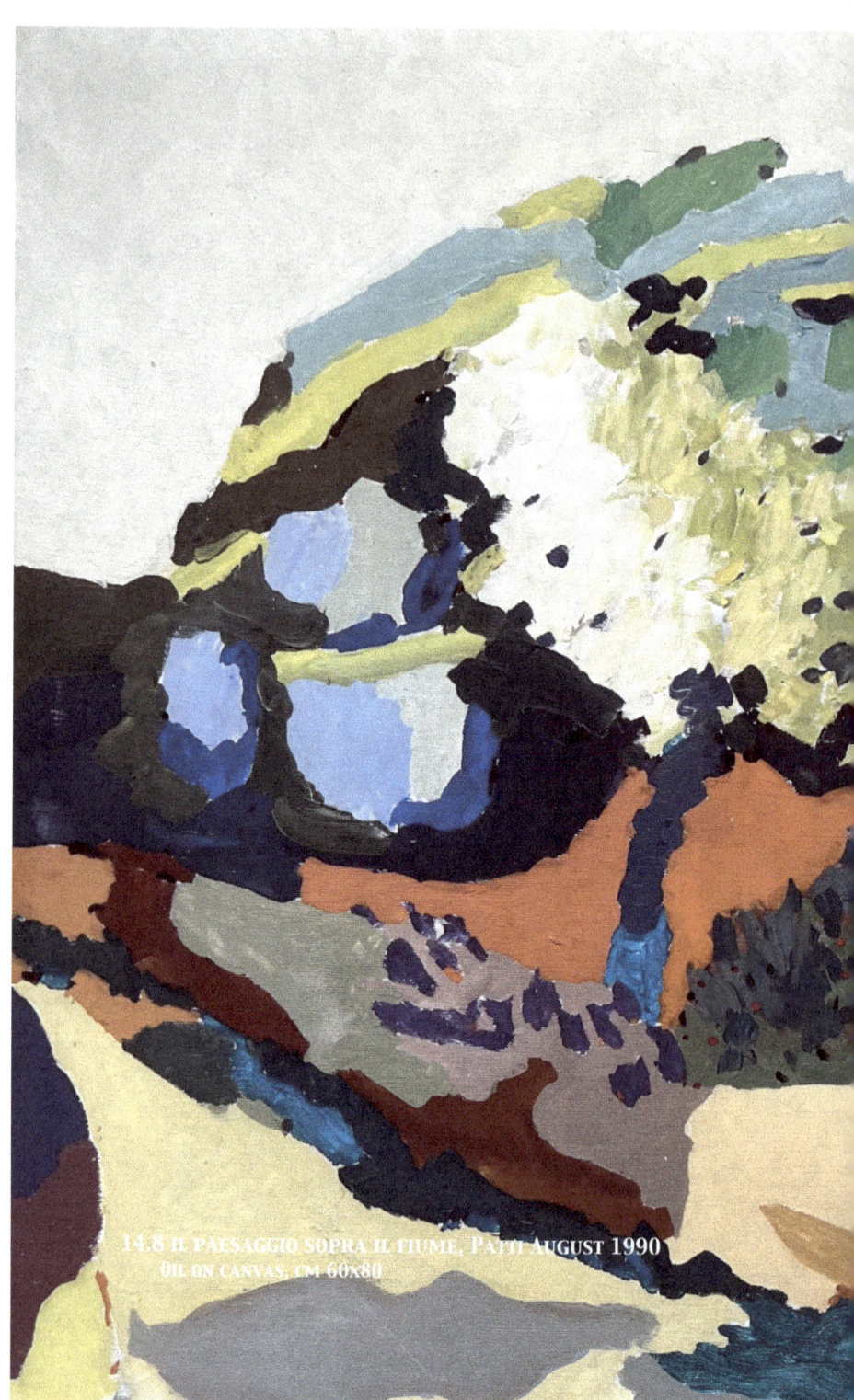

14.8 Il paesaggio sopra il fiume, Patti August 1990
oil on canvas, cm 60x80

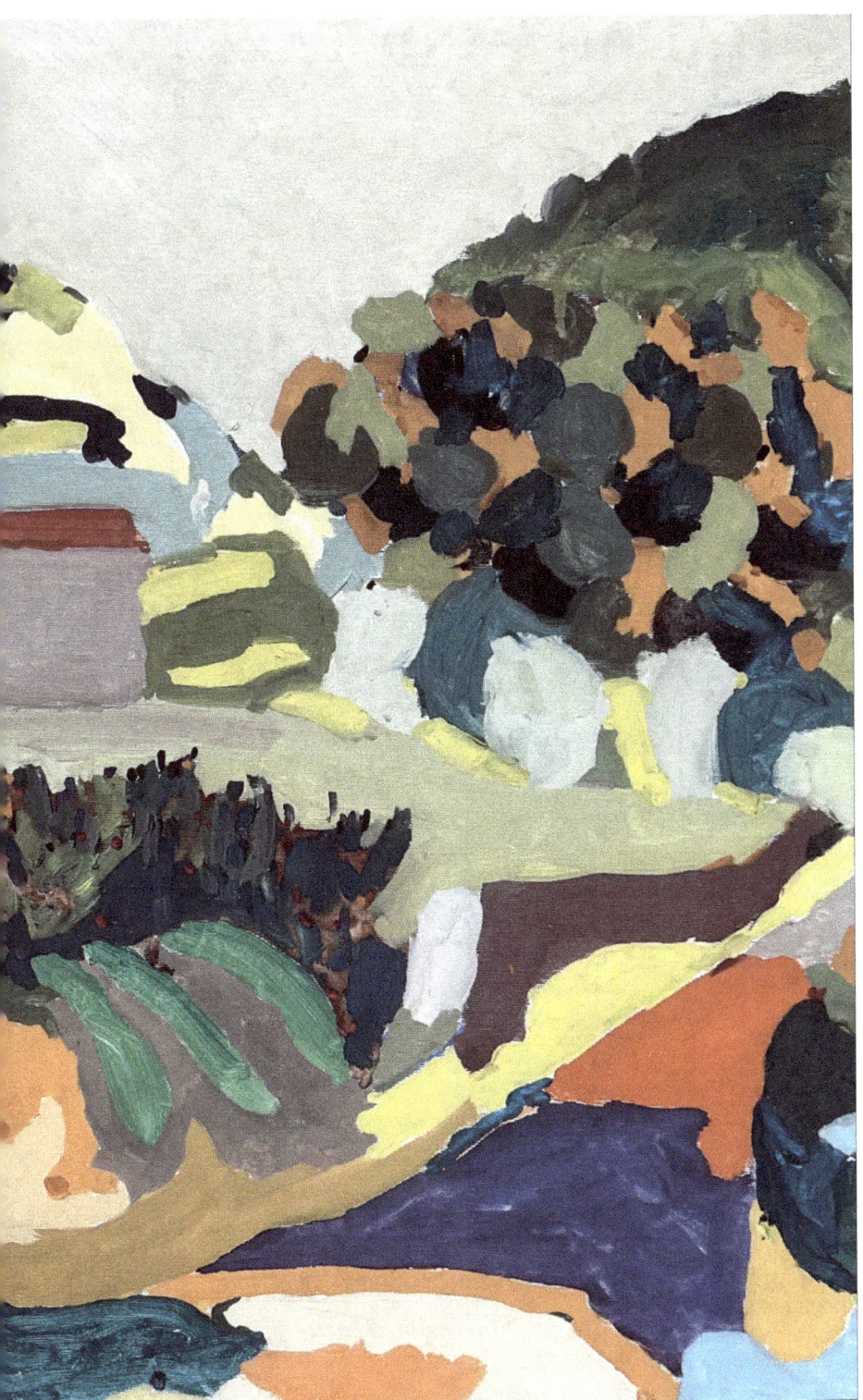

ITALIAN LANDSCAPES

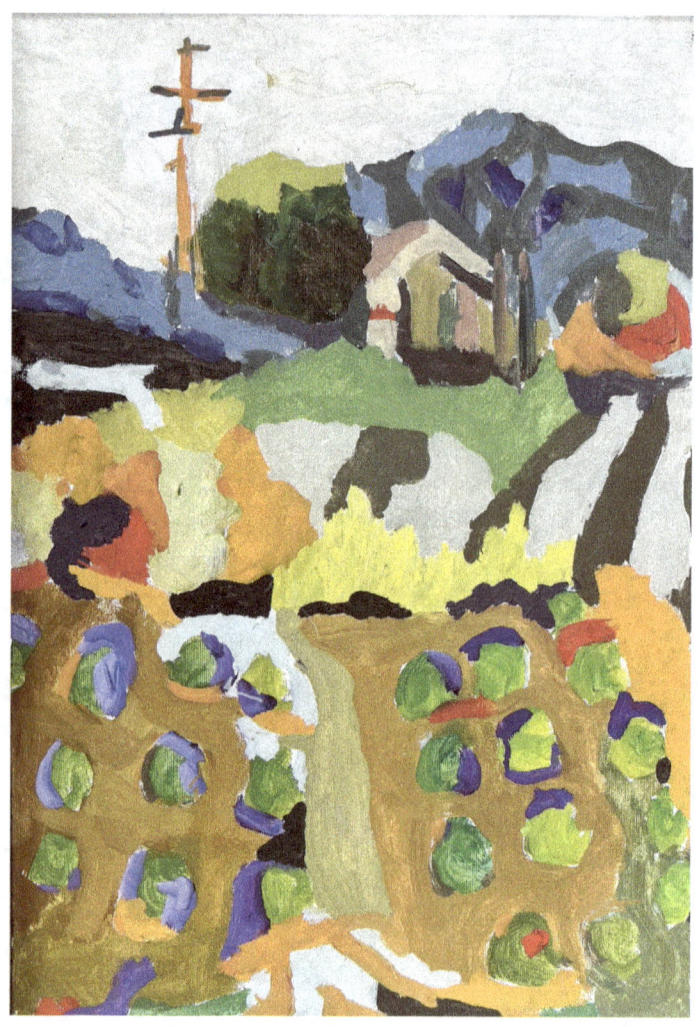

14.1 PAESAGGIO ITALIANO I 1983

15.1 ITALIAN LANDSCAPE INSPIRED BY KLEE. ROMA, 1985
    OIL ON CANVAS, CM 70X100
15.2 ITALIAN LANDSCAPE CLOSE TO RIGNANO, DECEMBER 1990
    OIL ON CANVAS, CM 35X50

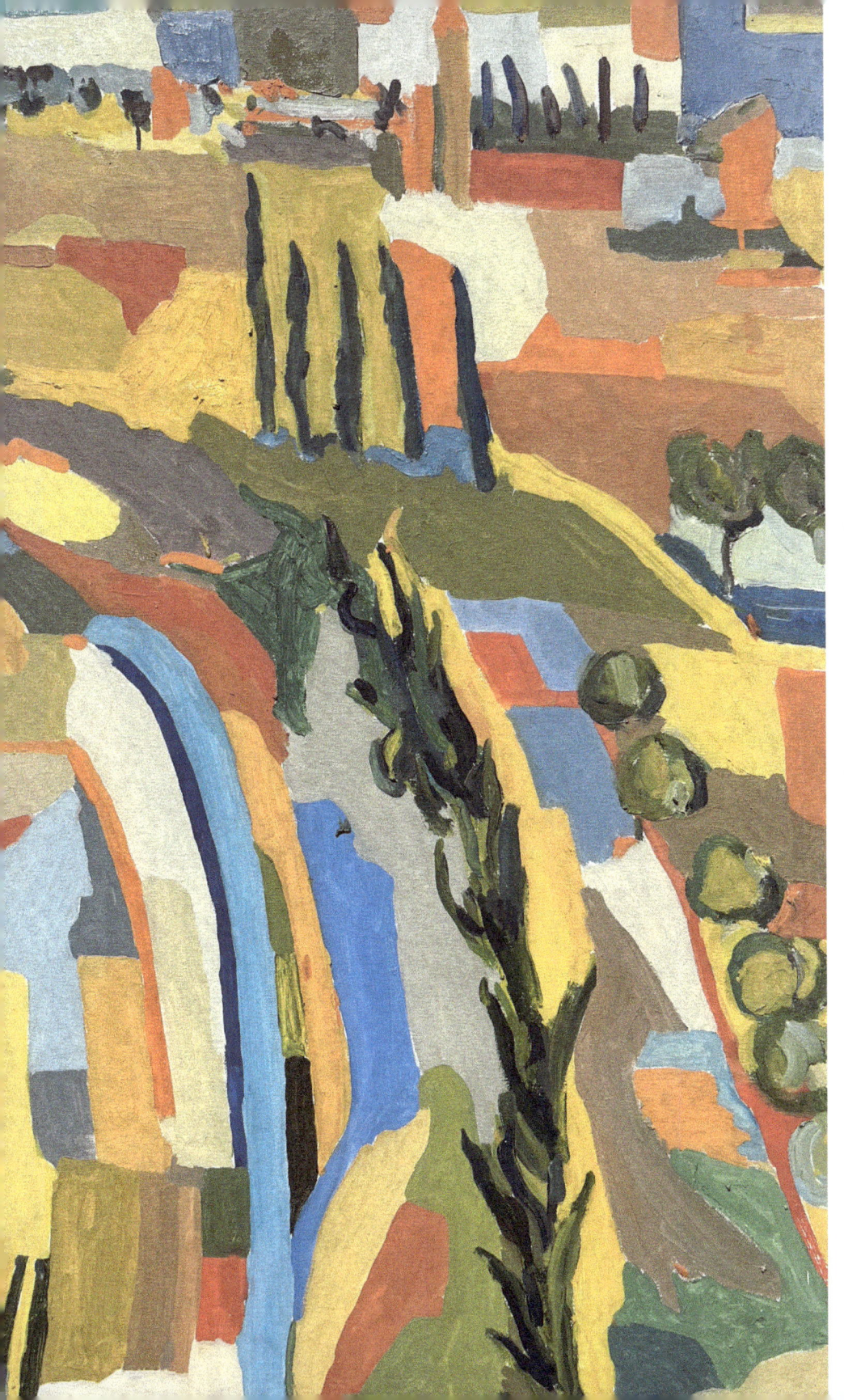

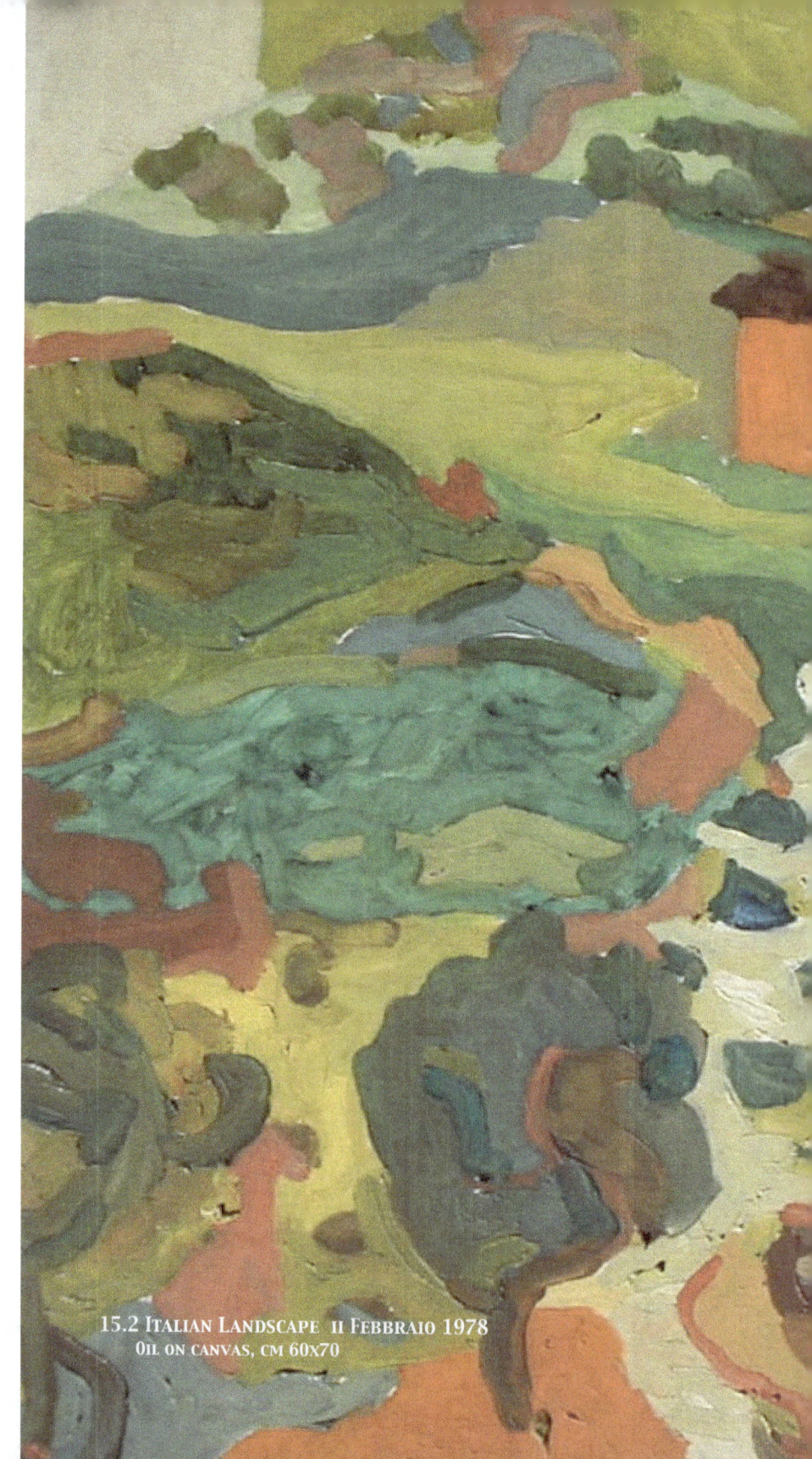

15.2 Italian Landscape II Febbraio 1978
Oil on canvas, cm 60x70

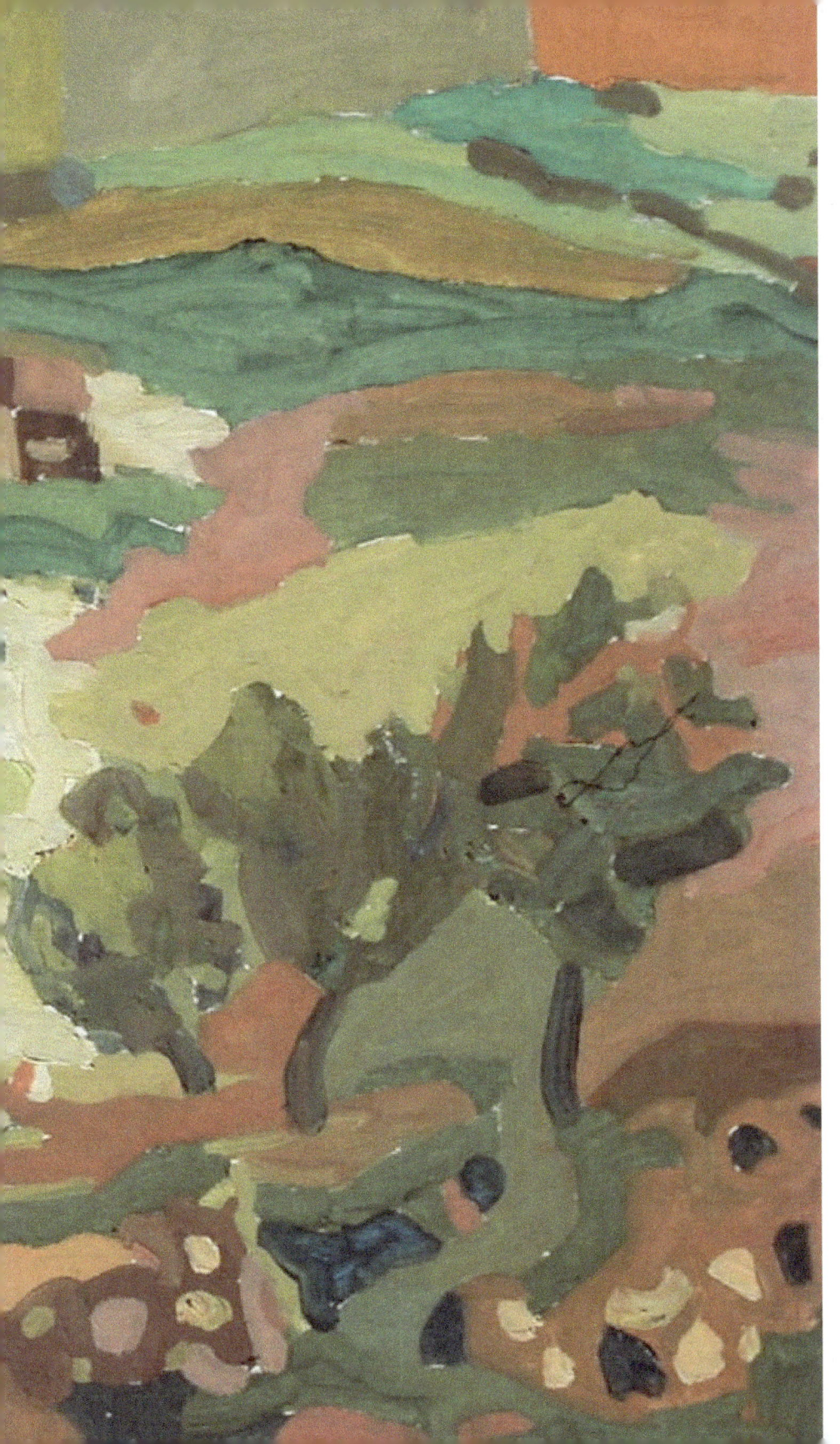

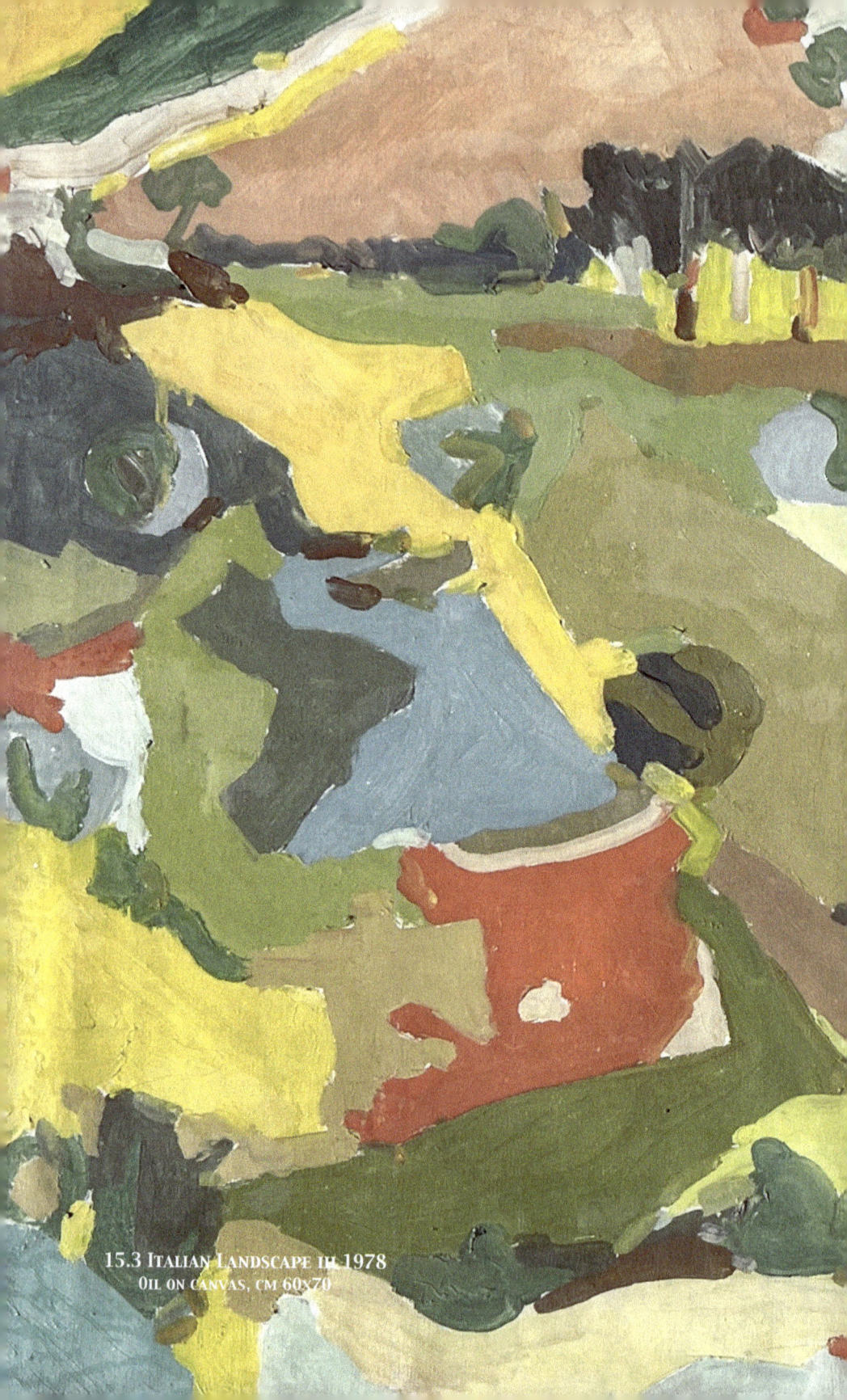

15.3 Italian Landscape iii, 1978
Oil on canvas, cm 60x70

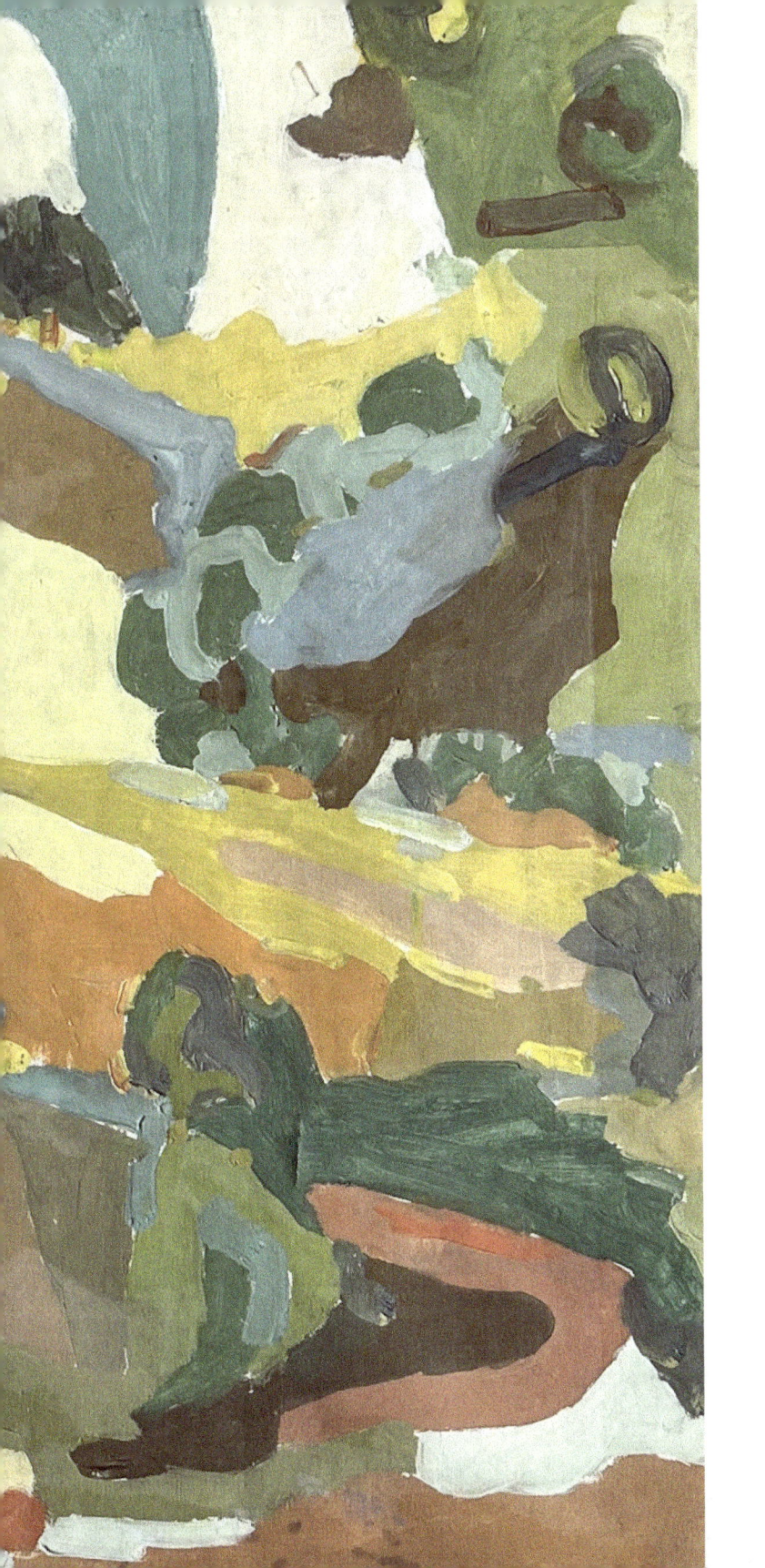

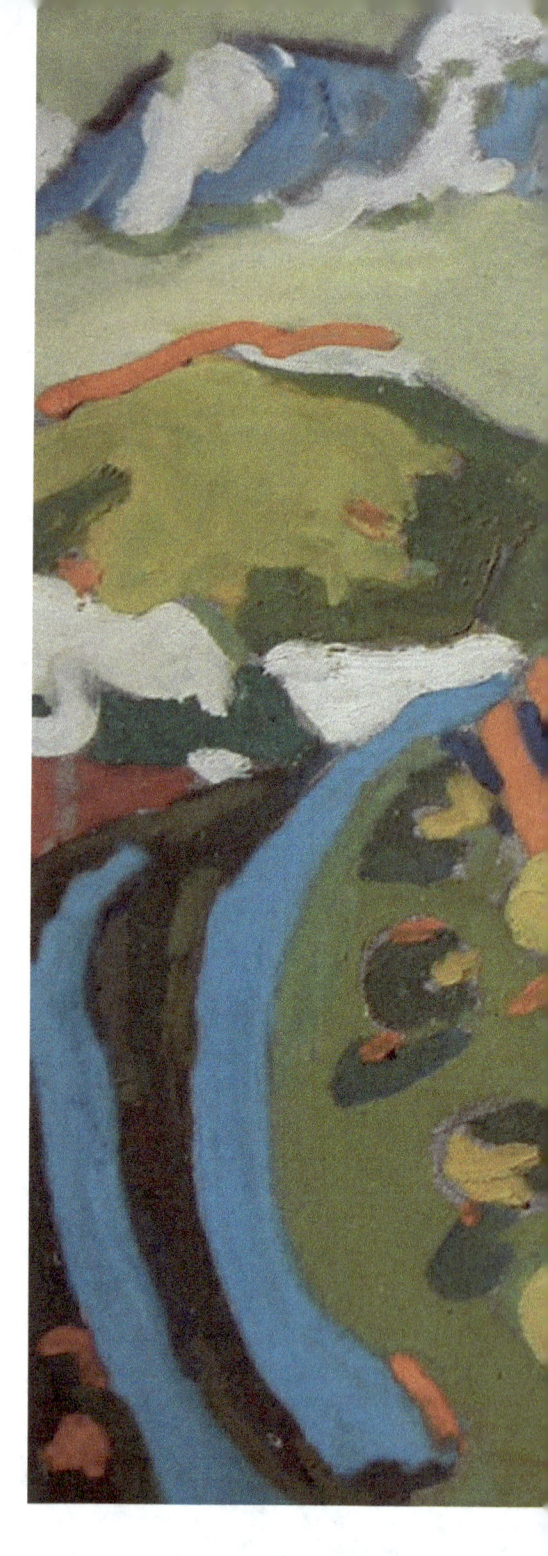

15.4 Italian Landscape IV 1980
Oil on canvas, cm 50x60

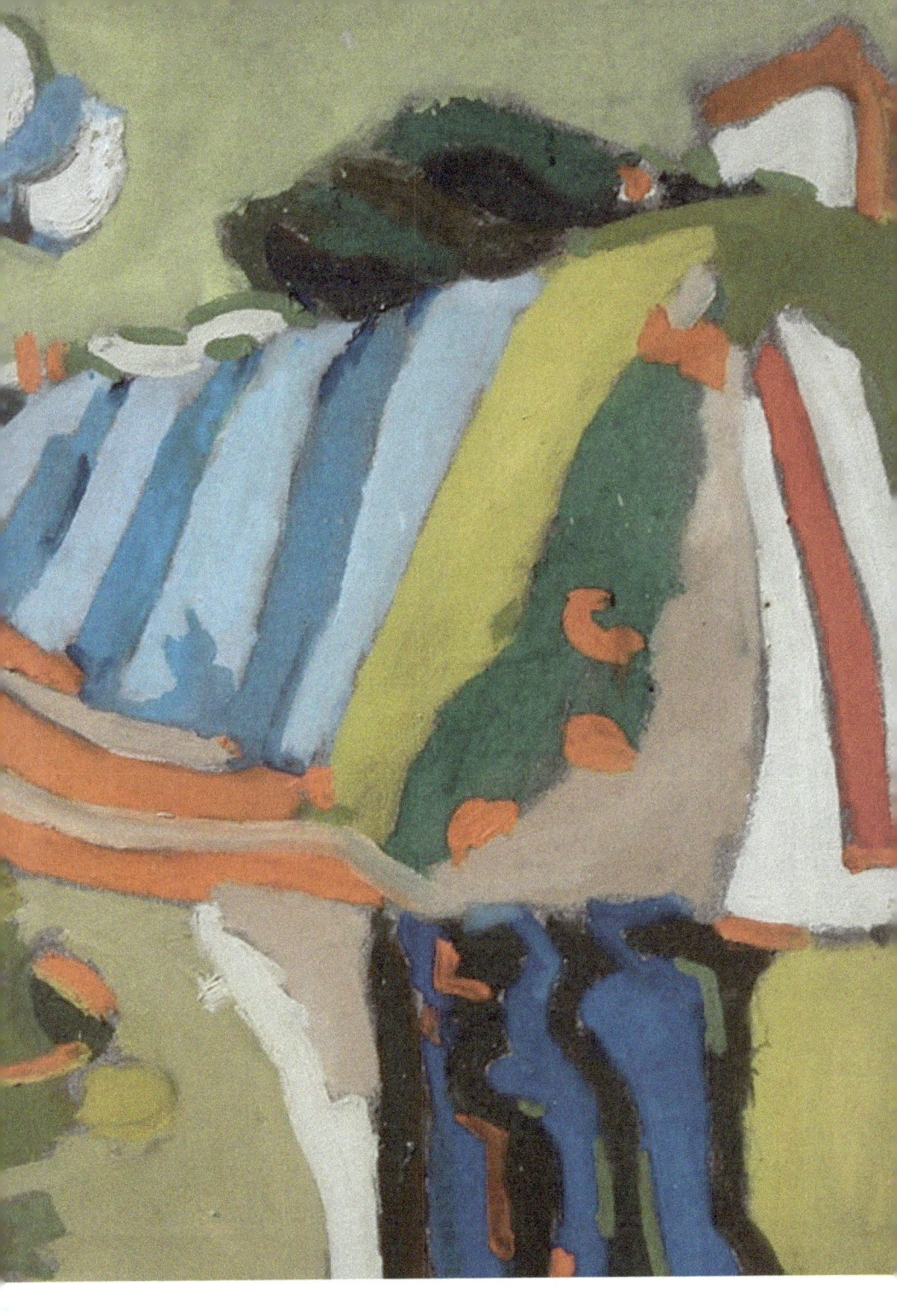

Sangu Miu!

16.1 Donatella, Roma, 1981
Oil on canvas, cm 30x40

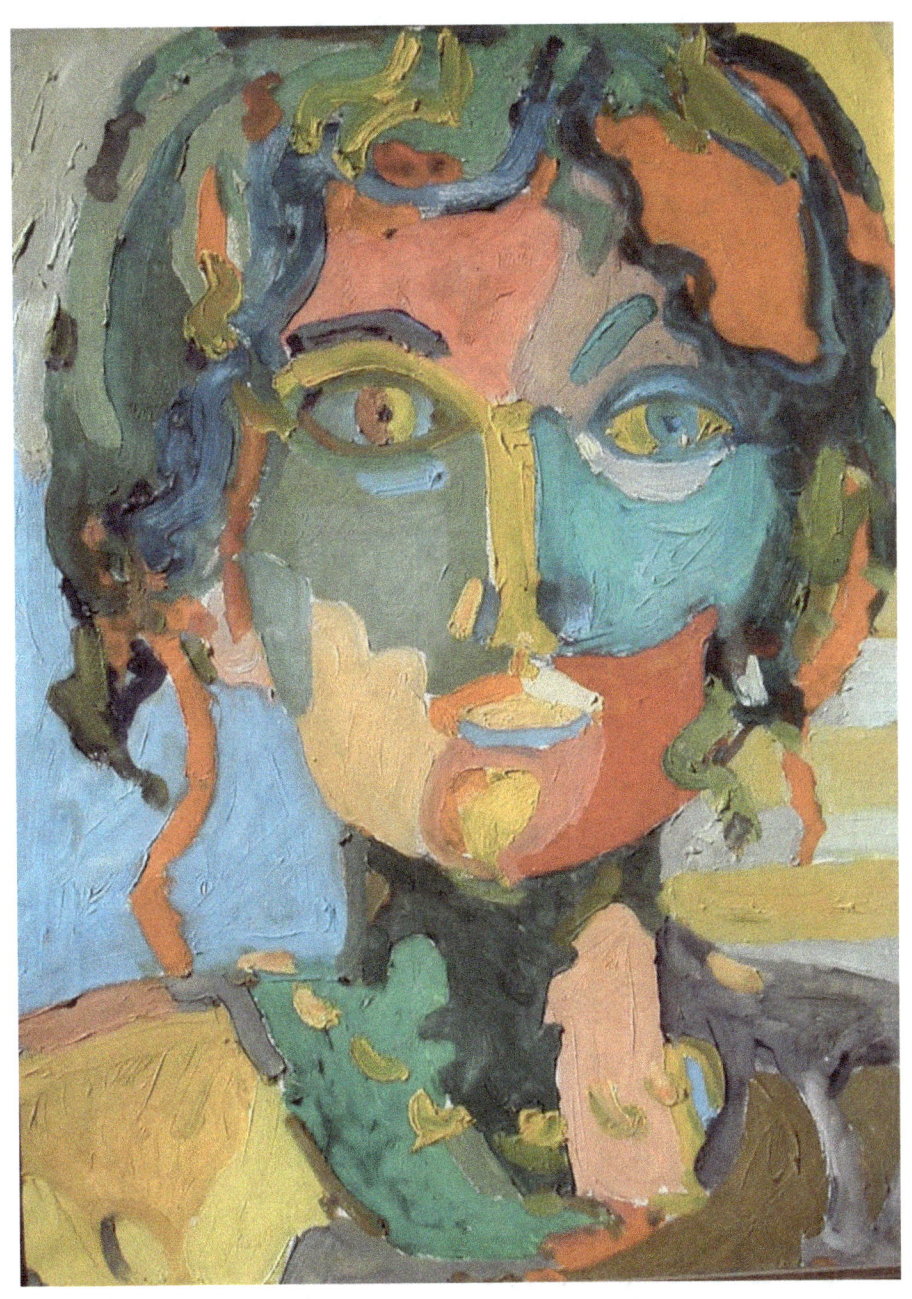

16.2 DONA AND FRICKY, ROMA, 1982
OIL ON CANVAS, CM 60X80

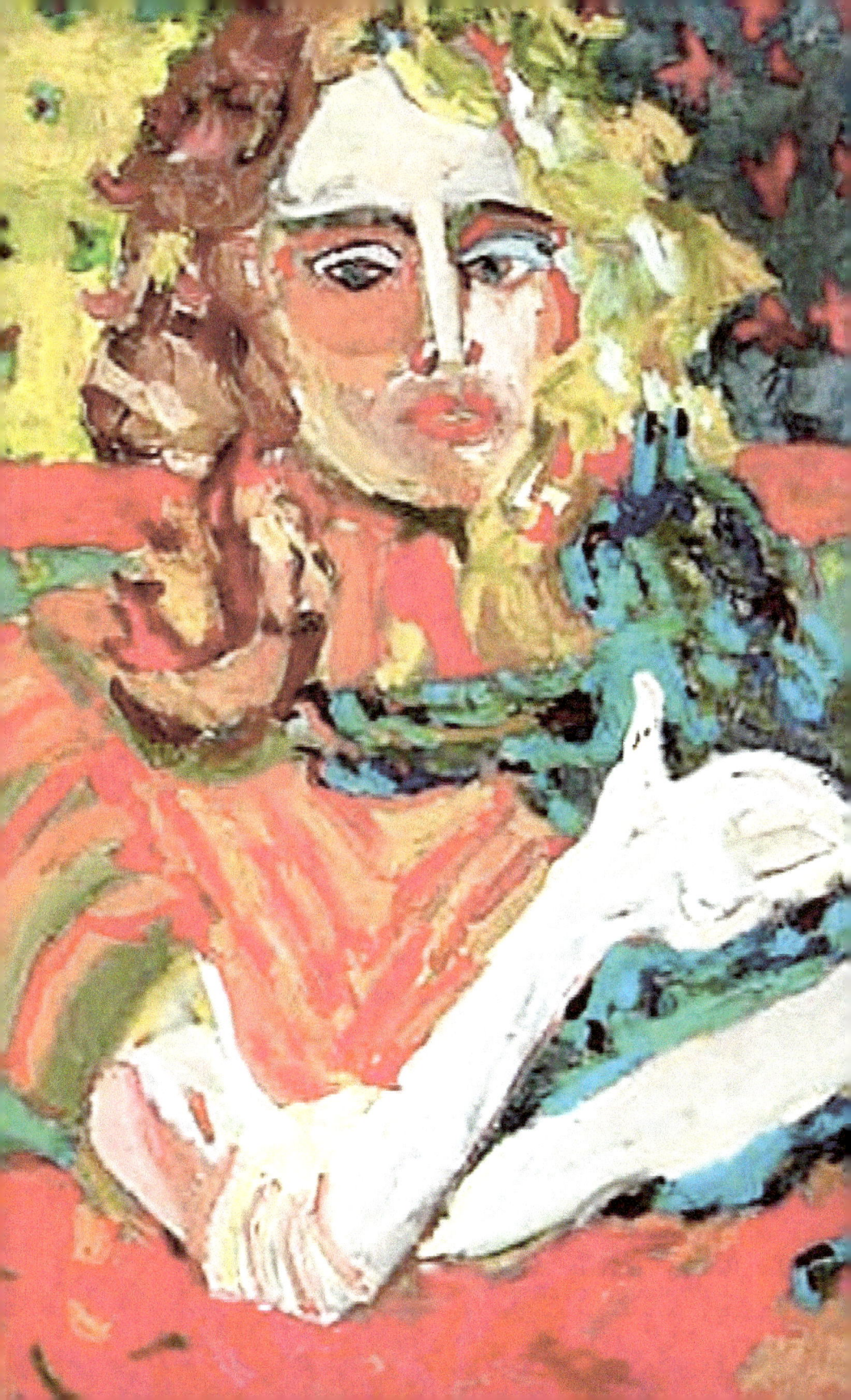

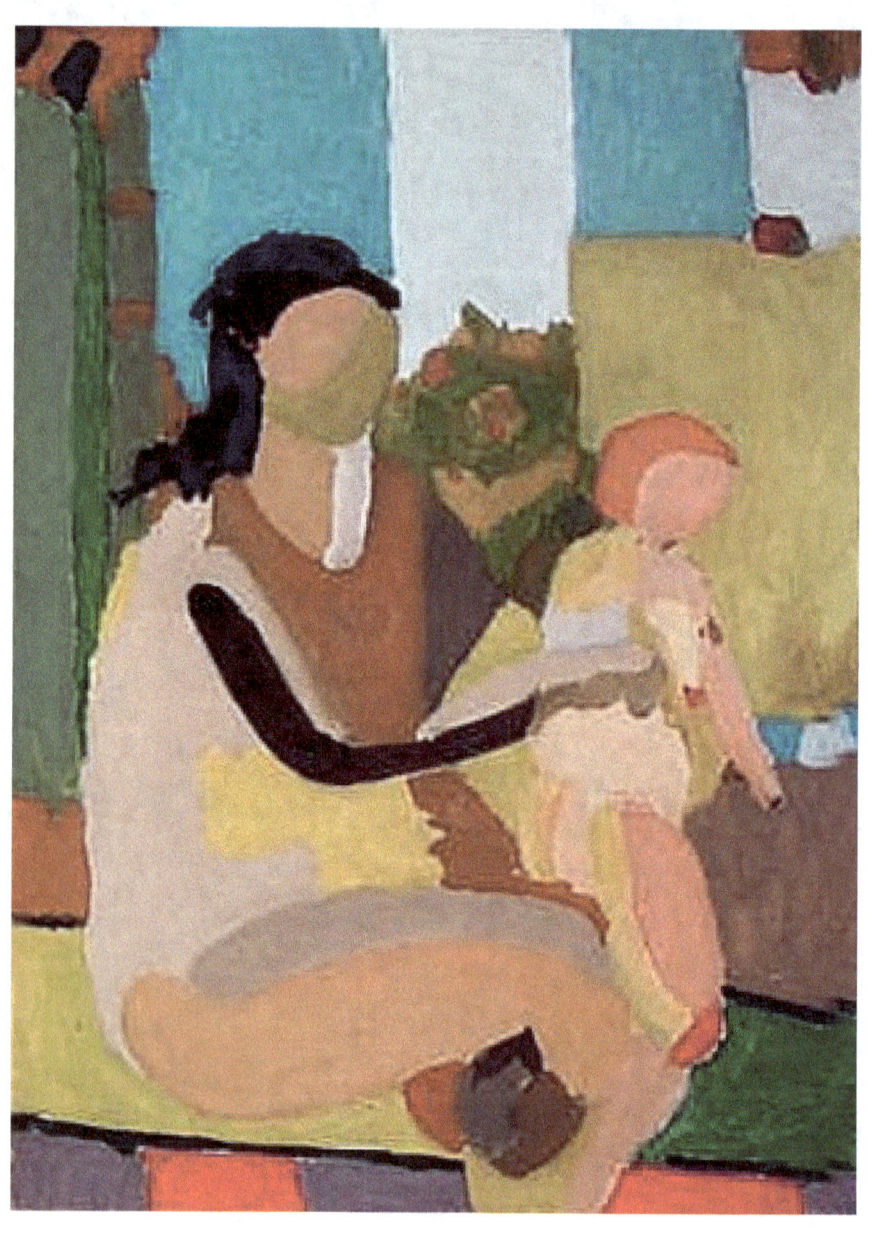

16.4 DONANO LELE, ROMA, AUGUST 1987
OIL ON CANVAS, CM 30X40

16.3 DONA AND LELE, ROMA, AUGUST 1987
OIL ON CANVAS, CM 25X30

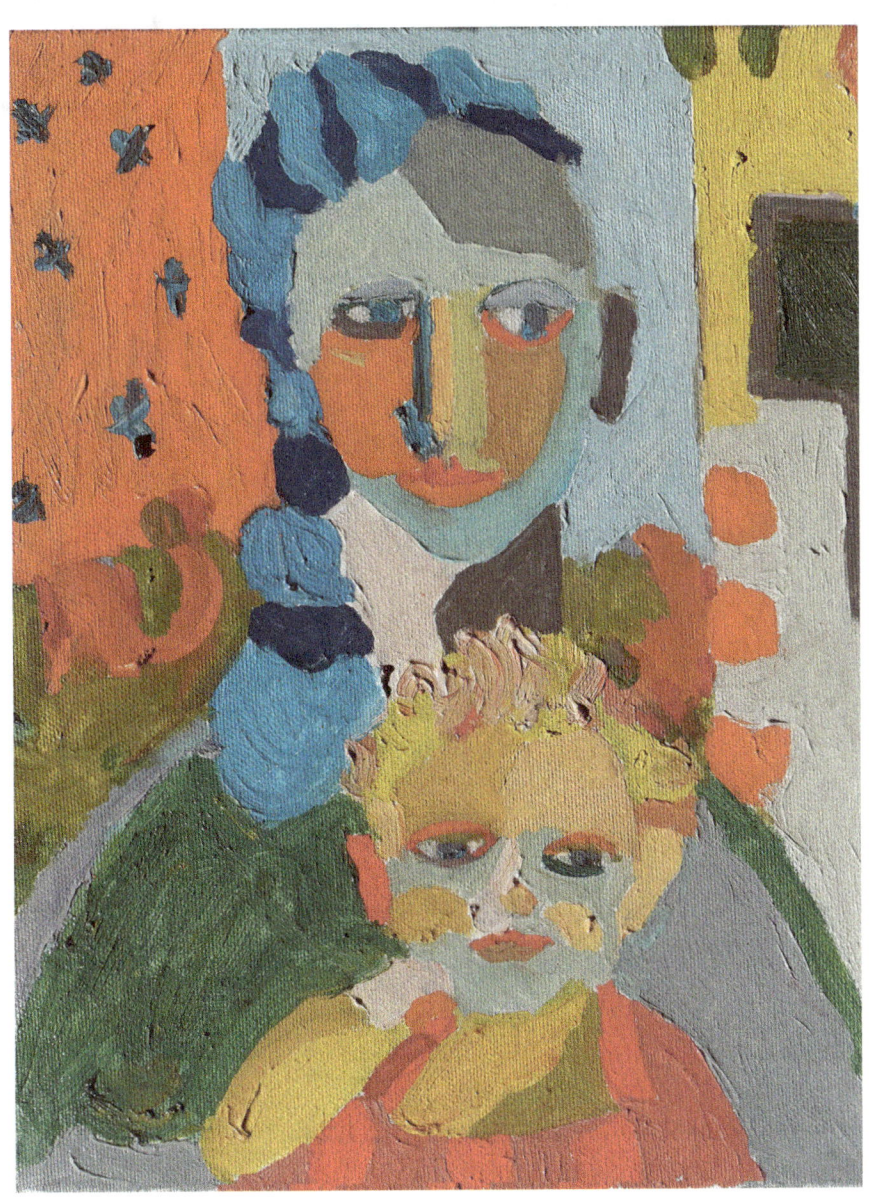

SEA OF SICILY

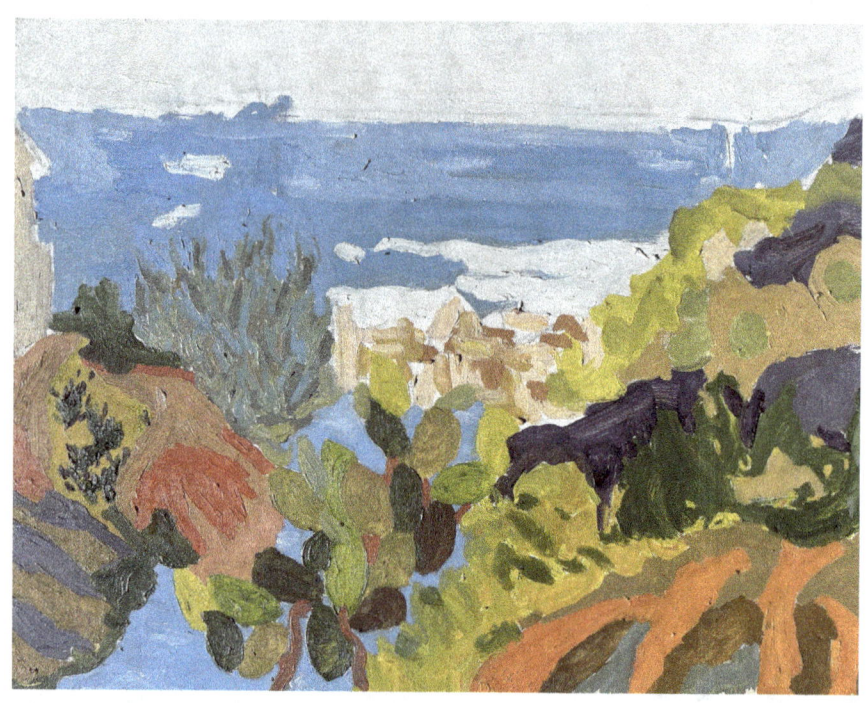

17.1 CLIFF AT CAPO CALAVÀ, GIOIOSA MAREA AUGUST 2003
   OIL ON CANVAS, CM 40X50

17.2 CAPO D'ORLANDO FROM GLIACA, GIOIOSA MAREA APRIL 2003
   OIL ON CANVAS, CM 40X50

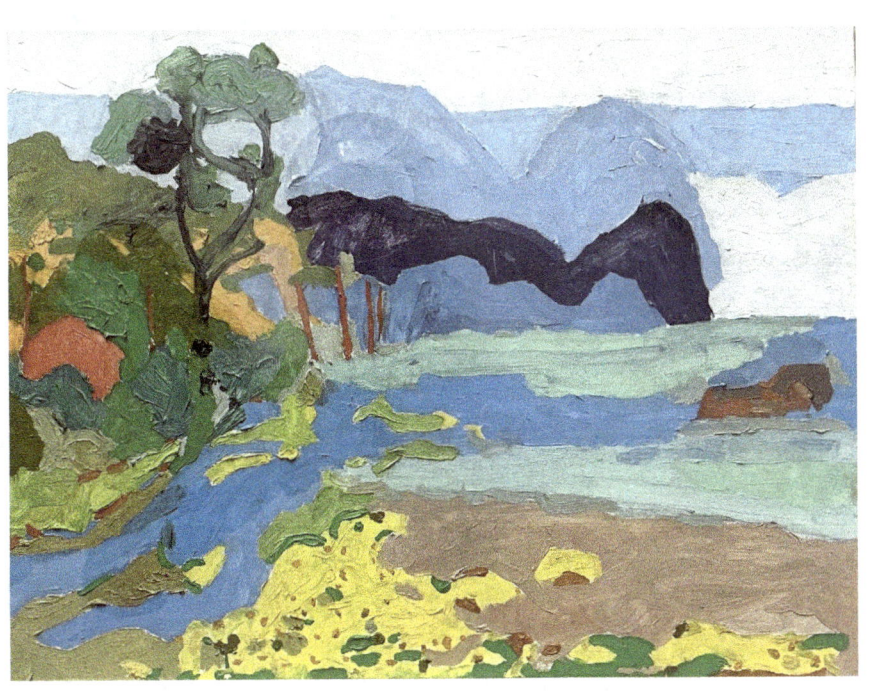

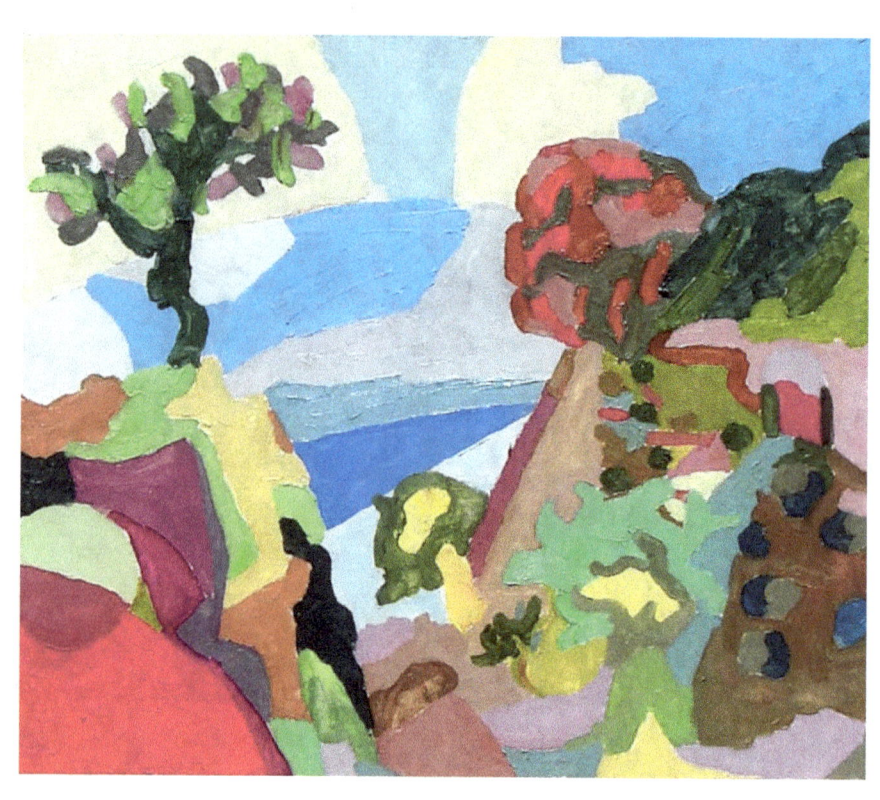

17.4 CAPO CALAVÀ, GIOIOSA MAREA JULY 2002
OIL ON CANVAS, CM 50X60

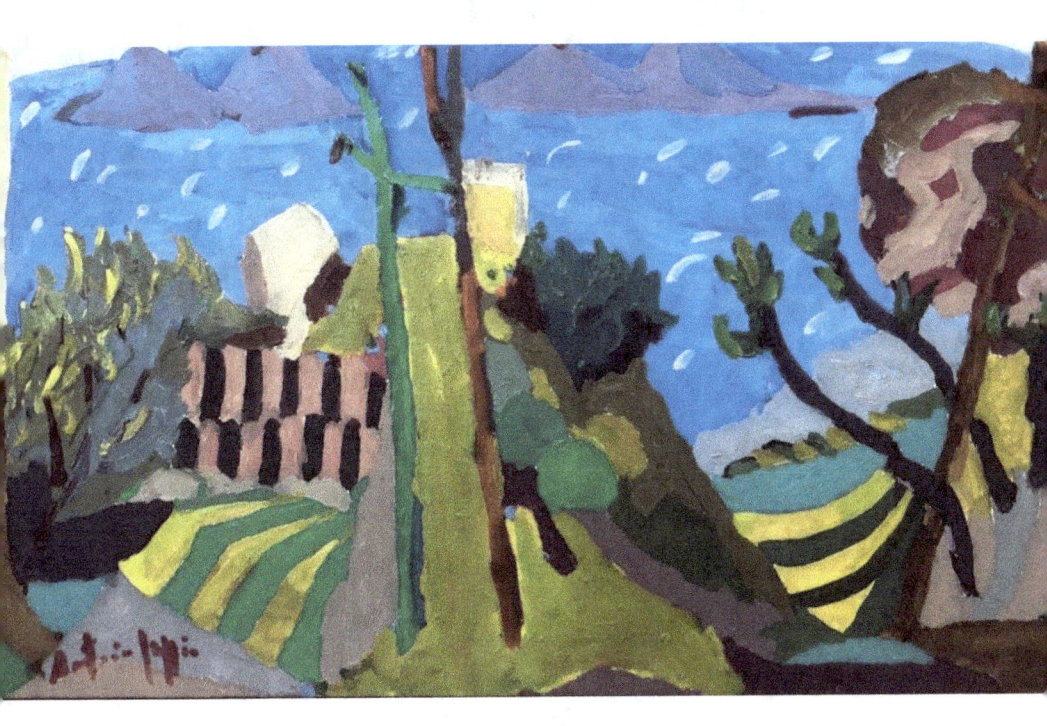

17.5 Skino district, Gioiosa Marea July 2008
Oil on canvas, cm 40x70

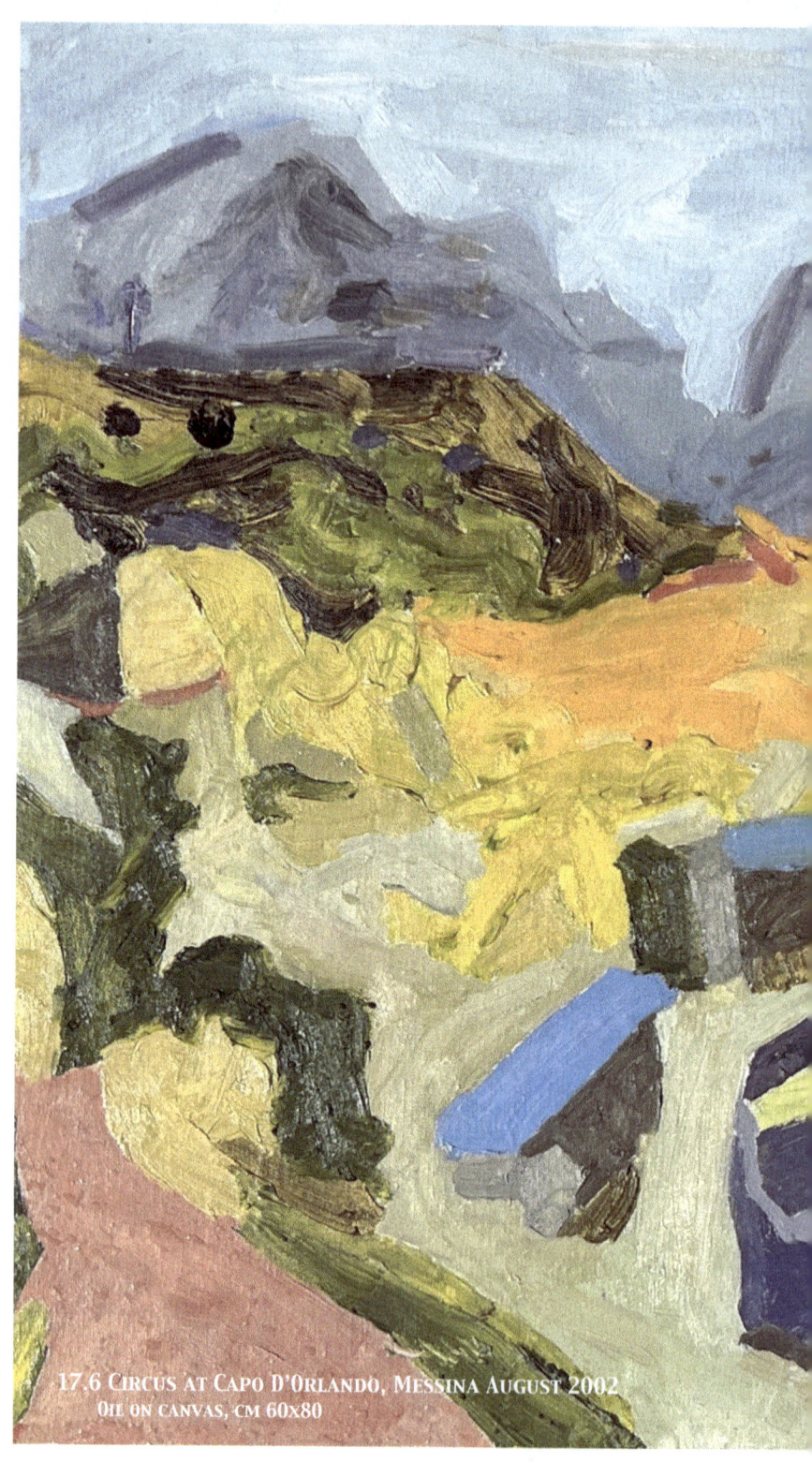

17.6 Circus at Capo D'Orlando, Messina August 2002
Oil on canvas, cm 60x80

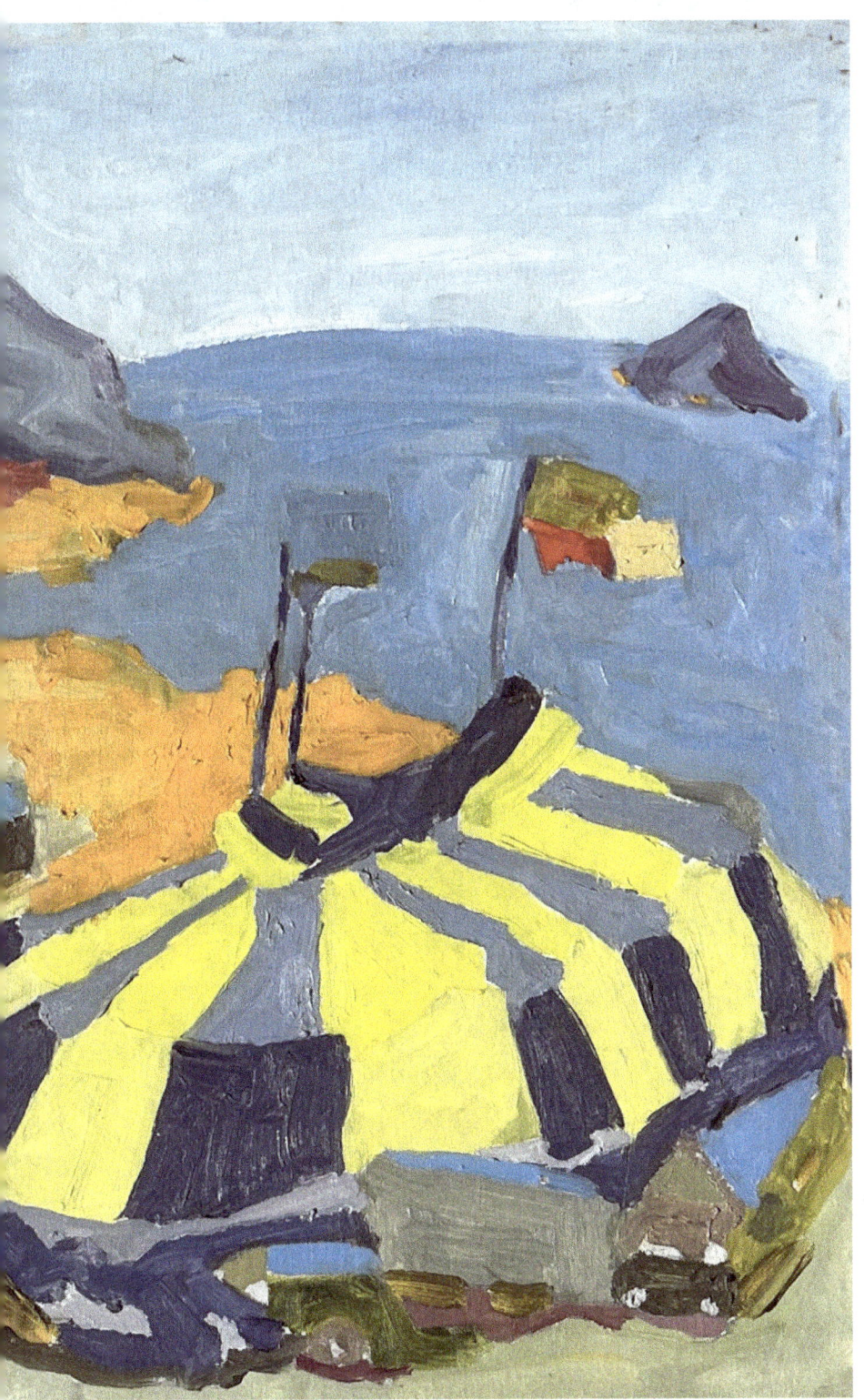

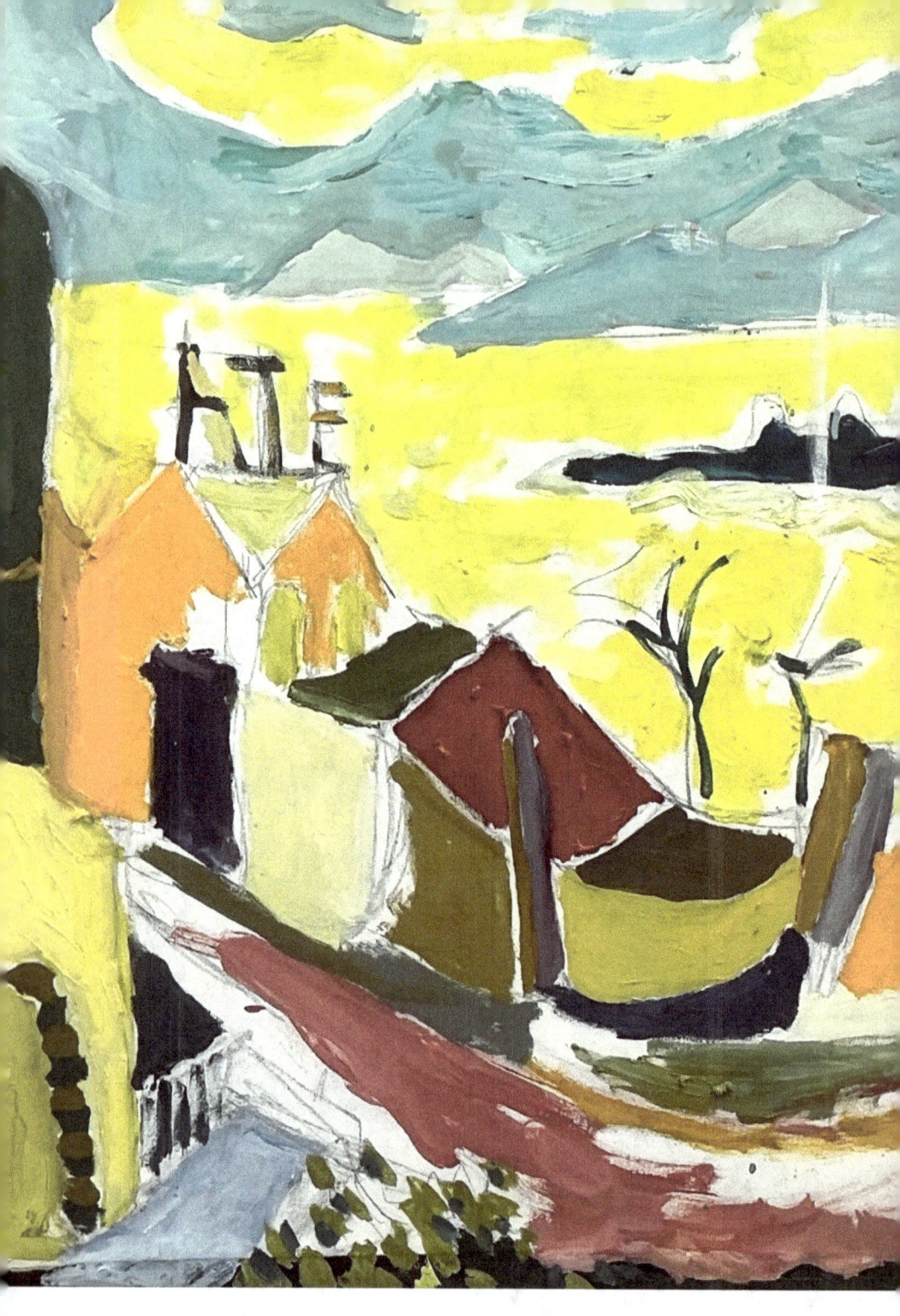

17.7 Tusa. Messina 2023
Oil on canvas, cm 70x100

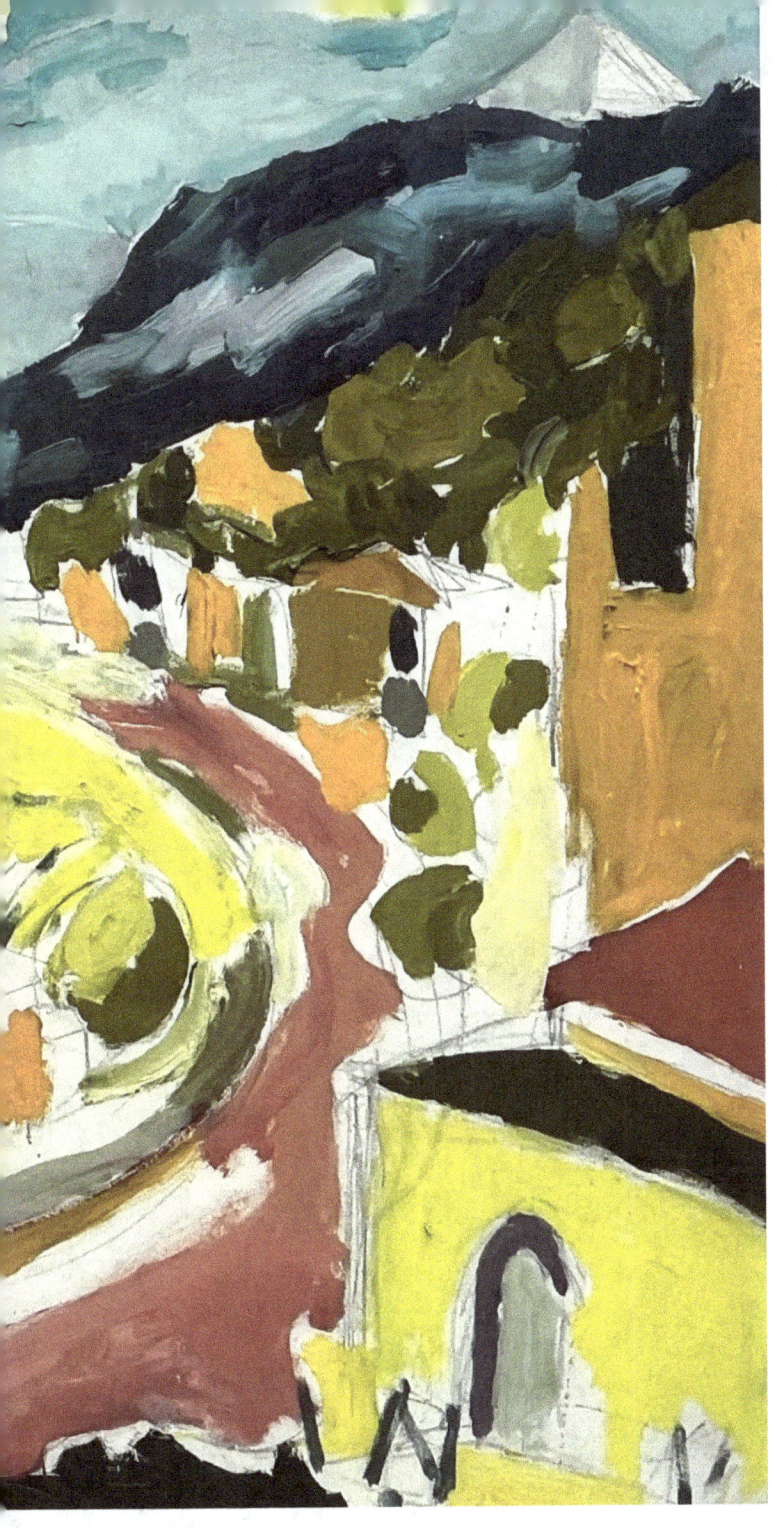

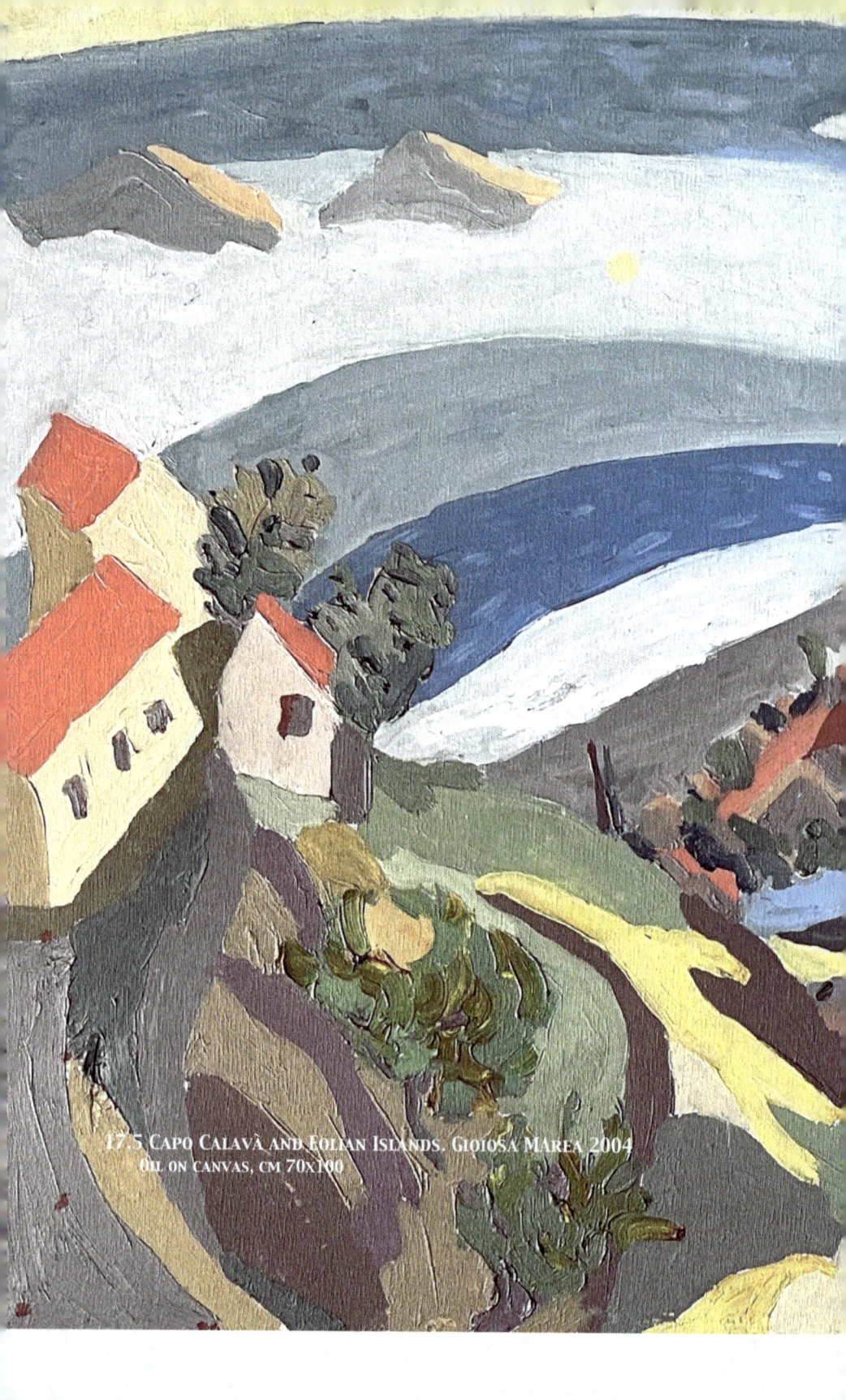

17.5 Capo Calavà and Eolian Islands. Gioiosa Marea 2004
Oil on canvas, cm 70x100

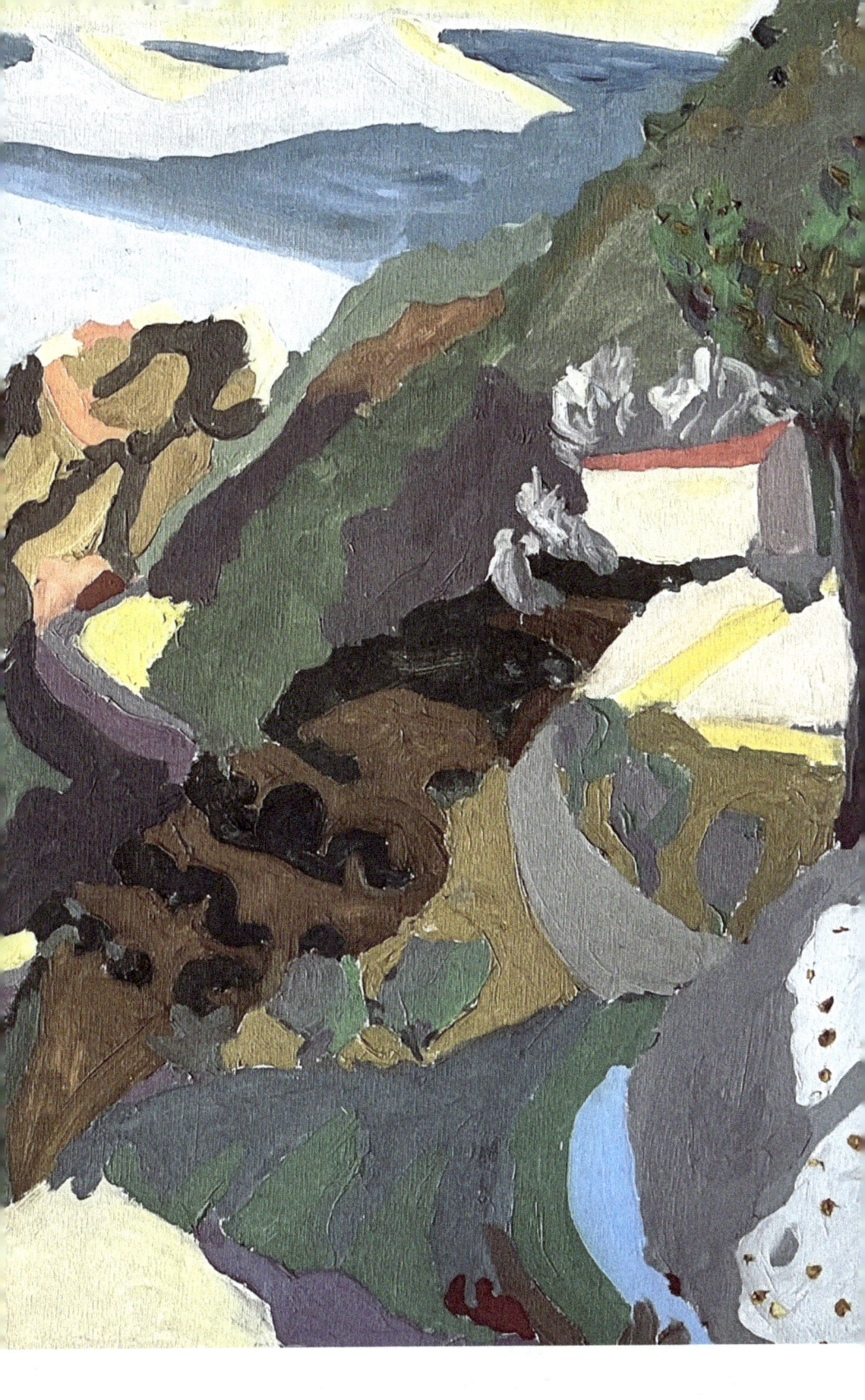

Santa Caterina

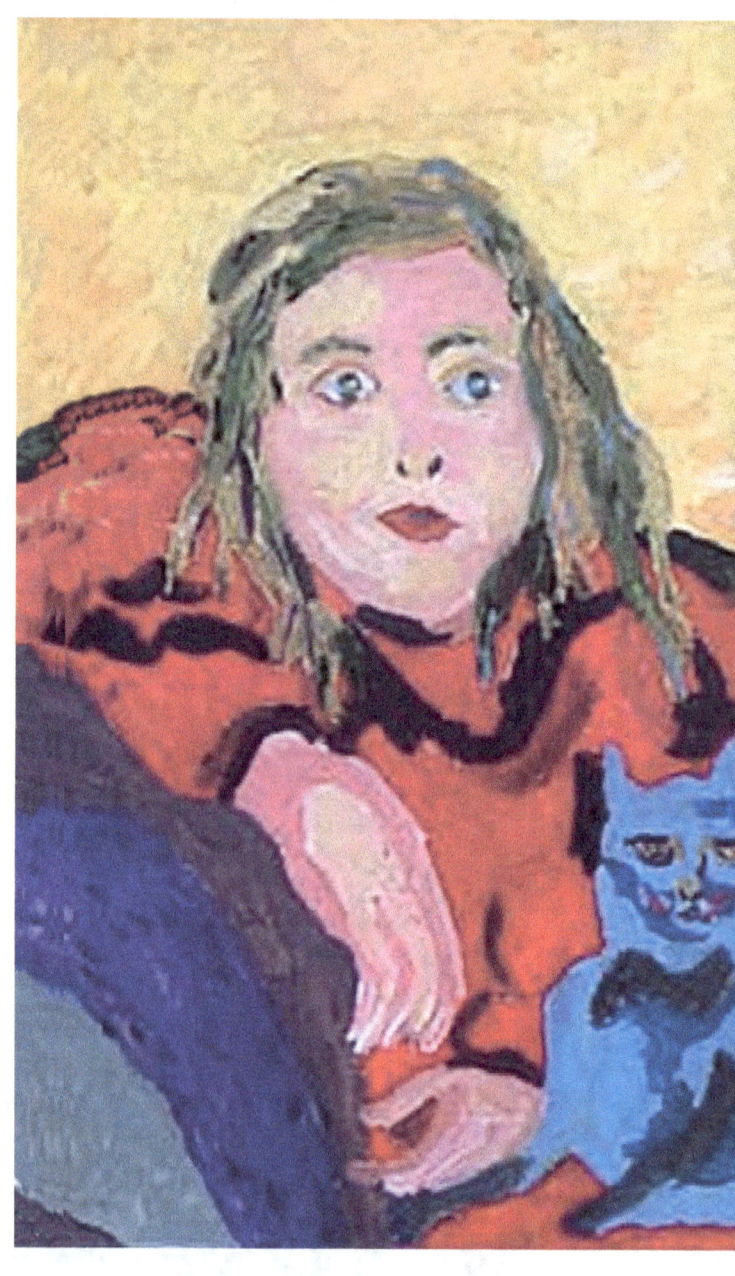

18.1 Caterina with Luna, July 2002
Oil on canvas, cm 70x90

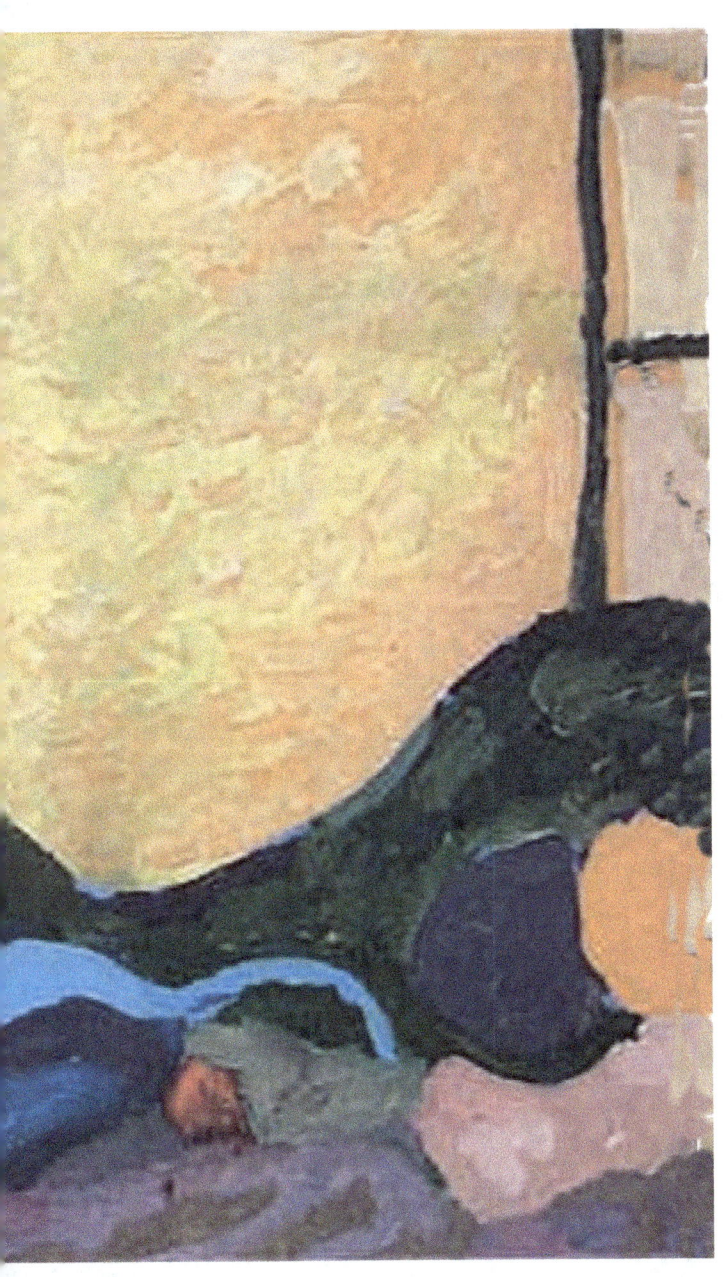

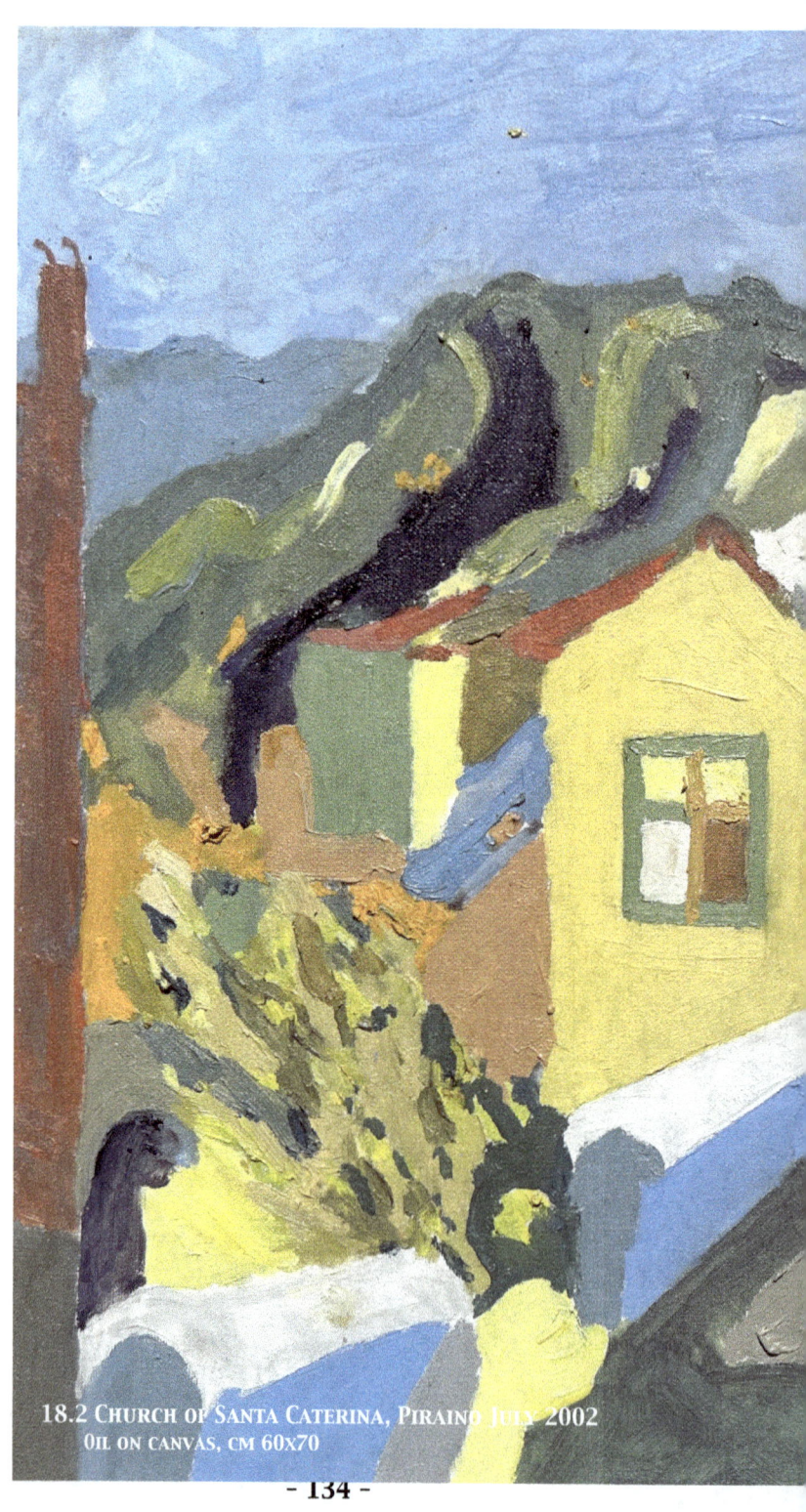

18.2 Church of Santa Caterina, Piraino July 2002
Oil on canvas, cm 60x70

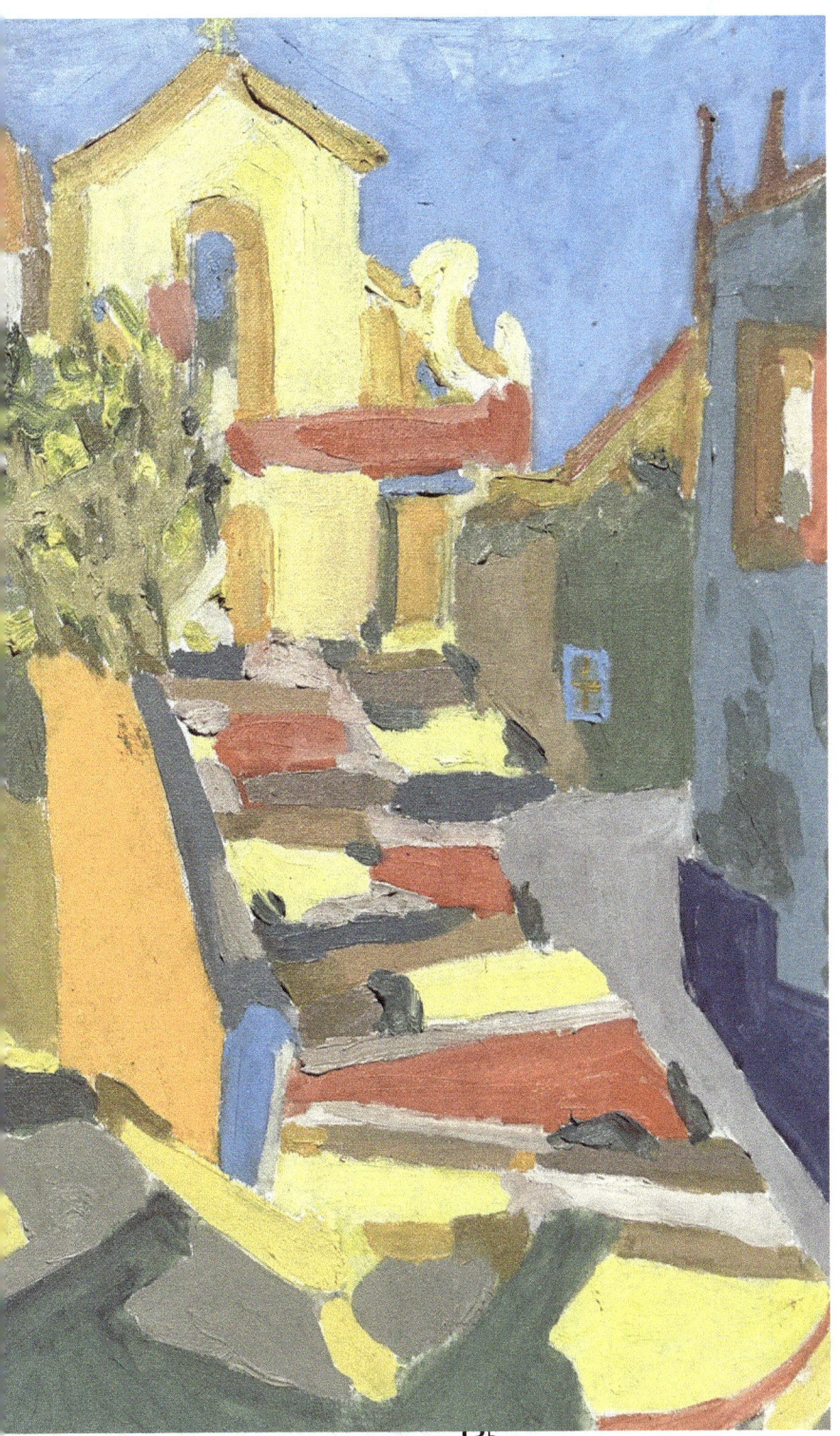

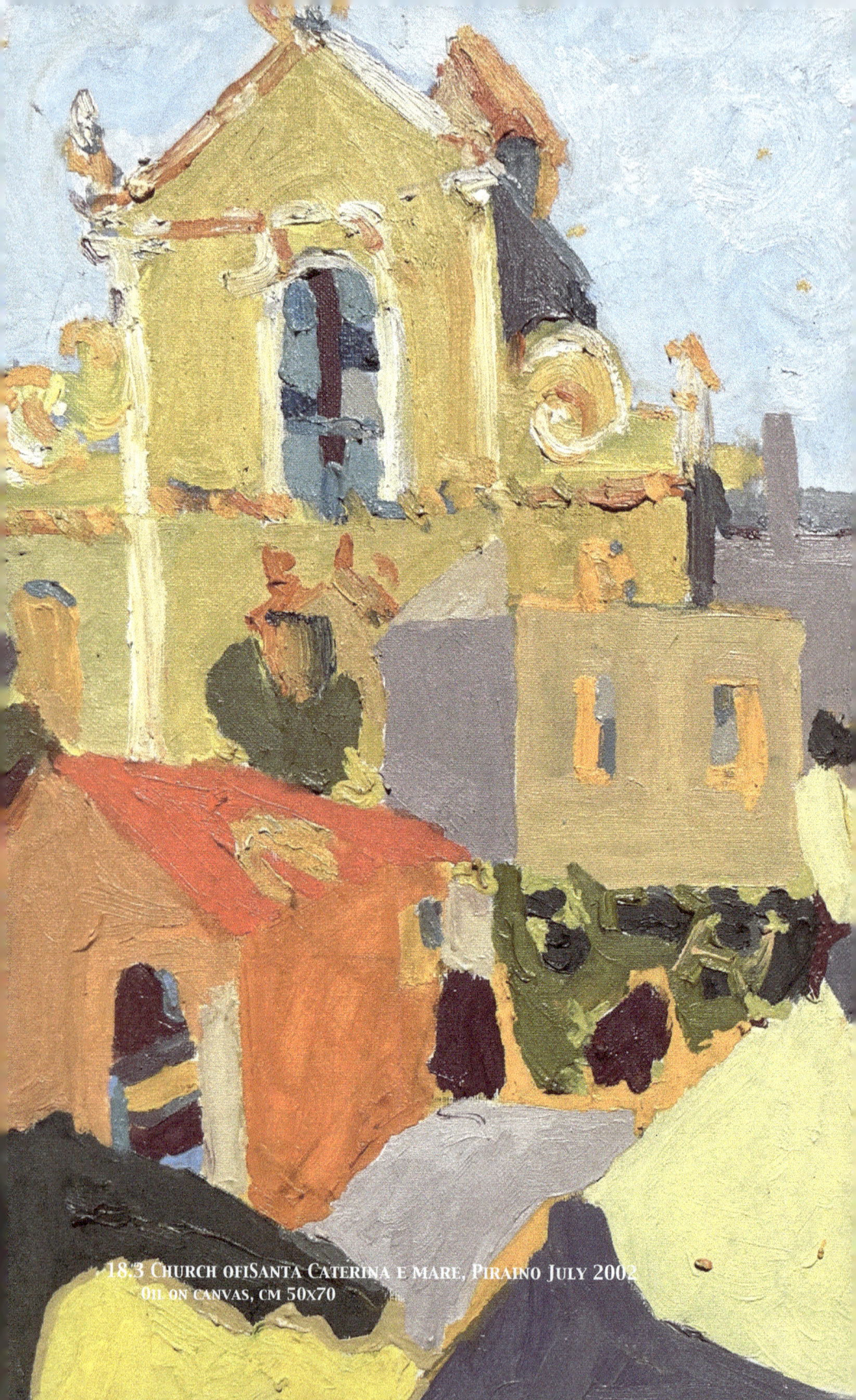

18.3 Church of Santa Caterina e mare, Piraino July 2002
Oil on canvas, cm 50x70

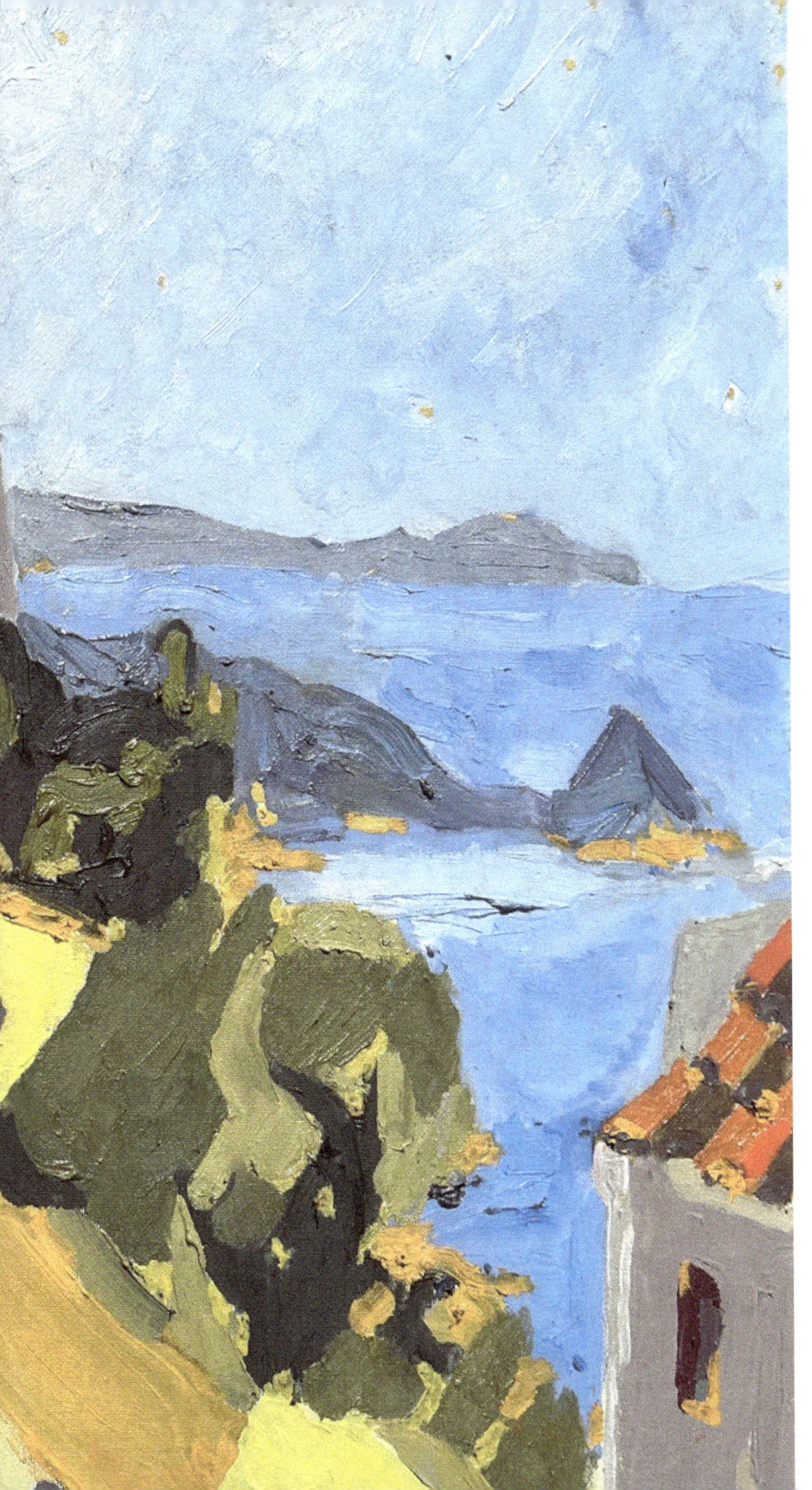

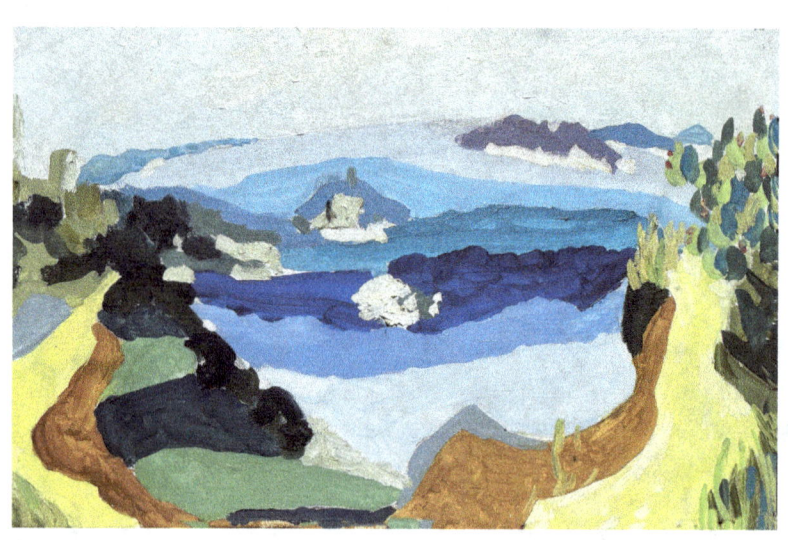

18.3 Eolian Islands, Piraino July 2022
Oil on canvas, cm 60x45

18.4 Church of Santa Caterina and sea, Piraino July 2013
Oil on canvas, cm 70x90

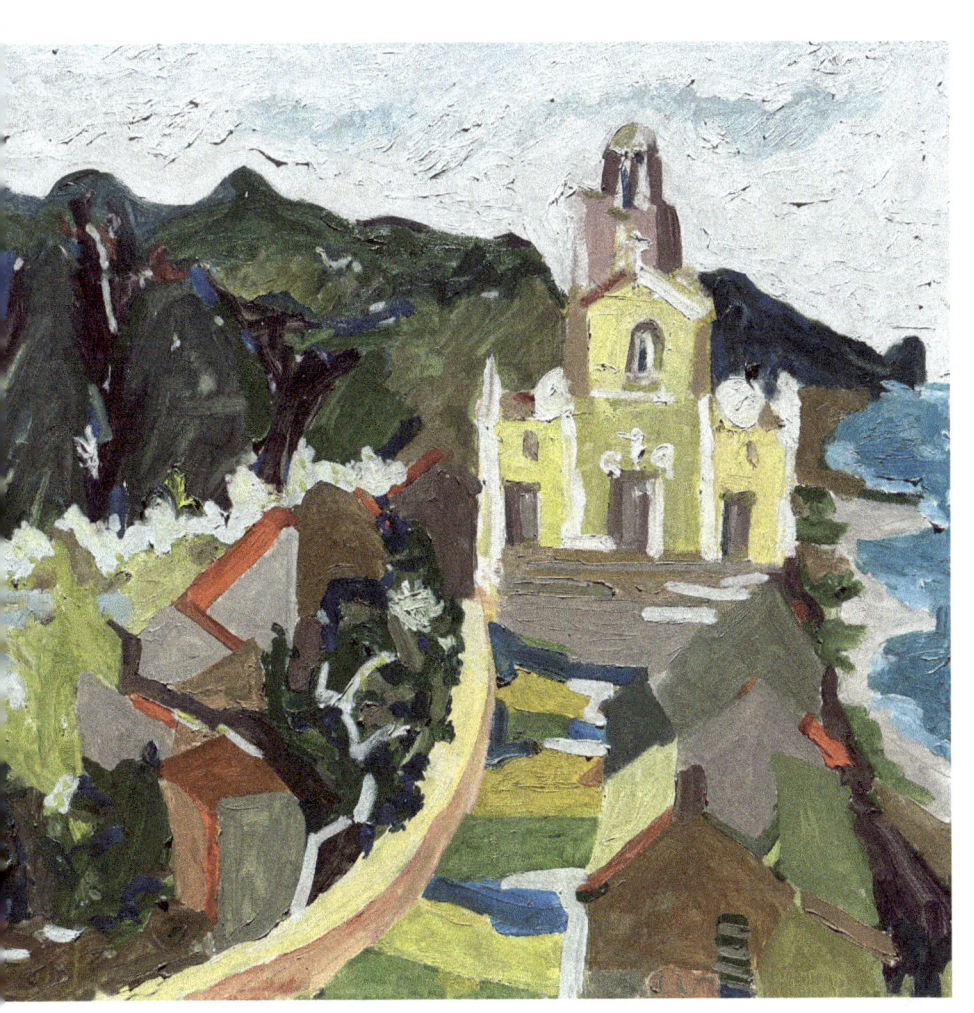

Sicilian Villages

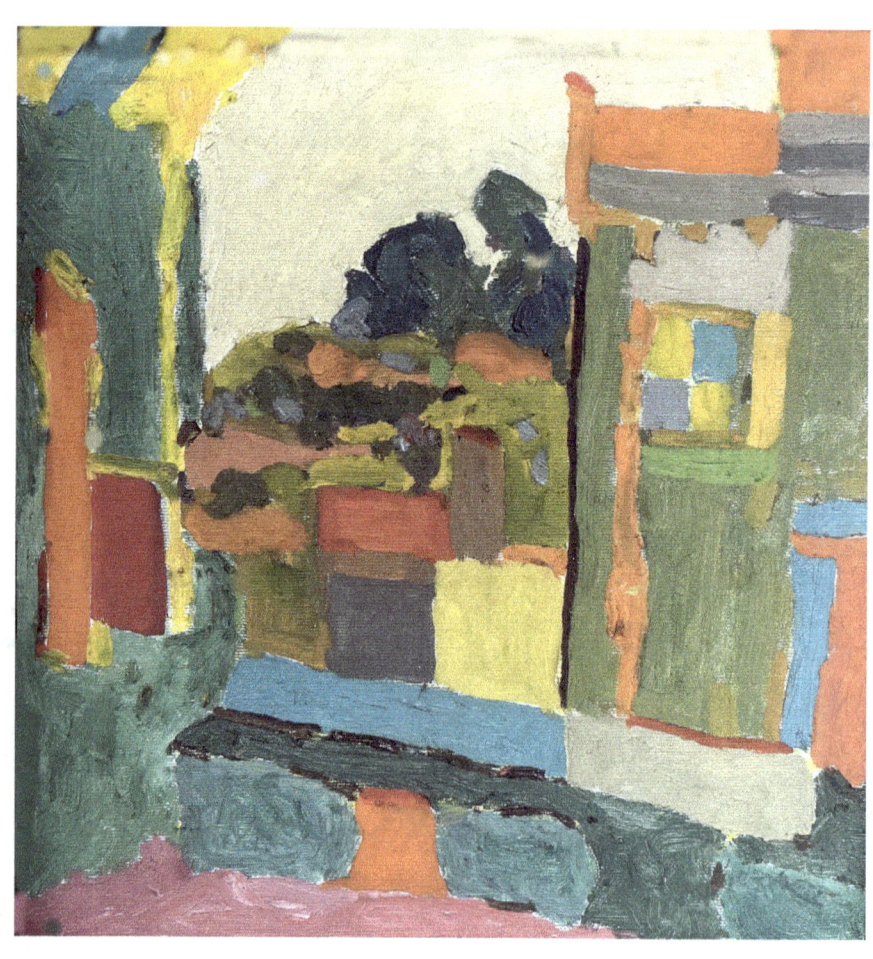

19.1 View from our house, Patti August 1985
Oil on canvas, cm 30x30

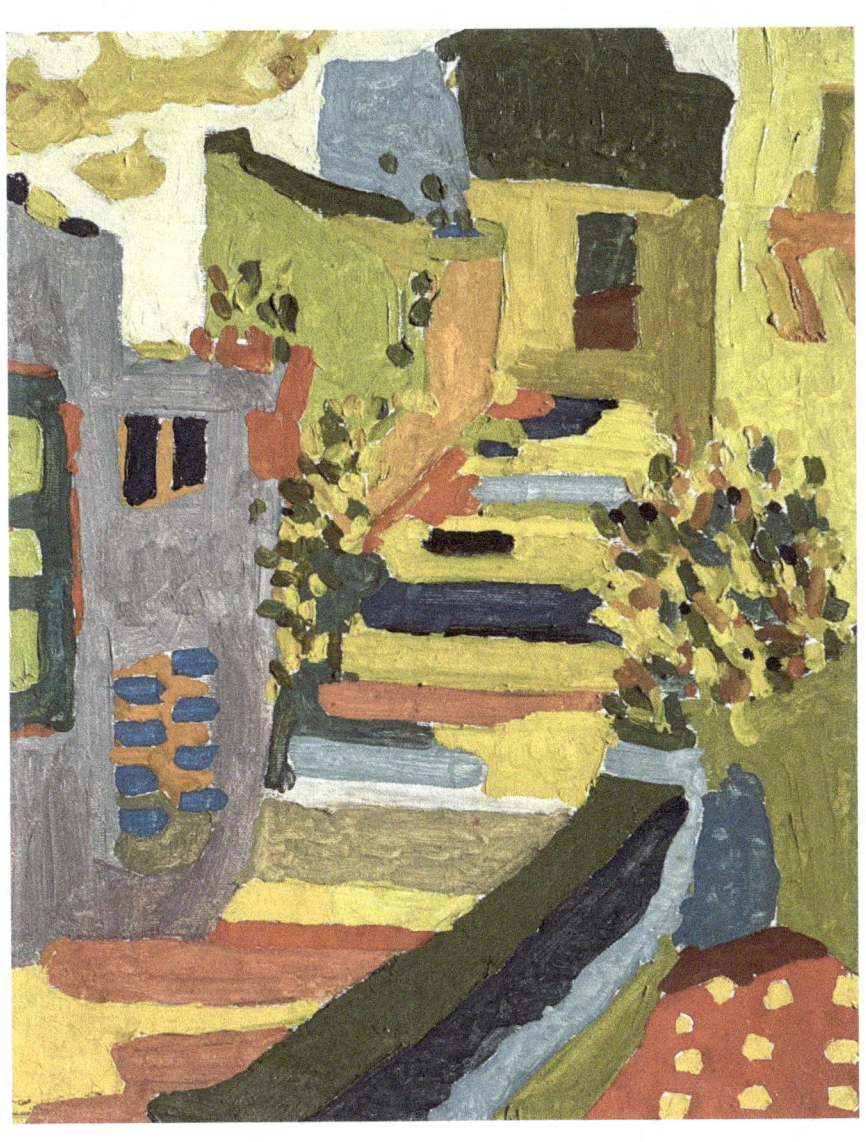

19.2 ARIMONDI HILL PATTI AUGUST 1985
  OIL ON CANVAS, CM 35X45

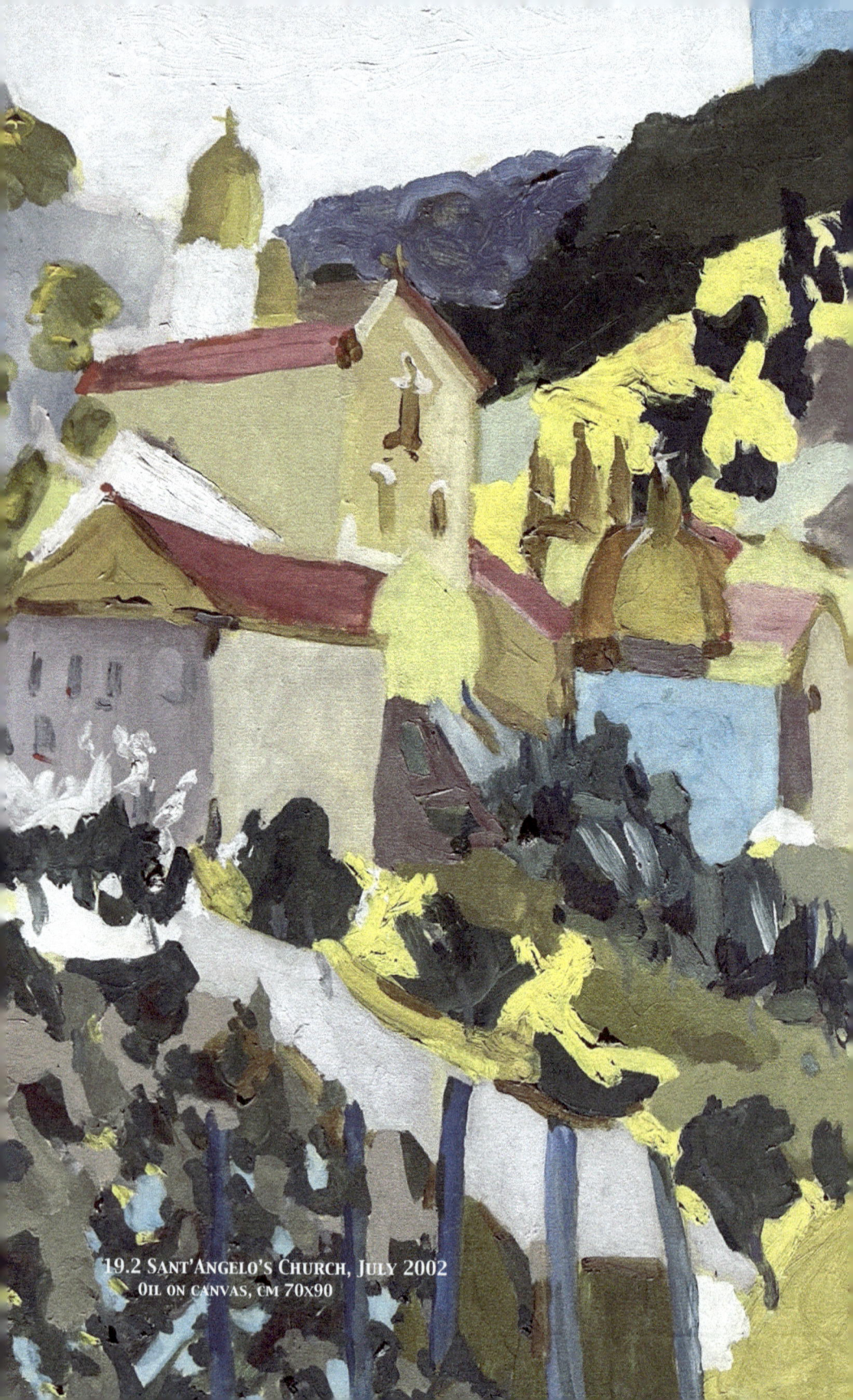

'19.2 Sant'Angelo's Church, July 2002
Oil on canvas, cm 70x90

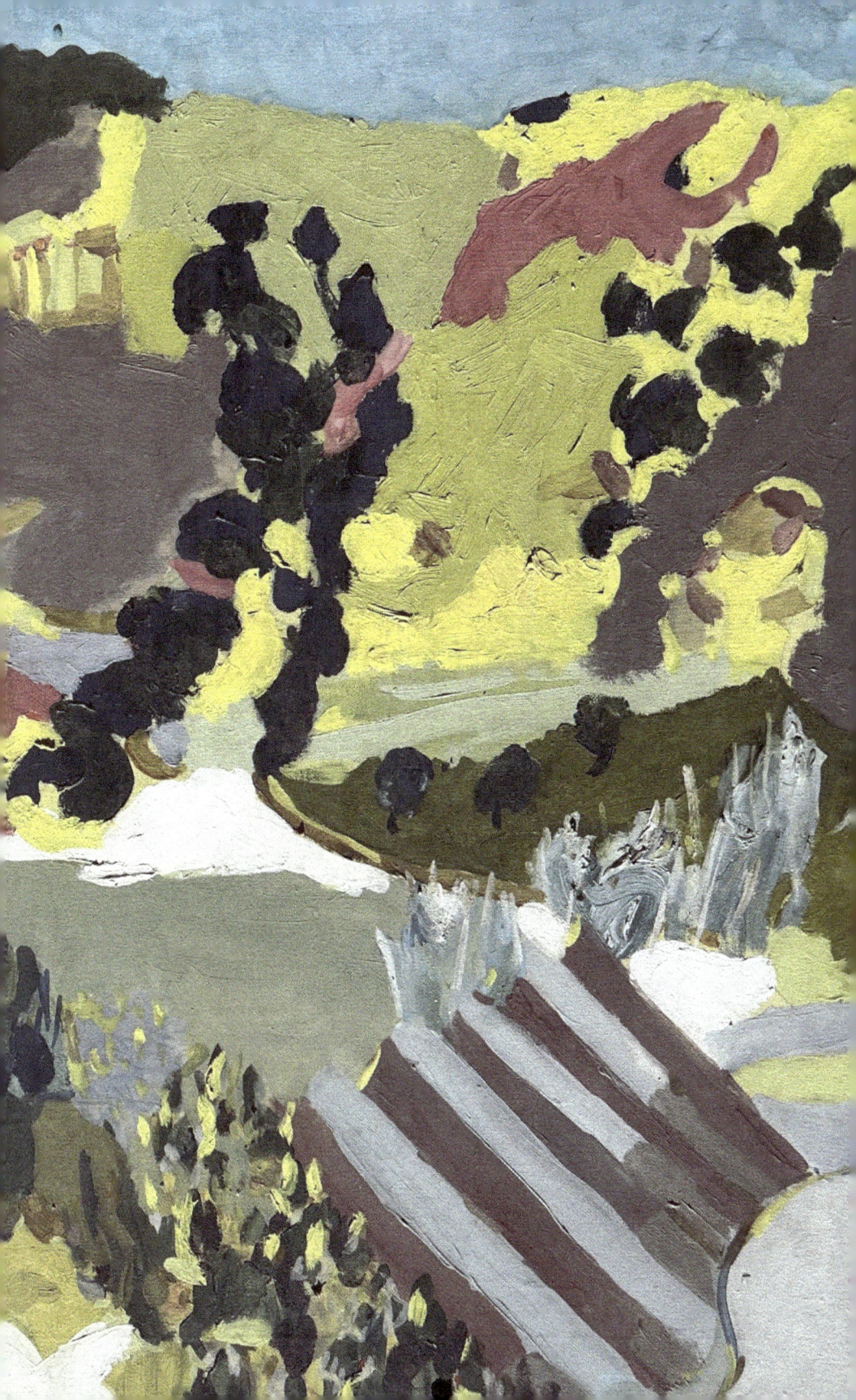

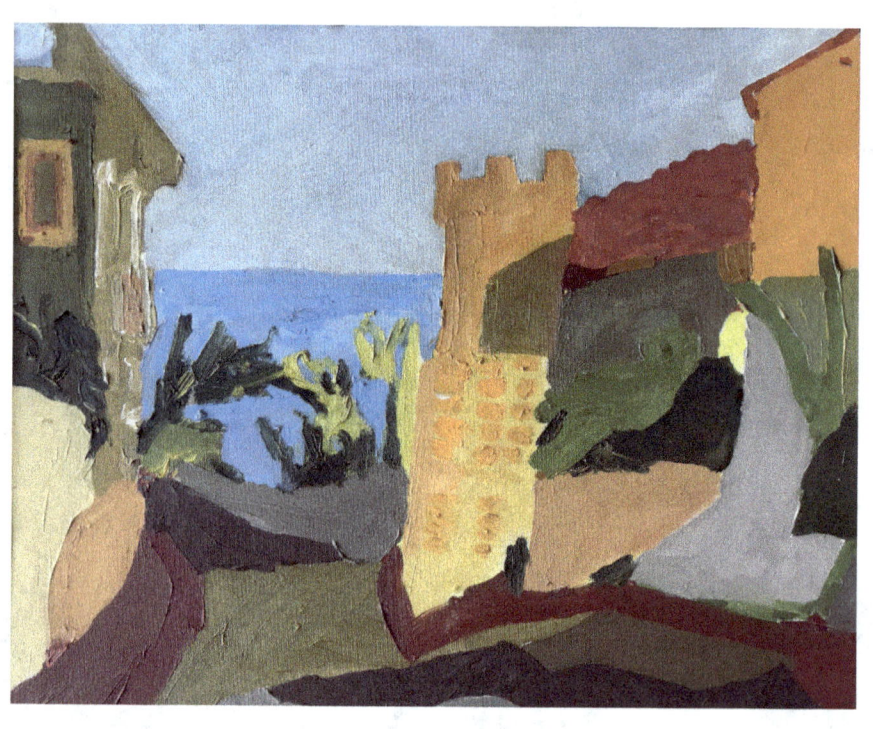

10.3 Gioiosa marea, December 26. 2016
Oil on canvas, cm 25x35

10.4 View from our terrace, Patti August 1987
Oil on canvas, cm 25x35

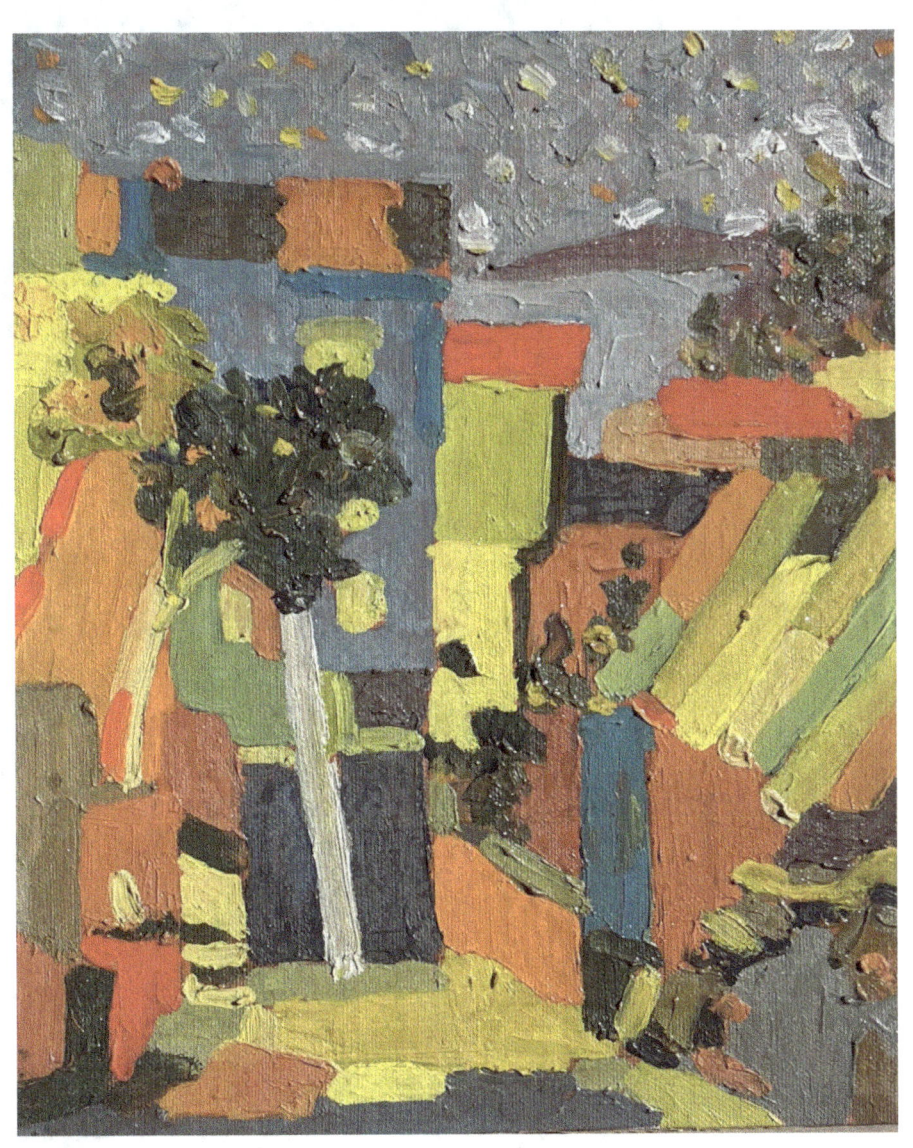

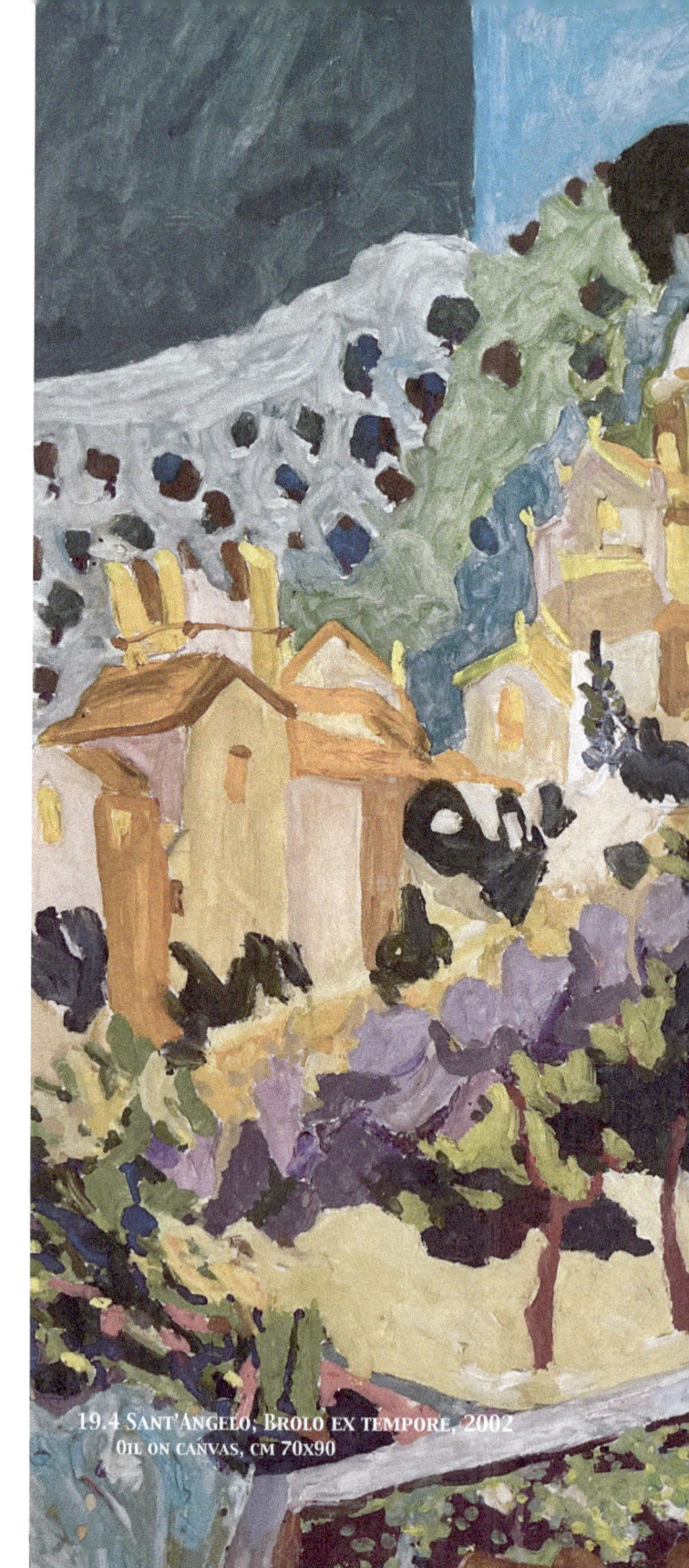

19.4 Sant'Angelo, Brolo ex tempore, 2002
Oil on canvas, cm 70x90

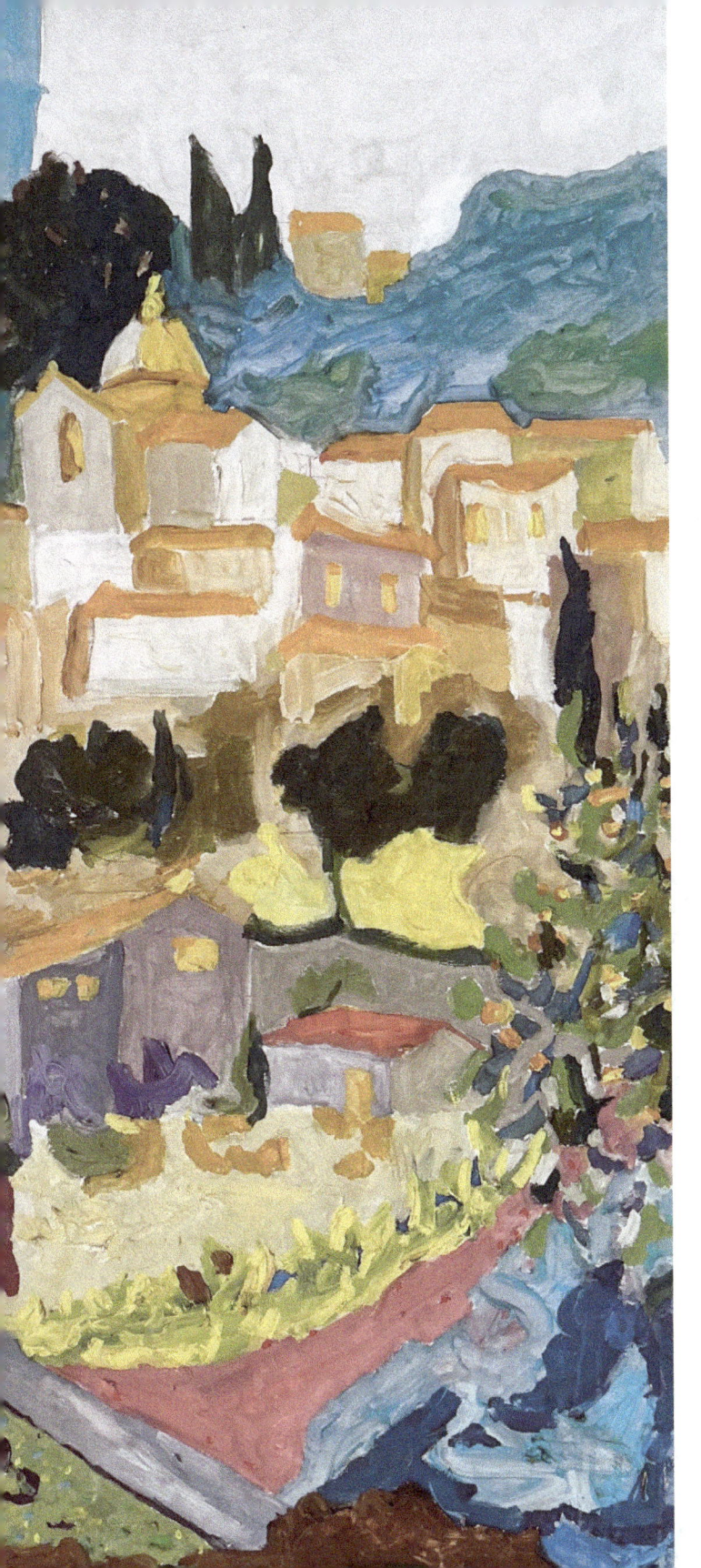

Abaué

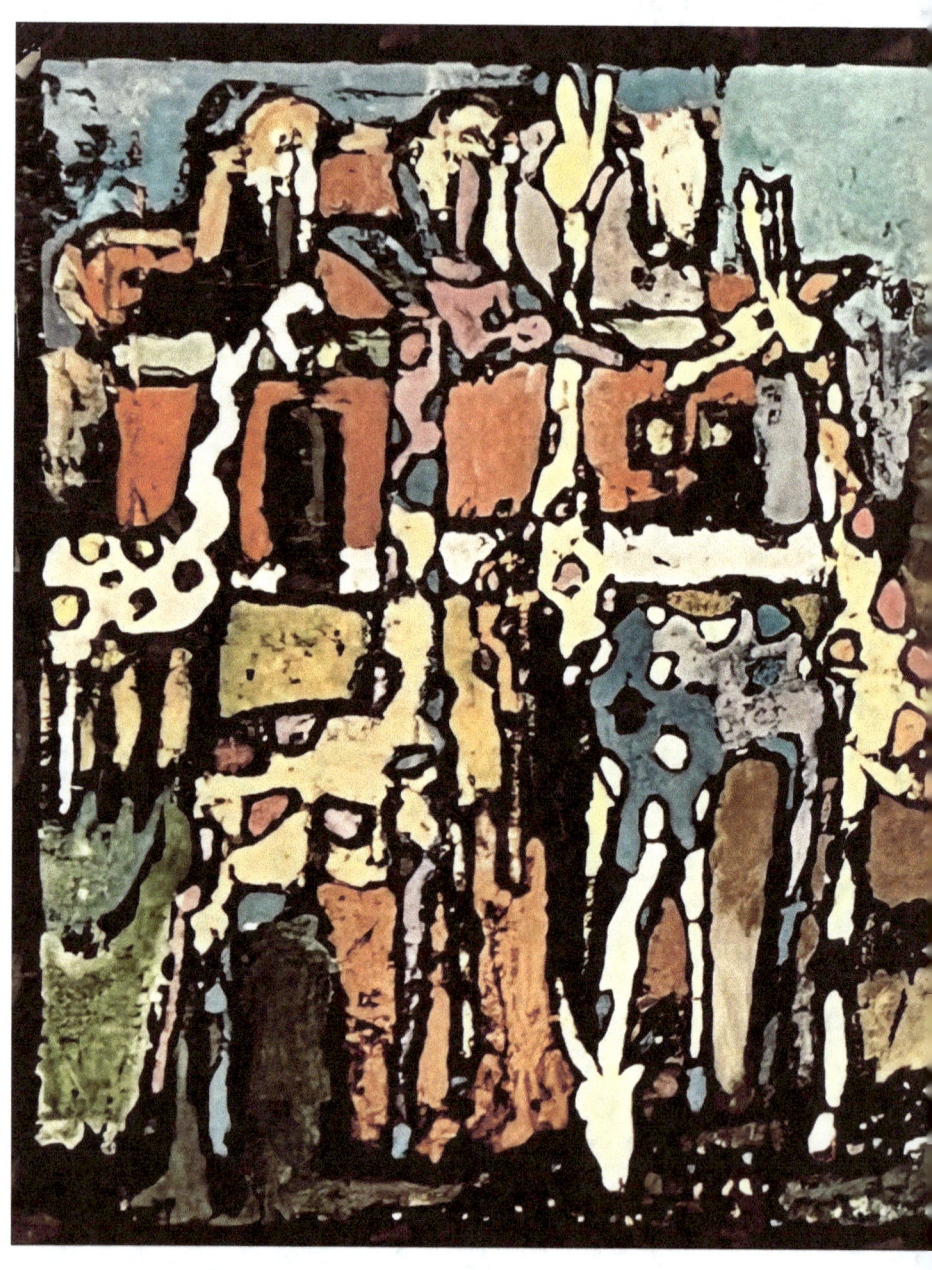

20.1 Zebra in Gioiosa, Maputo
acrylic on table (destroyed), cm 100x200

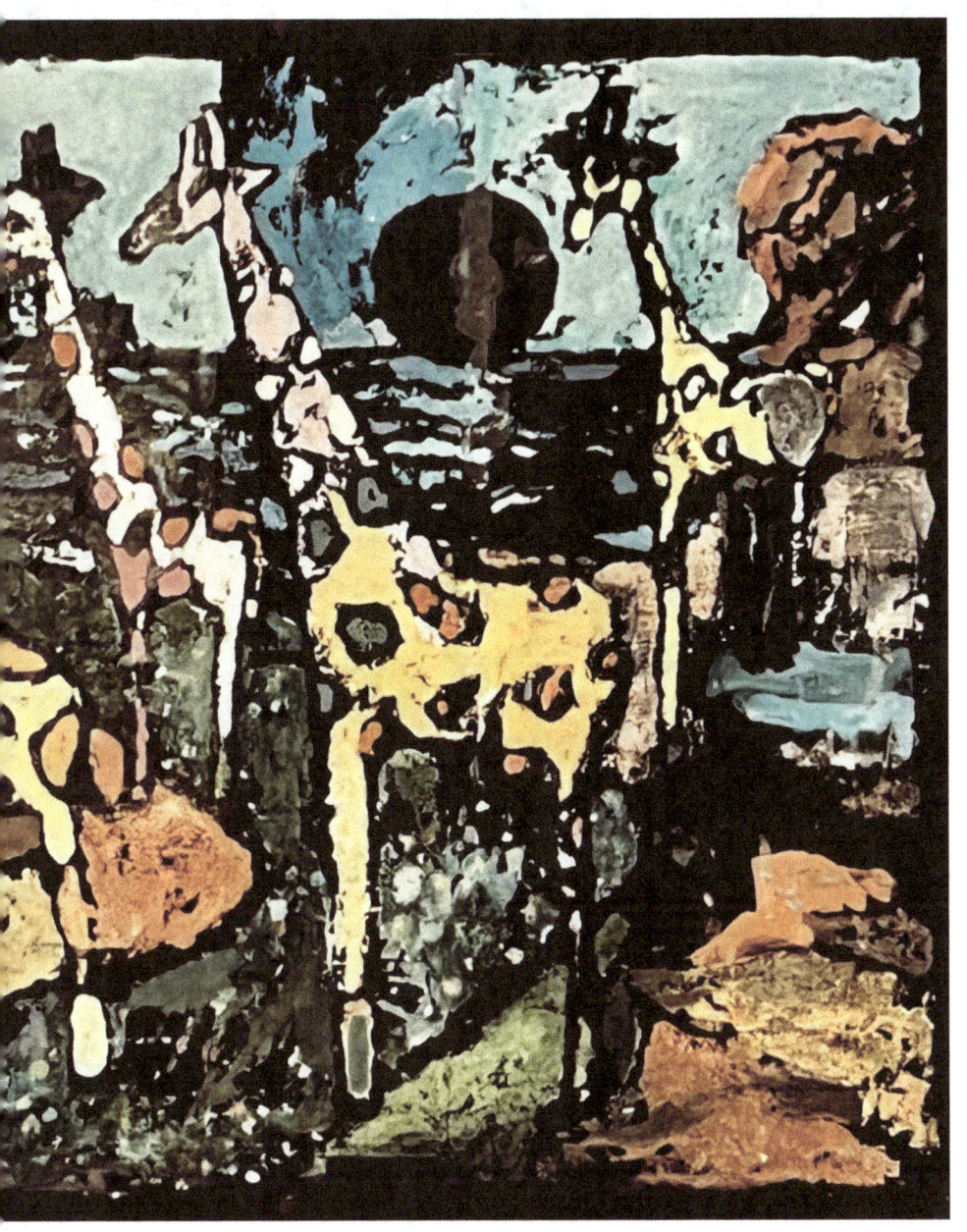

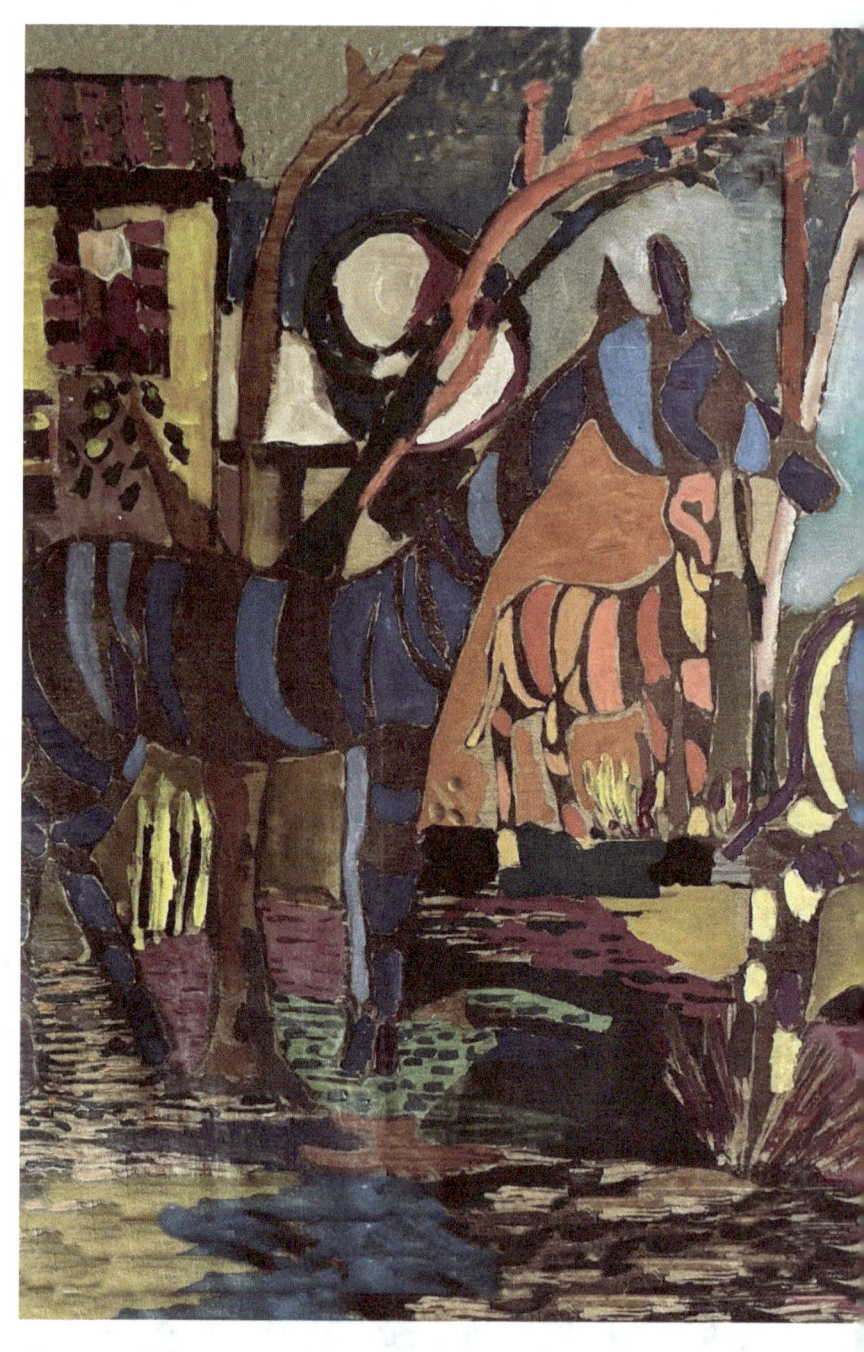

20.2 ZEBRAS IN ROMA,, MOZAMBIQUE MAY 1997
ACRYLIC ON BATIK, CM 100 x 210

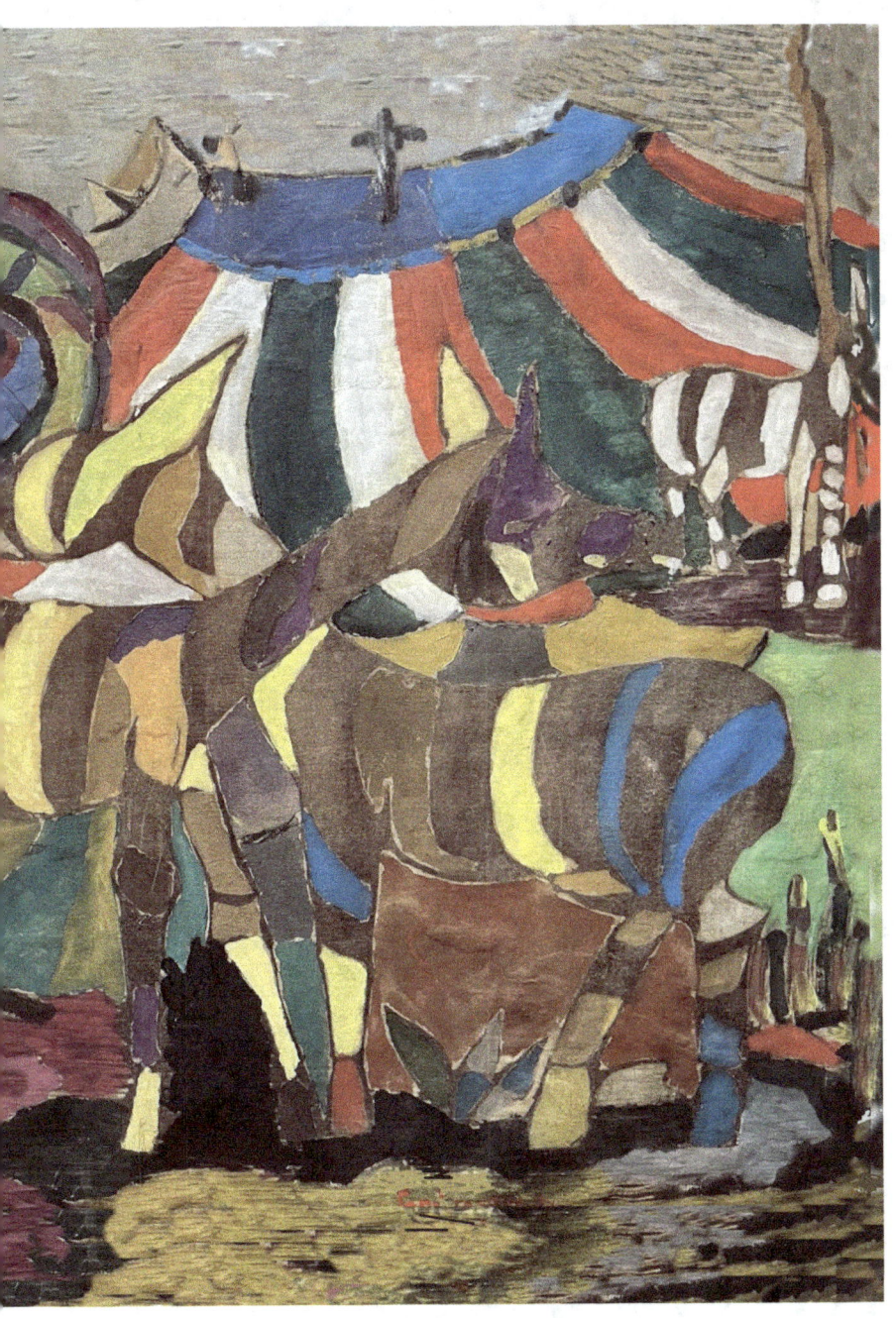

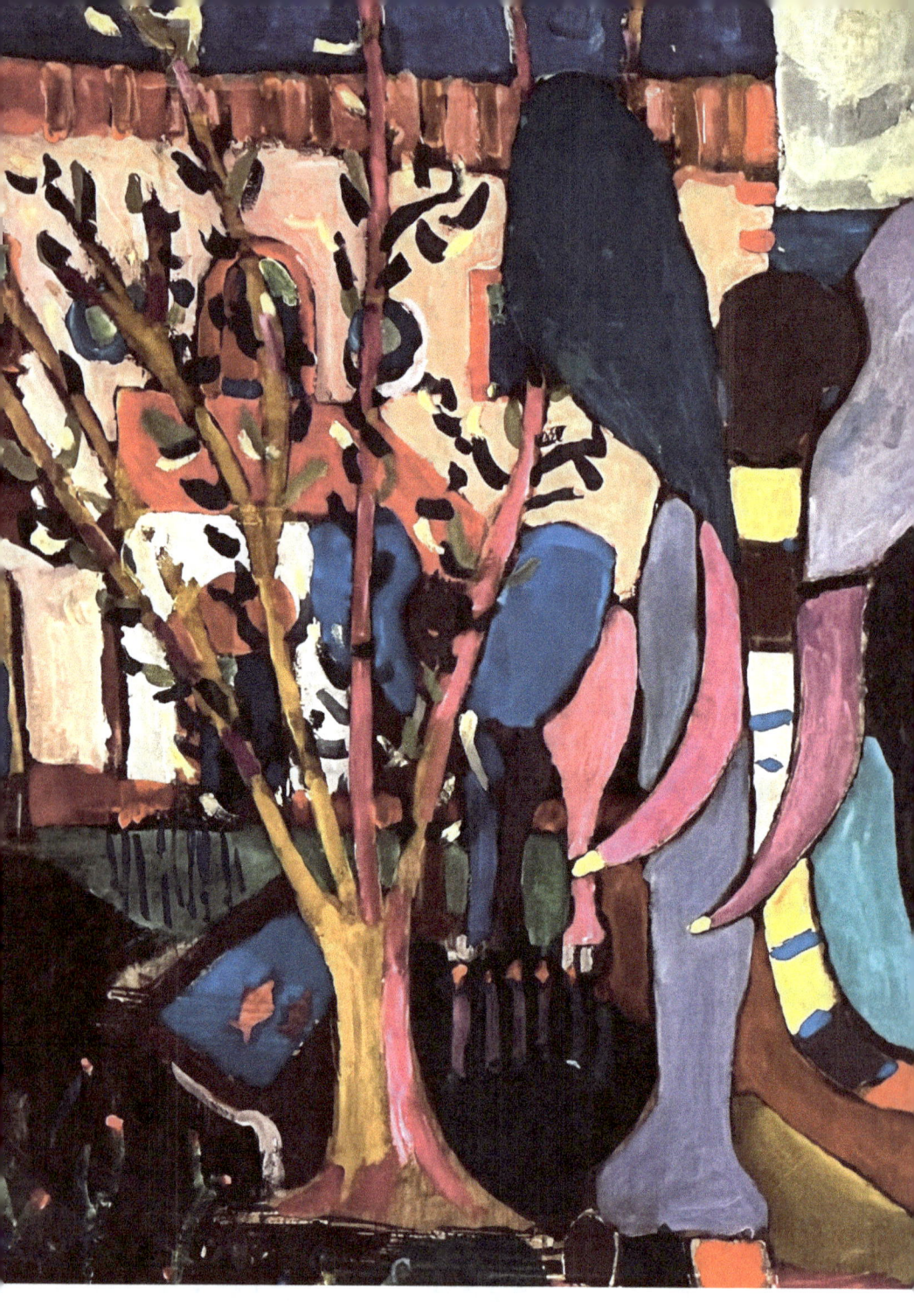

20.3 Elephants in Gioiosa, Mozambique May 1997
acrylic on Batik, cm 90x190

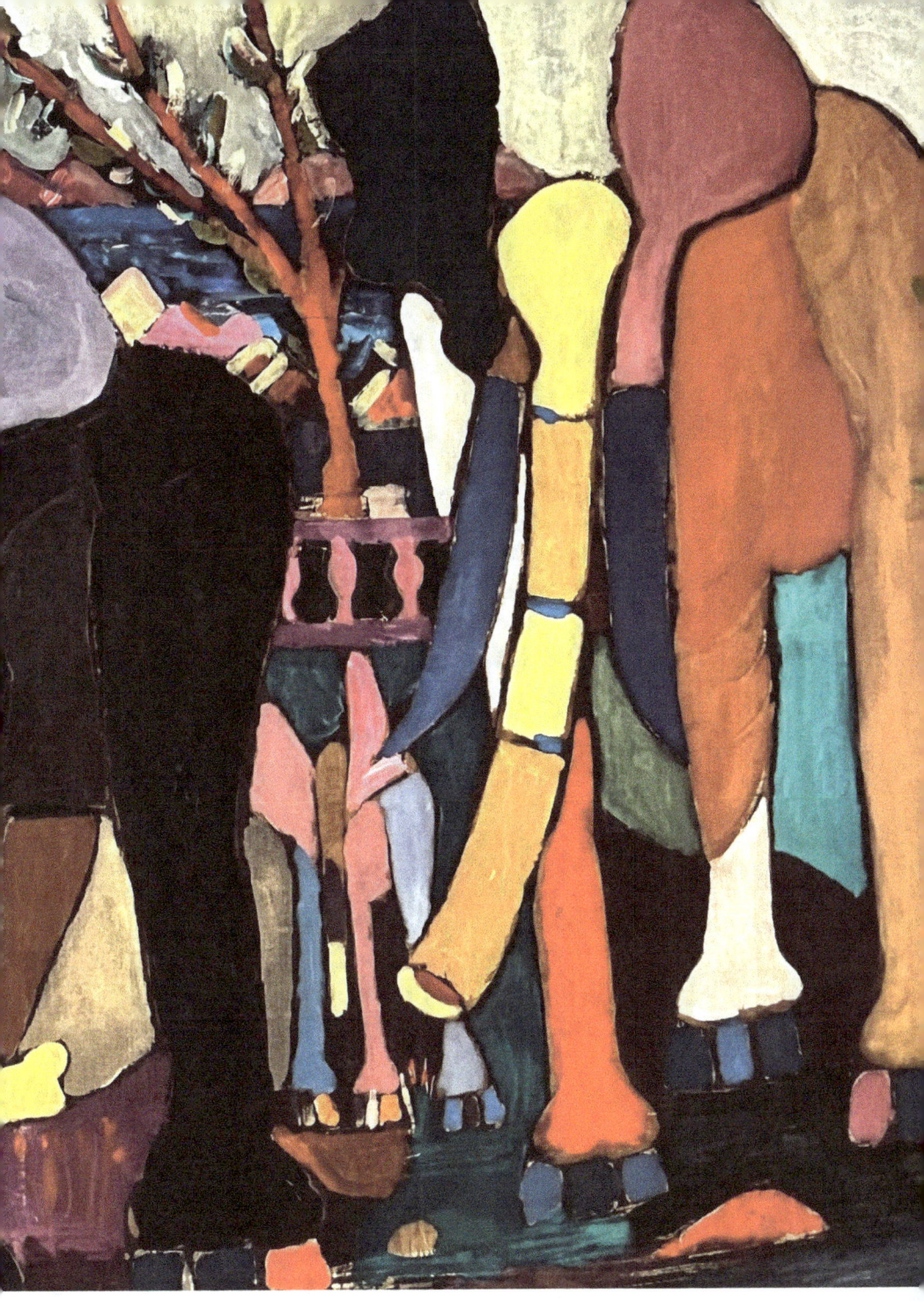

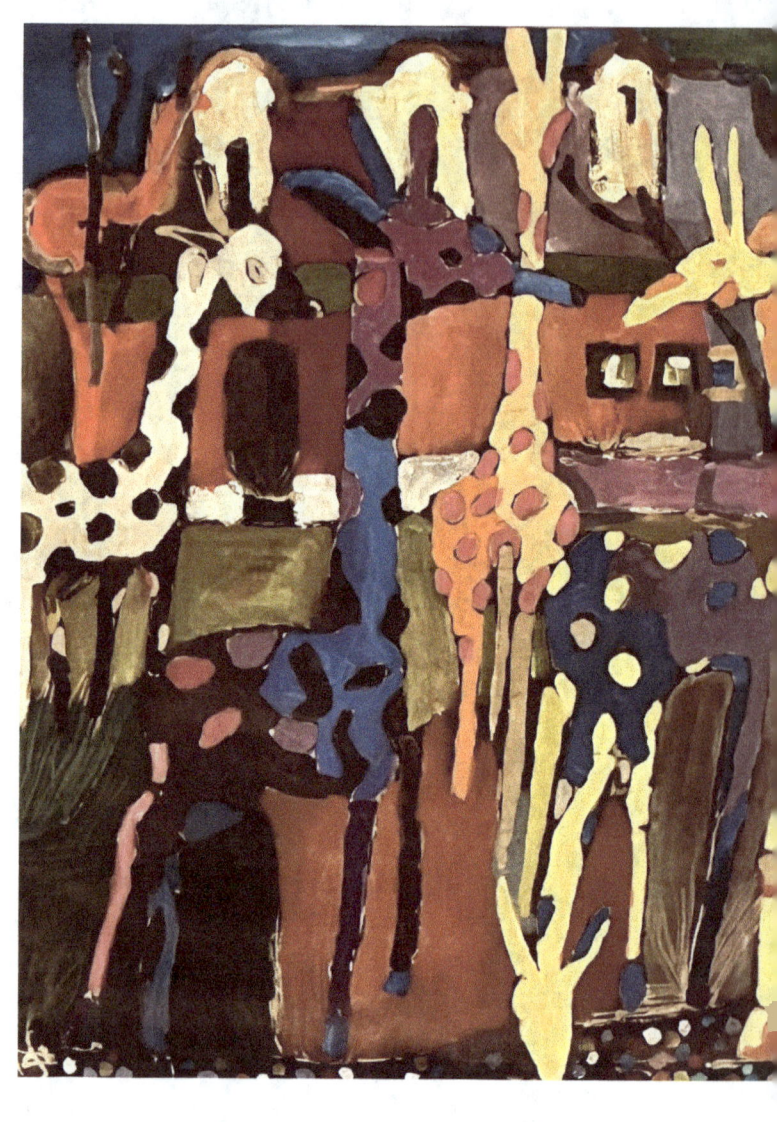

20.4 ZEBRAS AT CAPO CALAVÀ, MOZAMBIQUE APRIL 1997
ACRYLIC ON BATIK, CM 90x170

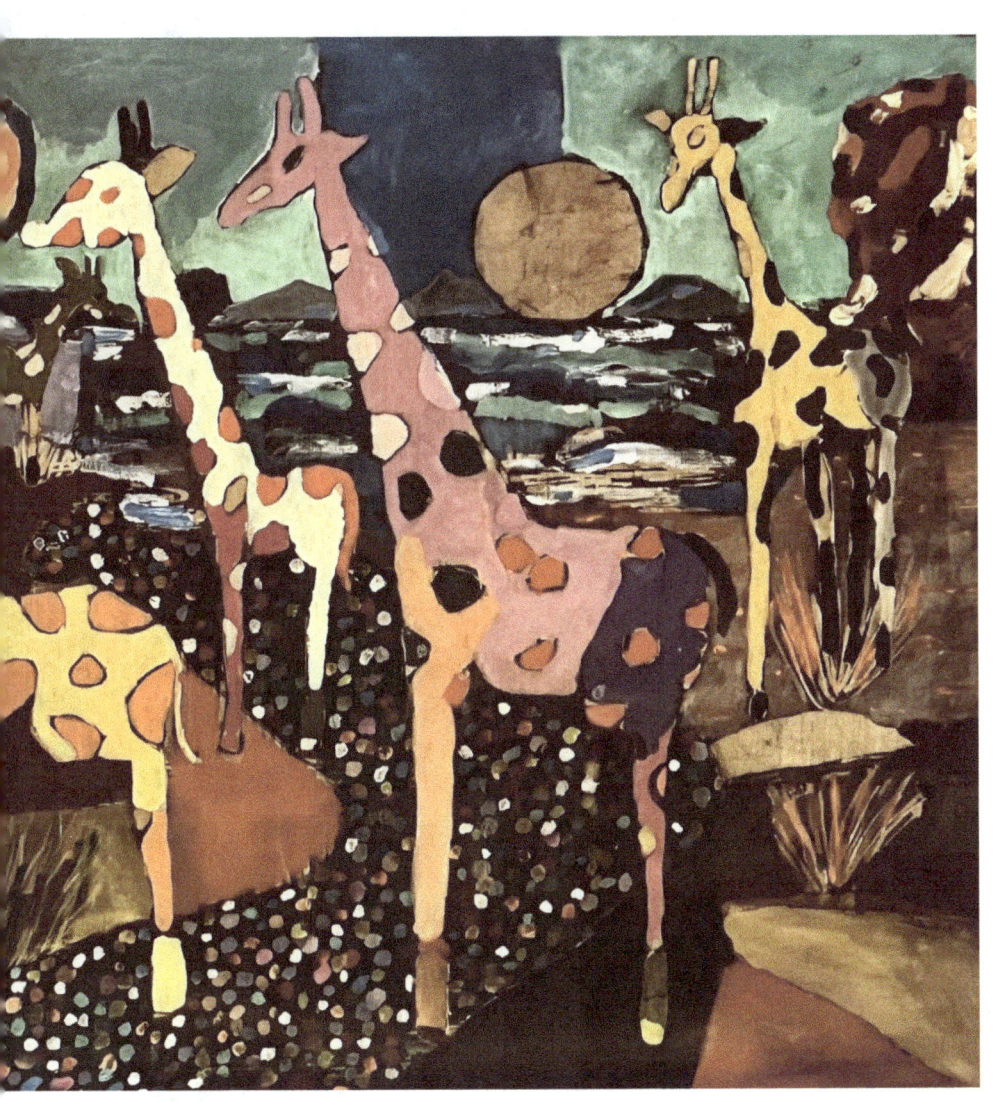

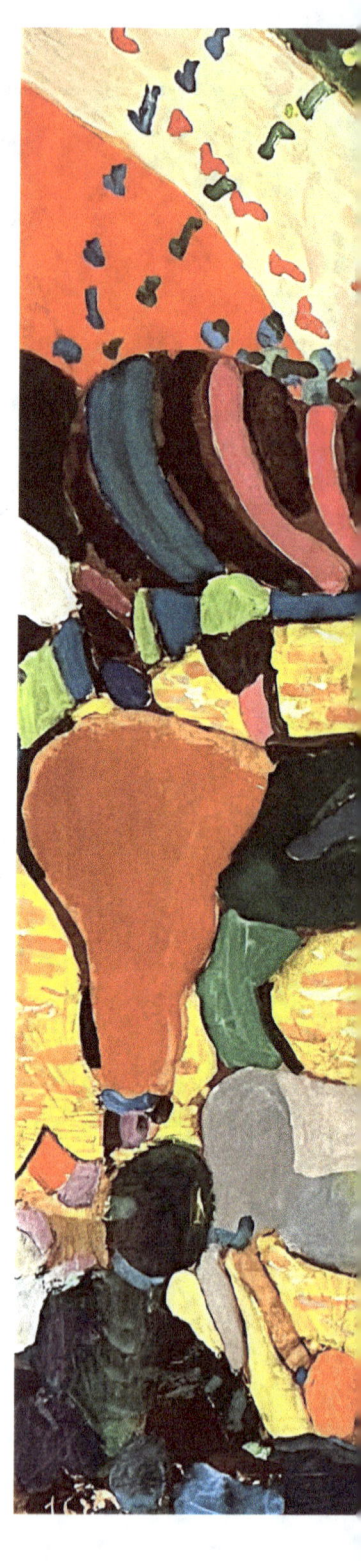

20.5 Circo arena with Raffaele, Mozambique
acrylic on Batik, cm 100x100

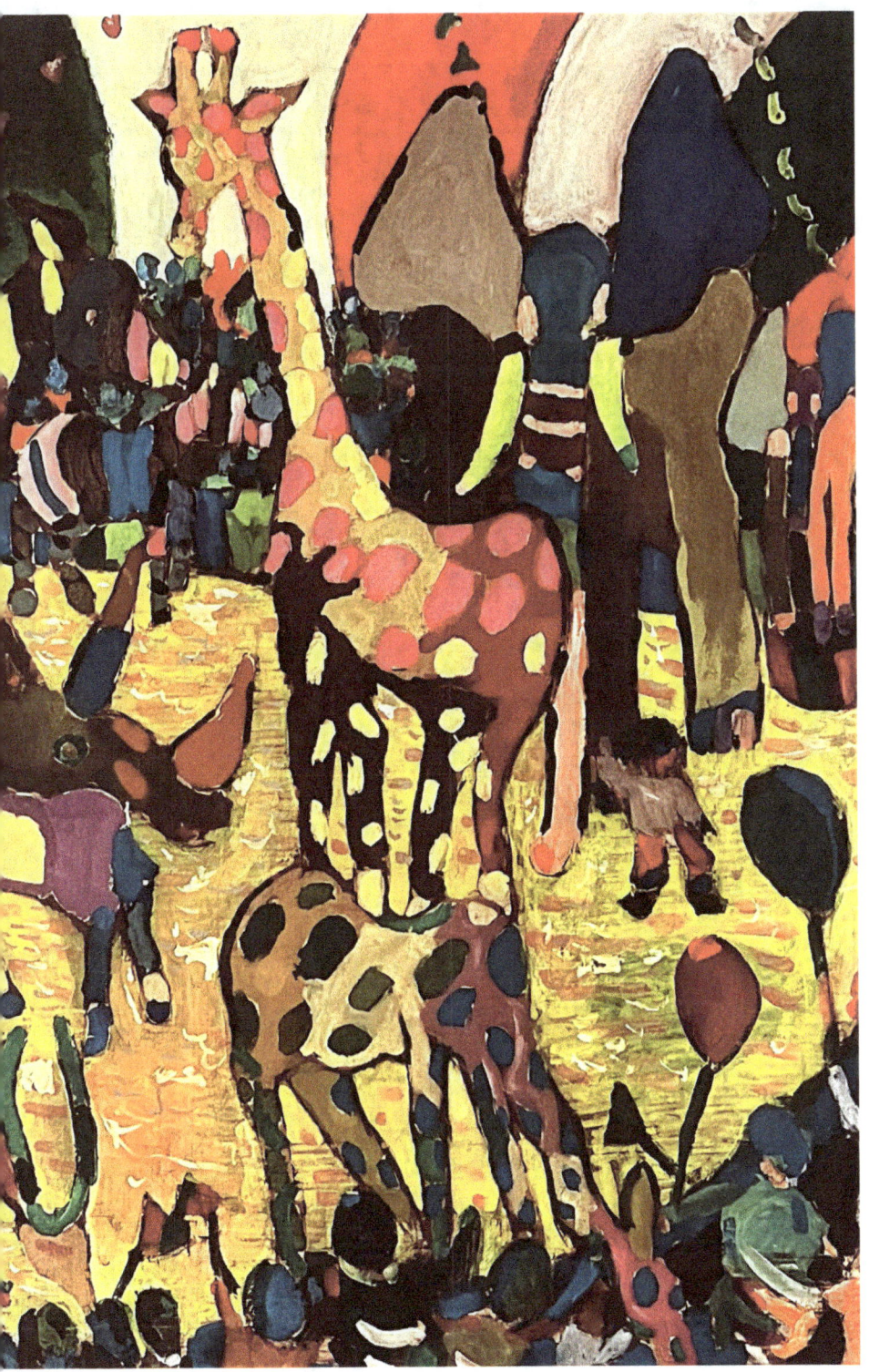

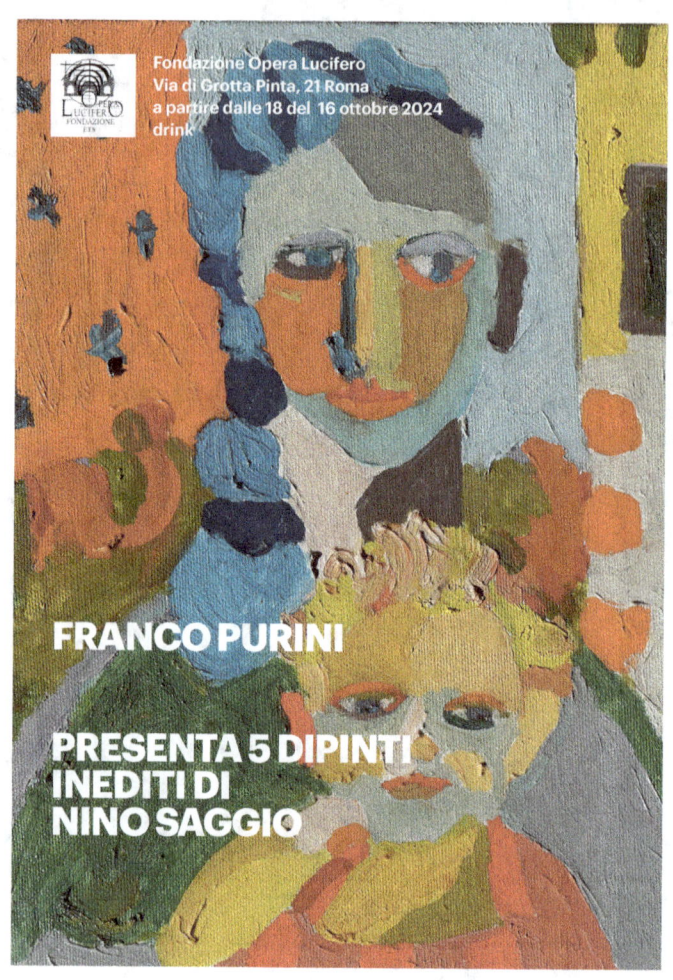

Note

Antonino Saggio (Rome, 1955) architect, scholar and professor at «Sapienza» has been painting since 1968 and has carried out more than five hundred works. He participated in only two exhibitions. None of his paintings have ever been sold, but many of them have been donated to his friends and closest family members:

- Milena Guarda
- Donatella Saggio Orazi
- Raffaele e Sole Saggio
- Caterina Saggio e Luca Virgilio
- Cristina e Marco Majoli
- Annamaria e Mario Napolitano
- Nicola e Tina Ingo
- Gisella Bonizi
- Luigi e Silvia Franciosini
- Luigi Prestinenza
- Giuseppe Prestipino
- Giovanna Natoli e Paolo Allegrezza
- Giancarlo e Loretta Guarda
- Angela, Rebecca e Paolo Guarda
- Antonio Presti
- Franco Purini e Laura Thermes
- Fernando Miglietta
- Giovanna De Sanctis Ricciardone
- Tonino Lepore e Laura Ottogalli
- Claudio Gabrielli
- Anna Maria D'Olimpio
- Tine Seybold
- Mauro e Liliana Poncetta
- Massimiliano Chialastri e Stefania Macori
- Pino Tabacco
- Eleonora Dolce
- Domenico Gangemi
- Fernando Recalde
- Ruggero Lenci

- Camilla Grassi
- Orazio Carpenzano
- Pro Loco Sinagra
- Luigi De Francesco
- Luciano Biancatelli
- Antonio e Joyce Tomaselli
- Gianni e Letizia Orazi
- Marcella Bolgi Orazi
- Giulia Natoli Forzano
- Rosa Saggio Pirrone
- Glenn Boornazian e Norma Barbacci
- Paolo e Stefania Meluzzi
- Carlo Melograni
- Elisa Montessori
- Francesco Tentori e Giovanna Alatri
- Marcello Panzarella
- SaraPatrizia Tortoriello
- MIchele Fasolo
- Marcello Sèstito
- SaraPatrizia Tortoriello
- Michele Fasolo
- Roberto Lucifero d'Aprigliano

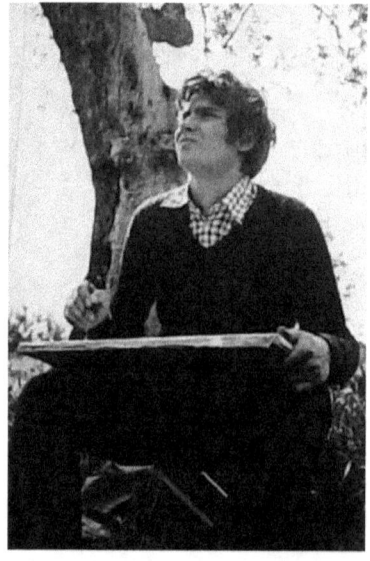

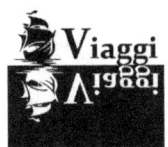

Book Series conceived and directed
by Antonino Saggio

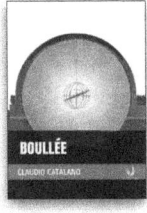
Claudio Catalano
Boullée
Isbn
979-8877546738

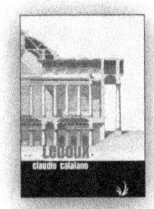
Claudio Catalano
Ledoux
Isbn
979-8340713834

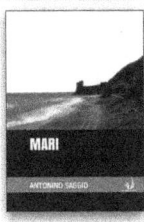
Antonino Saggio
Mari
Isbn
979-8878621458

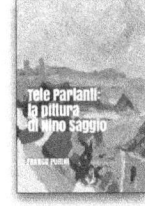
Franco Purini
Tele Perlanti:
La pittura d Nino Saggio
Isbn
979-8342839051

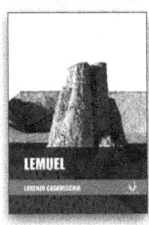
Lorenzo Casavecchia
Lemuel
Isbn
979-8323408450

This book can be purchased online at
www.amazon.com.

Scientific open access
www.academia.edu

Vita Nostra Edizioni
Roma, 2024

www.ingramcontent.com/pod-product-compliance
Lightning Source LLC
Chambersburg PA
CBHW071026240526
45469CB00006BD/2114